LOVE, LIFE & VODKA

NATASHA BLACK

Copyright © 2024 SisterScribe Publishing

All rights reserved. No part of this publication may be reproduced, distributed, or transmitted in any form or by any means, electronic or mechanical, including photocopy, recording, or any information storage and retrieval system, without the prior written permission of the publisher.

This book is a work of fiction. Names, characters, businesses, organisations, places, events, locales, and other incidents are either the product of the authors' imagination or used in a fictitious manner. Any resemblance to actual persons, living or dead, or actual events, is purely coincidental.

It was just one of the many rules and regulations that Kate concocted and David adhered to in order for their lives to stay on track.

Technically, Nigel and Ben were David's clients, but they were hysterical and whenever they had a new project for David's architectural genius, they'd combine it into a social evening.

As the first song ended, Kate couldn't help but peek at the clock on the treadmill. Huffing out loud, she flung her towel over the offending stopwatch that was clearly operating in slow motion. Kate peered around the gym, trying to distract herself. Did people really enjoy this? Perhaps she was missing something. But there wasn't a lot to distract her that day; the gym was remarkably empty. Out of the blue, she clocked a 'perfect body' dressed in some sort of sensational orange and black figure-hugging ensemble. The woman held her head high, majestic almost, and it bemused Kate to see that, unlike herself, she seemed to enjoy perusing herself in the mirrors. As she sashayed in Kate's direction, with a confidence that simply oozed out of her, Kate couldn't help but feel envious. *Bloody hell, her legs go up to her bloody armpits.* She suddenly felt awkward in David's baggy T-shirt and oversized tracksuit bottoms, especially whilst women like that graced the gym. In her defence, they were the first items she'd hastily thrown on to extricate herself from any more rabbit-focused duties. *Stop it.* Kate chastised herself. *Stop comparing yourself to these Spanish twenty-something-year-olds, who've probably never had children.* And she averted her eyes.

* * *

Stepping onto the treadmill, Jamie grabbed her AirPods and phone out of her small black gym tote and turned on her playlist. The energetic sounds of *She's Kerosene* by The Interrupters blared out, transporting her to another place. There was little else to look at, so she settled for her imagination. She recaptured Tomas's well-defined arms wrapped around her waist … his fingers running up her legs and sliding with intent down her back. As the chorus kicked in, the images grew more intense, and Jamie felt the need to push herself harder. Quickly increasing the speed on the treadmill until she was sprinting, she excitedly pounded away. Out of the corner of her eye, she couldn't help but notice that the woman next to her was flagging. She'd obviously been on the treadmill a long time.

* * *

Kate felt a wave of irritation that, in a near-empty gym, the 'perfect body' had chosen the treadmill right next to her to flaunt herself. Noticing that she was sprinting like a frickin' gazelle provoked a bizarre competitive surge within Kate, which led her to increase her own workout level to match. Clearly a big mistake. Huge in fact. As it became apparent that the speed at which Kate's legs moved did not correlate with that of the treadmill.

"Bloody hell, you stupid cow," Kate cried out as she nearly fell off the machine, frantically pressing both the speed and the incline arrows down to avoid complete and utter embarrassment. Visions of falling flat on her face and being carried out like a total imbecile flooded her mind.

"Excuse me?" Jamie glared at the red-faced lady, who was now walking rather cautiously on the treadmill whilst gripping hard onto the handrails.

"No whoops. Sorry. Crikey. Not you, ME."

"You're a stupid cow?" Jamie asked, amused, taking out her AirPods.

"Well, yes. You're not." Kate eyed Jamie up and down. "You're not a cow at all. Far from it. Me, I'm a cow. I was talking to myself." Kate felt mortified that not only had she made a total fool of herself, but her internal mutterings were also cringingly audible, and it was just her luck that this woman was also English.

"You're a talking stupid cow?" Jamie couldn't help but giggle as she decreased the speed of her machine, although still significantly faster than the two miles per hour 'the talking cow' seemed to be doing.

Kate smiled in acknowledgment as a little ripple of jealousy enveloped her; she still felt irked that this woman felt it necessary to get on the treadmill right next to her and show off how athletic and gorgeous she was. It just made Kate feel even more like a little short, fat Oompa Loompa. On the one hand, she recognised it wasn't this woman's fault that she was a bloody goddess and only trying to be friendly, but still.

"I'm Jamie. What brings you here?"

Oh god, she wants to chat. Just be polite, Kate thought, not wanting to engage in conversation, but it was impossible to ignore a direct question. "What, to the gym? Trying to alter the configuration of my wobbly bits. How about you? You don't appear to have any."

"Not to the gym. I mean to Mallorca. But now that you mention it, I do have wobbly bits, sadly."

Kate screwed up her face in confusion as she once again cast her eyes over head-to-toe perfection. "Are you sick?" Clearly, the 'perfect body' had to be on crack.

"No. Why do you ask?"

"Duh."

"Huh?"

"Never mind." Kate realised it wasn't a subject she should pursue with a stranger, who might not appreciate her blunt sense of humour. The island was small and the expat community even smaller. Everyone knew someone who knew someone, and Kate didn't want to get a reputation for being unfriendly. "I'm Kate. I live here." Then, worried she'd been rude but still not wanting to engage, quickly added, "You'll have to excuse me, I need to increase my speed; you've inspired me. I'm practically walking backwards, but I can't talk and walk." Kate chuckled as she increased the speed again.

Jamie laughed. "You go girl; I totally get it. I've done enough for today, anyway. See you around." She jumped off the treadmill before wandering out of the gym.

Kate listened to one more song before peeking at the stopwatch and realised with glee that she'd done twenty-two whole minutes. She quickly pressed her favourite big red stop button on the godforsaken machine. Thankfully, she'd barely broken a sweat and didn't need to shower. This way she could just collect the girls and take them straight to the market in the port and kill a few more hours, leaving David to work in peace.

As she plodded down the stairs, her legs still a little wobbly from the exercise, she wondered if she could have lunch with the girls at Cappuccino; it was nearly lunchtime after all. Kate salivated as thoughts of the famous Club Sandwich flooded her mind.

Reaching the crèche, Kate paused for a moment outside the glass door. Peering in, she immediately saw Tali sitting by herself doing some colouring. But where was Emily? Then she spotted her sitting on the brightly coloured rug with another girl who seemed around the same age. They appeared deep in conversation. Emily looked up as if sensing her mum was near and broke into a big smile. Her smile literally melted Kate's heart. It was as if a thousand lights had ignited and illuminated the world. Kate waved as she opened the door, making a beeline for Tali.

Emily intercepted, "Mum, this is Madison. Can she come back and play?"

"Not today, darling. I thought we'd go to the Portals market and have some lunch at Cappuccino, but your friend can join us if her mum's okay with that?" Kate turned to Madison. "Where's your mum? Let's find her and ask." Kate liked to be the good cop in situations like this and was bargaining on Madison's mum not being overly keen about letting her daughter go off with complete strangers.

Madison's eyes veered past Kate. "She's over there." Pointing down the corridor behind Kate.

Kate turned around to see the woman that had been next to her on the treadmill. *Fuck.* She was sauntering towards the crèche, having showered, looking even more disgustingly sensational in her non-gym clothes and high-heeled boots. Kate couldn't help but feel perplexed; how could that body possibly have given birth?

As Jamie appeared at Kate's side and smiled, Kate blurted out, "Please tell me this is your little sister." Even though she already knew it wasn't.

Jamie loved that and wondered, for a moment, whether she could lie. Since Jamie had passed the dreaded 'three-o,' although technically she'd never celebrated a thirtieth birthday, many people assumed Madison was her sister, and she didn't bother to correct them. It was easier than explaining how she had a ten-year-old, although a teenage pregnancy wouldn't be totally out of the question. Yet, Madison had already outed her. This was exactly why she didn't like bringing her to the gym. She cursed again that it was a fiesta that day. "Thank you for that. No, she's definitely mine, but you've made my day," Jamie said, still smiling.

"Did you have her when you were twelve?" Kate felt the need to continue the compliment, although, to be fair, she was genuinely confused how someone who looked like Jamie could have a ten-year-old.

"It's a long story," Jamie replied.

Madison and Emily ran off to the lockers at the far end of the crèche to retrieve their belongings. "I think our girls want to play," Kate said hesitantly, "We're going to the market in Puerto Portals, and happy to take Madison with us?" she added just as Emily and Madison returned.

Jamie, momentarily lost for words, hesitated. Whilst it would be amazing to have a child-free afternoon, she didn't know this woman. She couldn't just let Madison go off with a total stranger. "Erm," Jamie stalled.

"We live near Portals!" Madison piped up, "Can't we go too, Mum? You said we could go to the market together, and it's the last day today. Pleeeease."

Jamie hesitated, scrambling to come up with a credible excuse, but the lack of sleep and litres of alcohol the night before had slowed down her normally quick reflexes and she came up with bloody *nada*. Madison continued to stare, beseeching her to agree.

"How about we both join you?" Jamie offered, vying for the good cop position too.

Both girls were now looking at their mothers like puppies waiting to be given treats.

"Great," said Kate, feeling anything but great. What she felt was trapped, but her desire not to be left as the bad cop overcame her desire not to socialise. Suddenly feeling extremely self-conscious that she was still in her gym clothes whilst Jamie looked like she was about to pose for a fashion shoot, she quickly added, "I need to go home first to get changed. We live in Santa Maria. Shall we meet at Cappuccino in say, an hour? That way I can leave Tali with Juanita, our neighbour, and you can tell me this long story."

"Sounds like a plan. Why don't you give me your number, and we'll meet you there? Cappuccino is perfect!" Jamie said, thinking about the Cosmopolitans there, which were to die for. Despite the night before pickling, she had just sweated it all out, so she was actually detoxed and ready for a retox! In fact, if she dropped her car off at home, she could walk down, and the afternoon might not end up being a disaster after all.

Jamie tapped Kate's contact details into her phone, resisting the urge to tap in 'Talking Cow' and called it so that Kate had her number too. There was an uncomfortable moment of silence that made Kate feel even more uneasy. What on earth would they have to talk about?

Tali, aware that her mum was in the vicinity, looked up and immediately ran straight into her arms, nearly knocking her over. Kate was relieved for the interruption. Kissing the top of Tali's head, she smiled at Jamie. "See you in an hour, then!"

COSMOPOLITANS & CLUB SANDWICHES

As Kate arrived at Cappuccino, she glanced anxiously around, hoping to spot Jamie. Emily was fidgeting, excited at the prospect of seeing Madison again. Despite first impressions, Jamie seemed rather nice, and Kate felt a little more enthusiastic than before at the prospect of meeting someone new. She loved the island; she loved the way of life and especially the weather, but she really missed her London friends and had struggled to make connections on the island. Sure, Jamie wasn't the sort of person she'd automatically veer towards, and she was quite certain that she wasn't Jamie's usual cup of tea, but there was something about the island. It attracted a certain type of individual—those happy to step outside of their comfort zones and try a whole new life—which often meant they were open to getting to know new people too. Of course, there was always the possibility that Jamie was just lonely. The island, with all its magnificence, also had the power to create a solitary existence, and Kate felt this increasingly so. Whilst she had David, was it really enough just to have one person in your life, especially when that person wasn't around as often anymore? Kate wasn't so sure. She was going to be open-minded; at least they spoke the same language.

Inside, the lighting was dim, and dotted around the room were small round glass tables with dark mahogany chairs. Kate wasn't sure why she was even bothering to look inside, as virtually everybody congregated outside. Even in winter, large wrought iron heaters would create a warm and cosy atmosphere, even on the bitterest of days.

The popular coffee shop was in a prime location on the corner of buzzing Puerto Portals, with its shiny yachts and designer boutiques, and was the perfect place to watch the world go by. The problem for Kate at this precise moment, aside from the increasing discomfort of her too-tight jeans, was that Jamie and Madison were nowhere to be seen. It didn't help that the outside seating was on two different levels, making them easy to miss. Kate decided it was better to sit and wait rather than loiter around. Sinking down with Emily into an oversized chocolate brown sofa on the upper level, she gasped for breath as the offending jeans she'd somehow squeezed into were now violently digging into her.

"What's the matter, Mum?" Emily could see her mother looking uncomfortable.

"I'm fat." It slipped out before she could censor her words, conscious that it was bad parenting to use the word 'fat' with one's offspring. She made a mental note never to let those words escape her lips again.

Emily, however, with the face of a ten-year-old and the wisdom of an eighty-year-old, responded, "It's not that you're fat Mum, it's just that your jeans are too small."

As Kate sat uncomfortably, she agreed that Emily was indeed correct; the jeans were too small, so with a sigh of resignation, she discreetly undid the top button and eased the zipper down. Suddenly, her phone beeped. It was a text from Jamie. Kate prayed she wasn't cancelling at this late stage, especially as Emily was so excited and she'd now made room for the much-desired sandwich.

Jamie:	Where are you?
Kate:	Here
Jamie:	Very helpful. Top level or bottom?
Kate:	Top

Jamie appeared moments later, still dressed impeccably in skinny jeans, a tight-fitting T-shirt, and a cream silk wrap casually thrown around her shoulders. Only the high-heeled boots had been replaced with a pair of nude ballerina pumps, yet even in flats she was still annoyingly tall. Madison followed a few steps behind, but upon seeing Emily, ran ahead and the girls embraced. Kate noted that there wasn't a single person in the café that didn't follow Jamie with their eyes as she gracefully floated over. Jamie leaned down to give her the customary two kisses, and Kate noticed that Jamie barely wore a scrap of makeup and still looked stunning. Life was so unfair.

"Well, this is weird." Kate smiled awkwardly.

"Yeah, a little unusual, but I'm pleased," Jamie said, taking the armchair next to Kate while placing her grey designer bag on the little side table. She almost didn't recognise Kate in her slim jeans, and the black T-shirt really accentuated her vivid blue eyes, even if it was a little on the baggy side. Jamie would love to do a makeover on her; she could see a mass of potential just screaming to be developed.

"Mum, do we have to eat here? Can't Madison and I just get a hot dog and look around the stalls?" Emily said with her hands on her hips.

Kate hesitated, not that she was worried about the girls' safety. There was minimal crime on the island and children were always running around, but she was more concerned about what she and Jamie would have to talk about.

"Pleeeease!" Madison had now joined in. Both girls looked at their mothers imploringly.

Before Kate had a chance to figure out a valid reason why they couldn't, Jamie took it upon herself to decide. "Sure, why not? Here, take twenty euros." Passing the note to Madison as the girls ran off before Kate could voice any interference.

Jamie pushed a few curls away from her eyes. "We ought to get some drinks in." She figured a drink would help break the ice. "They do the best Cosmopolitans!"

Kate felt a little anxious. She never had alcohol at lunchtime and certainly not when she was driving, but it would certainly be easier if they lubricated the moment. David would pick them up if she needed him to.

"Great, a Cosmopolitan sounds fantastic." Kate nodded in agreement, although she didn't have a clue what a Cosmopolitan was and just prayed it was vodka-based and not whisky.

Jamie looked around for a waiter; she was near gagging for her drink now. Clocking one of the cuter members of staff, Jamie raised an eyebrow to alert his attention. Apparently, raising one's eyebrow was all it took for him to come scampering over. Kate was amused. The waiter hadn't taken his eyes off Jamie since her arrival; if it had been her trying to get his attention, she would've had to do impersonations of 'the wave' at a football match.

"*Dos* Cosmopolitans, *por favor,*" Jamie said to the young waiter, who was now standing there like a little puppy dog, hoping for any scraps of attention. Jamie smiled, and his face lit up as if she'd lifted her top and shown him her tits.

"What do you fancy eating?" Kate quickly interrupted, as it appeared Jamie had forgotten to order any food. "I've got to have the Club Sandwich; been thinking about it ever since we arranged to meet, but you look more like the salad type."

Jamie looked blankly at Kate. She didn't want to correct her that she was, in fact, the 'eat very little and only when she absolutely had to' type. A surge of panic swept over her. She'd already had a yogurt that morning, and besides, the Cosmopolitan had enough calories to sustain her for the rest of the day. Hadn't Kate heard of a liquid lunch?

"Sure, why not. Are they big? Maybe we can share one?" Jamie figured Kate could do most of the eating, and no one would be any the wiser.

"Great, yes, they're huge; I can never manage one on my own," Kate said, lying so convincingly she almost believed herself.

"*Y uno* Club Sandwich *tambien,*" Jamie said to the waiter, who was still hovering, before returning her eyes to Kate to signal he could leave.

Kate tried to stop her face from registering disappointment. She didn't want to share, but they were huge, and the desire not to look like a greedy pig in front of this woman overcame her desire to consume a whole one on her own.

"So, what do you do?" Kate said, fiddling with the top of her jeans through her T-shirt.

"You mean for work?"

"Yes. I mean, if you don't mind me asking?" Kate wanted to kick herself. Clearly, this woman must have more exciting things to do than she did. What if she returned the question? *Ummm, I'm a bored housewife with nothing better to do than go to the gym and stuff my face whenever I'm not there.*

"I'm a model."

"Of course you are," Kate mumbled with a touch of unintended sarcasm. *What else would she be?* The words once again poured out of her mouth before she had time to vet them.

"Excuse me?" Jamie's already magnetic green eyes widened as she looked Kate square in the face.

Shit. Bugger. "Sorry. Er ... er ... I mean, that must be exciting." Kate wanted to kick herself, desperate to extricate herself from her comment, when, thankfully, the young waiter was back, saving her. He was bearing two large Martini glasses filled almost to the rim with a blood red, clearly dangerous liquid, garnished with a slice of lemon and a glacé cherry. Kate eyed up the cherry, relieved that she could eat that too, seeing as Jamie was intent on starving her.

Jamie lifted up her glass. "Cheers! To crazy new gym friends!"

Kate chinked her glass against Jamie's, taking a giant swig as the strong liquid burned down her throat. Jamie took this as a signal to party and joined in with a large swig of her own.

"So what brings you to Mallorca, and how long have you been here? Oh, and I want to know about Madison, and are you married?" The questions were flowing into Kate's mind and out of her mouth at the most alarming speed, helped in part by the Spanish-strength cocktail.

"Steady on. This isn't an interview, is it?" Jamie winked as she took off her wrap, the alcohol warming her body, and carefully placed it on top of her bag.

Kate noticed how her smile nearly took over her face. It was very genuine. And her teeth annoyingly white.

"Well, I came on a shoot last summer, and I fell in love with the place, so I stayed."

It was a familiar story for most expats. There was something extremely captivating about the island. It was hard to put your finger on it, but the feeling of peace and tranquillity was so completely removed from life in London. For Jamie, just looking at the sea gave her joy, and it was the reason she was paying double to rent her front-line apartment in Bendinat; the privilege of having sea views as a back garden didn't come cheap.

"What, just as simple as that? Just liked it, and hey presto, moved here with your daughter?" Kate seemed in awe of this freedom, but wasn't that precisely what she and David had done too? Upped and gone?

"Actually, daughter and mother," Jamie said as she drained the last drops from her glass. She figured in for a penny, in for a pound; she might as well give Kate the whole low-down of her domestic life. "Want another one?" Jamie was already looking for the waiter.

"Go on then, although this one's gone to my head. Bloody strong, isn't it? David will definitely have to pick us up now."

Jamie signalled across to the waiter for two more drinks just as the Club Sandwich arrived. Perfect timing. Kate was going to need food to help soak up all the alcohol. She looked longingly at the four neat triangles of white bread stuffed with chicken, bacon, tomatoes, and salad; she could easily down the lot. Her stomach gurgled in anticipation. Consumed with regret that she'd pretended not to be the gluttonous pig that she was, Kate picked up a triangle and nibbled at it like one of her frickin' rabbits. If she was only going to have half, she was damn well going to make it last.

Mother? Had Jamie said, Mother? Kate's head was already

buzzing. Should she really have another drink? But it was too late. A strange adrenalin-type rush surged through her body, and she wanted to pinch herself. There she was, in the middle of the day, enjoying proper adult conversation with a glamorous model. She could get used to this.

"So, you mentioned your mother. How come she lives with you?"

Jamie indulged Kate with her story of how she'd fallen pregnant in Tokyo but then left … without the father, all whilst masterfully pushing her sandwich around the plate. Kate screwed up her eyes and listened with intent as they started on their next round of cocktails.

"Let's just say there weren't many fashion jobs that called for a bump the size of Japan, so the best place to go was Mum's. She was alone and wanted to help me, so it worked for both of us. I could earn more money, and she was better at looking after kids." Jamie let out a sigh. It felt like a lifetime ago.

Shit. How terrible. Jamie didn't seem too bothered though, or at least she wasn't letting on. Kate also wondered how anyone could go back to modelling after having given birth. She'd looked like a pregnant hippo for a good year after both of her pregnancies.

"Couldn't have been easy. So where's her father now? Does he ever see Madison?" Kate couldn't imagine not having David by her side.

"Well Jake, that's his name, had been seeing Madison maybe once or twice a year, but eighteen months ago he got married, and now he wants to play happy families and see her more often. I guess it's good for Madison not to feel abandoned, but who knows with men. They just fuck things up, don't they?" The words came out before Jamie realised how it might sound to Kate. "I didn't mean it like that … just that you don't need to have a man around. I never had my dad around either, and I turned out alright."

Kate noticed Jamie had started to pick at the polish on her nails. "So, what about your mum? What's it like living with her?"

"It's fine. Well, mostly." Jamie wanted to say it was, in fact, rather difficult. Her strict but fiery Italian mother didn't half give her a hard time. "Come on, Kate, I've told you my story now I want to know about you. What's it like being married so long? I'm presuming you must've been married for a while if David's Emily's dad?"

"Oh god yes, he's definitely Emily's dad." Kate wondered if now would be a good time to say that David had been her only 'proper' boyfriend too. "We've been married for fifteen years but met in our teens." Kate tried to ignore the almost horrified expression that appeared on Jamie's face.

"Fifteen years? Oh my god."

"Bloody hell, Jamie, it's not that bad. Well …" How honest could she be with someone she'd just met? "Okay, sometimes it is 'oh my god' but for the most part, it's amazing."

Jamie's face was sceptical.

"David's very special. I feel safe with him. Perhaps yes, it might've been nice to have had a few more boyfriends before settling down, but it's no sacrifice. Aren't we all just looking for Mr Right in the end? I'm just lucky I found mine earlier than most."

There was no such thing as Mr Right, of that Jamie was certain. The thought of only ever having one man was unimaginable. It was like a box of chocolates. Why would anyone want to just sample one? "I'm sorry, it's just that I have a very brief attention span when it comes to men. Jake, my ex, was the longest relationship I've ever had, but after him I reckon my longest has been, hmmmm … well, in all honesty, I reckon only a couple of weeks. In fact, I don't even call them relationships, just shag buddies. Actually, forget the buddies; they're just shags." Jamie creased up at the shocked expression now materialising on Kate's face.

"Oh my god," Kate said in jest as Jamie went to mock hit her.

Feeling light-headed and enjoying how easy it was to share with Kate, Jamie suddenly blurted out, "I slept with my spinning instructor last night."

"Oh my god!" Kate's jaw hit the table as Jamie laughed out loud. "Which instructor?" They'd only just met, but this was more fun than she'd had in ages, and Jamie was open and honest and nothing like she'd imagined.

"Tomás. You know, the super cute one."

"Can't say I do. I've never tried spinning. Can barely figure out the treadmill, as you know. But I'll take your word for it." Kate giggled; although the thought of exercise reminded her of food, and she'd already polished off her share of the sandwich.

"Maybe you can come with me one day!" Jamie winked, but Kate didn't look enthusiastic.

"David bought a rabbit," Kate said the first thing that came into her mind, not wanting to pry too much about Tomás, or be lured into going to a spinning class; she could just imagine herself falling off the bike.

"Woah, that's cool."

"Actually, two; my favourite one's called Floppy."

"Floppy? That's a terrible name for a rabbit. I've got a rabbit. It's called Stallion. Why on earth would you call your vibrator Floppy, and why do you need two?"

Kate looked at Jamie with open eyes, her hand hitting her forehead in despair. "Not a friggin' vibrator, a real rabbit. A pet."

Jamie had just taken a sip of her Cosmopolitan as it came spurting out of her mouth when she realised the misunderstanding. Kate burst out laughing too and the ice was officially broken.

"Another round? Shall we?" Jamie managed to squeeze out, once she'd wiped the tears from her eyes. Kate was hysterical; this was exactly what she needed.

"Why the bloody hell not. To be honest, I'd never had a Cosmopolitan before, I just didn't want you to think I don't get out too much. Actually, I don't. Not anymore. I haven't really made any proper friends here. The thing is, even if you do find someone that you connect with, eventually they leave."

"I know what you mean. Most people I've met are from my industry, so they're pretty transient. The thing is there's not much work on the island, so I get why people have to leave."

"Huh, bloody typical. That's what I mean; you meet someone, and then they bugger off," Kate said in mock indignation.

"Well, I haven't 'buggered off' yet, have I? And besides, I'm thrilled to introduce you to new things, especially if they're vodka-based. And dah-link"—Jamie put on her best fashionista voice—"you have so much to learn."

LONDON CALLING

"Nonna? Who's Mum on the phone to? She's been on it forever, and I want to call Isabella." Madison burst into the open-plan living room upon returning from school, throwing her stuffed rucksack to the ground, without a second thought. Maria scurried across to pick up the bag, which had been heavily customised by Madison herself, with numerous marker pen scribbles and further embellished by unidentifiable dangly objects. Who needed a maid, or manners, when you had a grandmother?

"*Bambolina,* Mamma talk to agent in London."

"Why?" Madison's already prominent eyebrows raised in alarm as she glanced across at her mother, who was pacing back and forth on their large balcony. Despite the two comfy rattan chairs, made even more inviting by plump ecru cushions, Jamie couldn't relax enough to sit down.

"I think she has job for her." Maria didn't want to be the one to break the news, but someone had to. The phone had been glued to Jamie's ear all day. Her agent was offering her a lucrative job back in London, and despite it not being as high-profile as she was used to, Jamie was grateful for the work. Her career had mainly been in high fashion: runway shows and editorials. But as she got older, those types of bookings had become thin on the ground. This job was for a car client. She would be filming a couple of TV commercials, along with some stills for their campaign. Commercial work, whilst not regarded as prestigious, paid rather well. The problem was that she'd be away from them for two whole weeks.

"So she's leaving us again?" Madison rolled her eyes as she looked over at her mother. Jamie's blue floral print mini dress swirled and twirled around her long, lean legs every time she turned.

"*Bambolina,* you know what it's like." Maria could sense the impending fallout. Any time now.

"London? Paris? Australia!"

"Mamma have to work. She here all winter but no much work. Normal for her to travel. *Figurati!* We have fun!" Maria reached out to hug Madison, but her granddaughter kept moving away. She didn't want reassurance; she wanted her mother. Every moment with Jamie, however stolen, was priceless. As there had been less work on the island, Madison had become used to having her mother around more often, and she liked it.

"Think of all cakes we make without get into trouble," Maria immediately offered, more jubilantly than she felt. Her English often got worse when a volcanic eruption was imminent. Whilst Madison was used to her mother being 'busy,' these last few months, she'd at least been in the same country.

"But it's not fair. Why does she have to go? I don't want her to go." Madison was inching closer and closer in the balcony's direction. Maria needed to think quickly.

"You wanna walk to beach to get ice cream? Nice place on corner do best gelato outside of *Firenze*." But her efforts were in vain. Madison's attention, now fully directed at her mother, would not be lured by images of cake, or ice cream, or even the beach. She wasn't even listening. Instead, she made a beeline for the balcony.

Horror swept over Jamie's face as she realised Madison was charging her way. She hated 'child' protests at the best of times and, whilst speaking to a top London agent, they were absolutely unacceptable. Frantically, she began waving her arms in an attempt to shoo her away.

"MUM, why do you have to go? Say you're not going. Pleeeease."

"Tabitha, I have to go. I'll call you tomorrow, but I'm on. Just email me the details. Bye." Jamie hurriedly made her exit. She knew drama was about to unfold, and she didn't need the snooty, child-free Tabitha to be privy to that particular outburst.

"Mum, are you going to London?" Madison's hands were now firmly on her hips; a stance she often took when she was angry. Hiding one's emotions was not practised in this household.

Jamie paused, her blood pressure now rising to tropical levels. She recalled someone once telling her, 'Having kids requires a totally different kind of love.' They weren't wrong.

"Yes I am. I have to work. It's only two weeks. You won't even notice that I'm gone." Jamie motioned towards the stairs. If she could just make it to her room.

Madison moved forward faster than Jamie could retreat, screeching, "But it's not fair. I don't want you to go. Tell them your daughter needs you. How is Nonna going to take me to my drama lessons? You know she can't drive." Appearing older than her ten years, Madison went to block the stairs, standing defiantly in her school uniform, which, like her rucksack, had also been altered, certainly shortened. Although Jamie was quite a few inches taller than her daughter—five foot ten in her bare feet—Madison held her gaze, as if by sheer will alone she might be able to change her mother's mind.

The drama lessons have paid off well, Jamie thought sarcastically. Whilst she recognised it wouldn't be easy for her mother to run around after Madison, she couldn't afford an au pair either. Their safety net was already at a dangerously low level. There were no other options. Therefore, no room for discussion.

"Madison, I have to go. That's all there is to it. Please don't wind me up about something I can't help."

"But Muuuuuuum, I don't want you to go. Nonna, tell her she can't," she said as her voice rose in panic.

Jamie admired her daughter's strong will. She knew it would hold her in good stead for the future, but a little more compliance at home wouldn't go amiss. The whining reached a glass shattering pitch, and Jamie needed to break free. What did they expect her to do? Turn it down? Was Maria going to work and support them all? At sixty-six and only ever having done small menial jobs, she figured probably not. And besides, there was a part of Jamie that was also quite excited—not that she'd ever verbalise it out loud. Two weeks of guilt-free pleasures. Two weeks of freedom and staying out until she wanted, with zero complaints from mother or daughter. The more she thought about it, the more the proposition became increasingly attractive. Madison would calm down.

But Madison did not calm down. Instead, Madison stomped around the bottom of the stairs in protest. Despite her slight frame, she'd easily put stampeding buffalo to shame.

"That's enough, Maddy. Enough. I said I have to work, and that's it. I'm going up to my room and I don't want to hear another peep out of you, understood?"

Feeling almost justified in her anger, with Madison's protests somehow giving her a licence to escape, Jamie vanished into the realms of her domain. Pulse racing, she walked over to her walk-in wardrobe and fished out the Dior box. Hidden beneath layers of white tissue was a Grey Goose miniature, inspired by her not-so-liquid lunch with Kate. Jamie had envisioned making a Cosmo at home but in absence of all the ingredients—and any semblance of calm—she took one look at the bottle and decided it was better than nothing. Kneeling down, she opened the lid, and swigged a large gulp directly from the tiny decanter. *Ugh, not exactly a Cosmo*, but she needed something to take the edge off. It was basically survival tonic and essential to her sanity.

As she sat there on the floor of her wardrobe, Jamie became mesmerised by just how many clothes she owned. It was like a giant dressing-up box, with every outfit possessing the ability to magically transform her into a different character. She ran her fingers along the bottom of the dresses: silk, satin, lace; every little girl's dream wardrobe, and most big girl's too. She spied a black lace basque. A gorgeous vintage piece she'd begged a stylist for after a shoot a couple of years back. Sure, she'd had to pay her a pretty penny for it, but Jamie smiled wickedly as she recalled that it was worth every last one of them. It had been Friday the thirteenth, and she'd been attending a Moulin Rouge themed party. The man in question—the man she'd had her eye on for quite some time, hadn't stood a chance. Not that he'd known it. Jamie was the hunter but always pretended to be the prey. It was formulaic. Men, in her experience, were easy game, and she knew just how to play them. Everyone else's unlucky day had become her signature fun one. Looking back at the brimming closet, Jamie contemplated how easy it might be to sell a few items of clothing; there were literally thousands and thousands of beautiful euros hanging all around her. The basque, however, could never be listed.

Walking away from the closet, Jamie turned on her CD player, which was set to 'shuffle.' *Shot at the Night* by The Killers came on. Jamie sighed. She loved that song. And goodness knows she needed a lifeline right now. She wasn't sure Tabitha's offer was really it, but at least it was something. Finally reclining on her daybed, her absolute favourite spot in the house, Jamie noticed the sea was totally flat, almost glass-like, and the most exquisite shade of aquamarine. She took a deep breath. Yes, she could be strong. Strong enough for them all. She had to be. Suddenly, Madison's face came into her mind. Damn it, she had been harsh. Should she go down and try to diffuse the situation? But wait, wouldn't that only encourage Madison to protest every time something didn't go her way? Perhaps she could offer to buy her something in London? Bring her back a new iPad perhaps? That would work. Teach Madison that luxuries like iPads required money and the more she worked, the more lovely surprises she could have. Hell, it was tough being a parent. Yes, she'd done the right thing. Even Maria hadn't commented, and Maria always commented.

Thinking about parenting reminded Jamie of Kate. *Shit.* They'd arranged a lunch for the following week, and now she wouldn't be able to make it. She ought to call as soon as possible and reschedule. Turning the volume down on The Killers, she reached for her phone. She needed to get everything in order if she was leaving. She speed-dialled Kate's number.

"Hello?" Kate sounded flustered.

"Hey, Kate. It's Jamie."

"Oh, hey. Sorry, I was juggling kids and the rabbits. Didn't see who was calling. How are you?" Kate sounded distracted, but Jamie could almost hear her smiling through the line.

"Well, stressed, actually. Just had a major row with Madison."

Although thoughts of luscious men and dirty deeds had ebbed much of it away.

"Oh dear, why?" Kate sounded genuinely concerned.

"Had my agent from London on the phone. I have a shoot in London next week. Well, a two-week shoot to be exact and Madison isn't happy about it."

"Poor thing. I bet she isn't. Great news about the job though."

"Oh goodness, it really is. And to be honest, I'm beyond excited about getting away too. I could certainly do with a few fun nights out, a little shopping, or should I say 'window' shopping? I do miss the Kings Road." The thought of a naughty little purchase made Jamie smile, even if it had to be a teeny-weeny purchase this time.

"God yeah. I really miss shopping in London. Especially Marks and Spencer." Just as the words slipped out of Kate's mouth, Jamie laughed out loud, thinking she must be joking.

"Don't you knock my Marks & Spencer, missy," Kate was quick to retort in jest. So what if she didn't shop at Harvey Nicks, not even Mussolini would stop her little Marks & Spencer's guilty pleasure.

"Okay hun, you can have your Marks & Spencer, but I'm heading straight to Agent Provocateur. Ooh, I'm so excited. But listen, that's why I'm calling. I won't be able to make our lunch date." The silence on the other end of the phone lingered.

"That's a shame," Kate eventually said with a sigh. Then in a moment of uncharacteristic impulsiveness, her brain almost audibly ticking over, she burst out, "What about tonight then?" Remembering that David was taking the girls to the tennis club for supper, Kate realised she had a rare evening to herself. It was either that or spend it with the bunnies, and she knew which option she preferred.

"Tonight?" Why hadn't Jamie thought of it before? It was her lucky day. A genuine get-out clause from the family plus the opportunity to sip guilt-free cocktails with her Marks-and-Spencer-clad new buddy.

"Yeah, why not? I just need five minutes to get dressed and about half an hour to get there." Kate was on a roll. She liked this new version of herself.

"Wow, you surprise me, Kate. Can't say I know many women that can be ready in five minutes. But absolutely. I'll meet you at the beach bar at Portals, beside the little church."

"Say around seven?"

"See you there." Jamie was so elated when she put down the phone that she quickly slipped on the sexy basque before getting dressed. Turning on her large ring light, she decided to film a little reel for her Instagram followers, and who knows, maybe she could shift some of her pieces for more money. Dancing around her bedroom as she addressed her adoring fans, Jamie practised her own version of Burlesque, whilst imagining a potentially delicious audience. There was a god.

TITS N' NITS

Kate shifted her weight from one foot to the other, waiting for the kettle to boil. Gazing out the kitchen window, she observed her two girls out in the distance, towards the far end of the garden. They scrambled through the hedge, no doubt heading back towards their camp site. Kate smiled as she revelled in the freedom and simplicity of their island lifestyle. It would be hours before the girls made another appearance, undoubtedly when their stomachs required refuelling. She was still thinking about how spontaneous she was about asking Jamie to go for cocktails the other night. Maybe she liked this version of herself? Maybe Jamie could be a good influence; besides, it felt good to have some carefree hours away from the house.

Kate glanced towards the two large pine trees near the swimming pool. It was no surprise that David was in his customary Sunday position—swinging casually on the double Aztec-printed hammock. Sunday was Kate's least favourite day. She often felt at a loss. It was true David wasn't around much during the week, but she just wished they could do more together on the weekend. Instead, he appeared to spend the vast majority of the day on the hammock. And why was it necessary to read several articles all on the same subject? He was obsessed with the war and had downloaded several newspaper apps. It wasn't as if the news differed in each one. Perhaps she was being unreasonable, she knew it wasn't his job to entertain her.

Kettle boiled, Kate made tea and slurped it with pleasure. It was already her third cup that day. She loved tea but needed to stop drinking so much and start doing something more constructive with her time. But what? She could, of course, go to the gym, but she'd already been twice that week. Besides, she was on her period and her breasts appeared to have grown to even greater proportions, if that were possible.

Gazing down at her tits, Kate breathed an enormous sigh. They were huge, and it wasn't just because she had her period; they seemed to be growing. What was even more exasperating was that the right one was definitely growing at a faster pace than the left. She was practically walking lopsided. Everybody else she knew seemed to have wonderful little happy upright tits, whilst hers … well, she didn't have any recollection of there ever being anything remotely upright about her breasts. They were, from the moment that they sprouted—almost overnight at thirteen—just huge, big, droopy things, pointing south. And then breastfeeding two babies had done little to enhance their general appearance.

Still gazing out of the window, Kate stopped sipping her tea when she saw her little one, Tali, racing towards the house. Her budding naturalist, now naked other than her *Minions* knickers, was bolting towards her, faster than normal.

"Mamá, I have *animales*."

Kate felt confused. What animals? What was Tali on about? She prayed they hadn't captured some revolting reptile or insect, or worse still, found some stray pet; they had enough pets with the rabbits. Tali must be referring to the rabbits. Kate grinned. How sweet. Squatting down so she was at eye level with Tali, she planted a kiss on her forehead, lingering for just a moment as she inhaled her daughter's unique smell. Pure nectar.

"Ah, darling, that's so lovely, yes you do have two little bunnies. Floppy and Fluffy. Do you love your little bunny wunnies?"

"No, *aqui*." Tali seemed nonplussed whilst pointing and then itching her head. "Emily say *yo tengo animales* in me hair."

As if in slow motion, the penny dropped. *Fuck. Fuuuuck.*

"Come here and let me check." Kate leaned over to survey Tali's hair. It was difficult to tell whether there were any nits, as there appeared to be several other alien objects residing in there: leaves, twigs, and was that a piece of cheese? Tali continued her itching, and with a groan, Kate speculated that her initial assessment was accurate. It was therefore reasonable to presume that Emily may also be afflicted. Which meant, horror of all horrors, she might have them too. Pushing open the solid oak door that led from the kitchen to the back garden in order to retrieve Emily, she spotted her eldest sauntering towards her, also itching her head. Kate cursed herself for wishing for something to do just moments earlier. If there were indeed little blood-sucking creatures in her children's hair, she'd hunt them out and destroy them. But as their hair was so long, it could take hours.

Kate's brain shifted into gear as she considered the job at hand. The girls' hair was less of a problem, but if she also had them, who on earth would spend hours picking them out for her? She couldn't do it herself and doubted David would have either the inclination or the patience. She'd better hope she hadn't already contracted them and would focus on prevention instead.

Kate remembered hearing that a mixture of lemon juice, vinegar and olive oil was a good deterrent and decided the answer was to douse herself with the concoction and pray it was more than just an old wives' tale. So, before starting on her children, she poured the mixture all over her hair and, upon feeling it drip down her back, ingeniously wrapped it all in cellophane. She stunk to high heaven, and she was well aware, it wasn't a good look.

* * *

Emily and Tali were finally—hopefully—nit-free and headed back to their camp to resume play. Kate observed that true to form, David had not moved from the hammock during all the commotion. Enough was enough. She needed some adult stimulation after singing a thousand renditions of 'ten green bottles sitting on the wall,' adapted to, 'one hundred naughty nits sitting in Tali and Emily's hair.'

As Kate sauntered towards David, she vowed not to snap, despite a burning desire to do precisely that. David deserved some time out. After all, he'd just secured the commission to design and refurbish an old building in Palma and had hardly stepped foot out of his office since. Yes, David needed his downtime and so she would bite her tongue. Approaching him quietly, Kate stood beside him, waiting for him to notice her hovering like an alien spaceship, but even the chip shop aroma failed to stir him. Moments later, the wiggling of his nose suggested he had at the very least smelt her presence. Eventually tearing his eyes away from his phone. "You stink." David burst into laughter as he registered his wife's new look.

"You think, huh?"

"Really bad, actually. I suppose there's a good reason you've got your hair wrapped in cellophane?"

"Nits." Monosyllabic responses may help accentuate her terrible plight.

"You've got nits?"

"Well, no, but the girls did. I've just spent the last two hours delousing them. You didn't miss me then?" Kate, unable to contain herself despite her good intentions.

"And the cellophane is … to intercept them jumping into your hair?"

"No, the cellophane is to stop the vinegar and olive oil dripping down my back."

David, whilst perplexed, decided not to pursue the topic and turned his attention once again to his phone. Kate lingered for a fraction longer. Realising that she wasn't going to engage him in any sort of conversation before he had fully read the news, gave up. As she turned to make her way back to the house, he called out, "New tits or a new car?"

"Excuse me?" His question momentarily startled Kate. How on earth had he known that she was having a bad boob day? The man was surely psychic.

"New tits or a new car?" David was being serious.

"Are you speaking to me? Are you actually talking to me, and on a Sunday?" She walked back to stand in front of him.

"Don't be funny Kate, I'm being serious."

"What on earth made you ask that? And what do you mean?"

"If you had to choose between getting a new pair of tits or a new car, which would you go for?"

"Is this another one of your hypothetical questions?"

"No really, I'm being serious. You're constantly going on about how you detest your tits and you're always going on about how much you hate your car, so I'm just wondering, if you had the choice, which one would you pick?"

Totally ignoring the question, Kate wondered if that was all she'd become—some saggy-boobed, moaning excuse of a woman with a cellophane-clad head. How on earth could he still fancy her? As images of her being single and forty, with two children and droopy tits, sped through her head. "Not sure. Why are you asking?"

David held his hand out to her and moved up, making room for her to join him. Kate sat down next to him, plonking her feet in his lap. Without even having to ask, he started to give her a foot massage, and she melted. She turned her attention to the report he was reading on his phone. "Low body image results in low female libido."

Kate looked at him, eyes opening wide; he must have exhausted the war articles then and went in search of his next favourite subject. On some level, it was rather comical; she should've realised his question would ultimately refer back to sex. Did that man have anything else going on in his head?

"New tits or new car?" David looked at Kate quizzically, searching for any signs that might indicate a preference.

"Sorry, I was miles away. I honestly think it'll take more than a new pair of tits to get my libido activated."

"You should read the article. It's very interesting," David enthused, offering her his phone.

She swiped his hand away. "I'm sure it is, but I don't think it's my tits which are stopping us from having the sort of sex that you want. I think it's because we've been with each other for eternity and have two kids," Kate said as part of her counter defence. "And why is it all my fault, anyway? Perhaps you could take some responsibility as well?"

"Me? You think it's my fault?" David now on the defensive.

Kate knew she was being oversensitive, but she didn't want to discuss it. David was still playing with her feet and she didn't want that to stop. It felt so good. She closed her eyes, turning her face up to the sun, feeling the warmth wash over her like warm water. The rhythmic swaying of the hammock almost lulled her to sleep.

"I'm thinking about it," she murmured, her eyes still shut, to suspend the moment and encourage more foot rubbing. David turned back to the article, whilst continuing his soft stroking. Who said men couldn't multi-task?

The heavenly combination swaying in the hammock whilst having her feet stroked was Kate's definition of an orgasm. Who needed sex when you could have 'strokey' in the sunshine? She felt like purring. Her thoughts drifted. She cast her mind back to the previous Tuesday again, where she'd met Jamie by the beach. Jamie was excited about the prospect of her trip to London, and as they sat watching the sunset, she regaled Kate with stories of sexual conquests, of which there seemed many.

Kate had sat mesmerised; fascinated by Jamie's love of sex. How she ached for it, sought it out even. Perhaps sex and Kate had just gotten off on the wrong foot? If sex was so bloody amazing, then surely, with a little effort, Kate could discover its pleasures as well? Obviously, the sort of sex Jamie talked about was different, non-married sex. But, did that mean if Kate were to experience this, she'd have to experience it without David? The thought of not being with him filled her with horror; she'd rather live her entire life without Jamie-sex than be without David.

"David, I'm sorry. I know I'm crap at the moment. It's just that I'm so tired, and we've been over this. Honestly, even if I had upright breasts, I doubt you'd get any more out of me. Anyway, let's not talk about our sex life or lack of it for a minute and go back to the tits versus car debate.

Kate thought about the Volvo she'd had for many years; it was nothing short of a miracle that it was still functioning. They'd brought it over from the UK, so it really had done some mileage … but then again, so had her tits!

David seemed aware that Kate was trying to process between the two things she so desperately wanted to change. Car? Tits? Car? Tits?

"I'm thinking about it. New tits would be nice. New tits would be amazing. New tits and new tummy would be the best," Kate finally announced.

"Go on then, do it." David smiled cheekily, dimples forming on his clean-shaven face.

"Do what?" Kate was lost.

"Check it out. The new tits and the new tummy."

"Are you being serious?"

"Absolutely, go on. Why don't you investigate it and see what's involved? You've been moaning about how much you hate your body for as long as I've known you, so why not change it? And despite what you think, I reckon it'll definitely increase your sex drive."

Kate thought he was being funny until she looked at his earnest face and then sighed with pleasure. *Hmmmm, plastic surgery. New tummy and new tits.* Why the hell not? No harm in finding out what's involved; besides, the Volvo was sure to die soon and then he'd have to buy her a new car as well.

Kate slid off the hammock and ambled back to the house. She'd message Jamie; if anyone knew about looking good, it was her. In her profession, she must know loads of people who've had work done. Yes, Jamie would know the names of some good surgeons. Yippee! Kate finally had something proper to do with her time that didn't involve picking out live animals from her children's hair.

IN THE DRIVING SEAT
London, England

Jamie had her own dressing room for the day. She was always amused to see the 'STAR' sign on the door. It rarely happened in fashion unless you were one of the 'Supers,' but the commercial world of modelling was actually far kinder to its talent. They'd even sent a car for her at the crack of dawn, so she didn't have to worry about getting to Elstree Studios that early. Perhaps she'd been wrong to turn her nose up at this side of the industry for all those years.

Beth, her designated assistant, was ready to tend to her every need. She couldn't have been more than twenty-two, an intern for sure, hoping to work her way up the industry ladder. Beth was tiny in every way possible. Even her face was so petite that her black-rimmed glasses dwarfed her features except for her eyes, now magnified to resemble a street artist's caricature of herself.

"Would you like a coffee?" Beth lingered by the door. Jamie noticed she was wearing white Converse sneakers and smiled, reminded of Madison.

"I'm okay for now, thanks." Jamie looked no older than Beth at that moment, standing bare-faced, her damp hair pulled back into a loose ponytail, all bony shoulders and collarbones poking out beneath her white cotton vest top, worn over blue jeans.

"Just let me know. I'll be right outside. There's food too, if you want to eat. I heard the catering company they're using today is excellent." Beth's enthusiasm was wasted on Jamie. She obviously didn't realise that Jamie didn't eat. There was a joke in the industry that these huge spreads would be put on, but they may as well come with a sign saying, 'Don't feed the models.'

Jamie took a seat on the slightly shabby green fabric sofa, the only real colour in a very grey room. Laurence Llewelyn-Bowen clearly hadn't been let loose here. Nevertheless, she had the room all to herself and grabbed a copy of the latest Condé Nast Traveller from the pile of glossies on the table, settling into what would inevitably be a very long day. Kicking off her chunky black biker boots and curling her legs up on the sofa, Jamie began flicking through the pages. She found herself drawn to a particular article on Italy's free wine fountain and smiled to herself. Italy had always been one of her favourite places, not least because it was her mother's home country, and of course Milan often called for work. But whether it was the Amalfi Coast, Tuscany, Lake Como or Venice, it was all magical and easily would have been her second choice if they hadn't moved to Spain.

Having spent the entire winter vegetating in Mallorca, Jamie was considerably larger than usual. A full UK size eight now. These days, girls were coming in at size zero—US sizing perhaps—but even so, only a UK size four. Madison was bigger than that! Yes, some of them were also dying, but still, 'it's fashun, dah-link.' Tabitha had measured her with disdain at the agency as soon as she'd landed in London. Jamie hated those days. The days when the tape measure came out, and on occasion, the scales too, determining her worth. Whilst Jamie recognised that she was far from fat in the real world, she didn't work there. Her world was filled with models whose statistics made up just one percent of the population. Half an inch in the wrong direction, and she'd be destined for the reject pile.

Finishing the magazine, Jamie felt bored and turned to her phone; it might as well have been an extension of her body; when she wasn't working, or with some tasty specimen, she was usually glued to it. *Shit. Kate!* It had been nearly a week since their wonderful sunset meeting in Portals and she suddenly felt bad that she hadn't been in contact since. Kate had been overjoyed to have finally found someone living permanently on the island, which was now making Jamie uneasy. There was no way around it. She'd have to come clean and tell Kate she was leaving. She just couldn't afford to live there without work any longer. She also needed to respond to Kate's enquiry about plastic surgeons; Malcolm Barnes was the best by far. Frantically typing away on her phone, Jamie composed the apologetic email and prayed Kate wouldn't be too upset that she was buggering off.

Just as she pressed send, she noticed Beth had entered sheepishly. "Sorry, sorry, I just wanted to let you know Hair and Makeup will be here in thirty mins. You still have time for a quick snack before they come. Want me to grab you something?" Bless her, she really didn't get it.

"Don't worry Beth. I'll grab something later," Jamie lied as she smiled back. She could almost feel the disappointment that was now on its way through cyberspace to Kate. She wondered if Kate would understand or just add her to the pile of other almost-friends who'd also left the island. She hoped not.

Popping her head out the door, Jamie called out to Beth, "Actually, I might grab something, but I don't mind getting it myself. Need to stretch my legs. Where did you say catering was set up?"

"Just follow the corridor along until you see an exit door to the right. Shall I take you?" Beth spurred into action, only too happy to be of use.

"No no, it's fine. I've been here before; I can find it. Thanks Beth." Jamie was happy to wander unsupervised, especially as she had no intention of actually eating.

Walking around the huge building through long, cold, echoing corridors, Jamie noticed there were teams of crew milling around, albeit very quietly. Noise had to be at an absolute minimum during filming. She scanned the crowd in seconds, just in case there happened to be a cutie in her midst.

Suddenly, out of a puff of smoke. "Jamie!"

Jamie turned around. *Shit.* Was she due back already? But she'd only just left and Beth did say thirty minutes.

"Oh my god, hey gorgeous," Jamie whispered back more quietly, aware of any noise being amplified tenfold. It was India; one of Jamie's closest model friends, appearing in a haze of Marlboro Gold. India liked to do things old-school, inspired by Hollywood starlets of times gone by, albeit in her own grungier, wilder version. India was probably the closest thing Jamie had to a 'best' friend in London, although their friendship rarely extended beyond the party scene. Unless it involved India crashing at Jamie's after a night out, which happened rather frequently.

"Oh gosh sorry, babe, I didn't see you. What are you doing here? Ooh, love the new hair." Jamie air-kissed India on each cheek, whilst trying to keep her voice as low as possible.

"Yeah, just had it done. Luke did it for me," enthused India, pushing her short blonde hair behind her right ear for the third time already. Her new 'edgy' crop—which was supposed to look like she'd cut it herself and the epitome of cool—was actually courtesy of Luke Hersheson, one of London's hottest celebrity Hair Stylists, and cost a whopping three hundred and ninety-five pounds. Clearly it was more irritating than edgy as the overly long fringe designed to be swept to one side kept tumbling over her feline eyes, weighed down today by lashings of thick black mascara.

"Shooting an ad for Vivienne Westwood," India drawled as she sucked the last traces of tobacco from her cigarette. Dark shadows had taken up residence under her equally grey eyes. Her late night escapades were showing. Judging by her 'cold,' she'd probably been on the coke too. But neither seemed to affect her adversely. India worked non-stop. In fact, clients couldn't get enough of her revived heroin chic-come-Lolita looks. But she was still just twenty-six, and in real years.

"What are you shooting?" India was dressed in the sexiest bustier top, over a lace-up corset mini skirt, showing off pencil thin legs.

"An ad for Volvo haha!" Jamie rolled her eyes as she pulled India further down the hall. She didn't want to risk upsetting the people paying her bills by making too much noise.

"Lovely," India said with more than a touch of sarcasm. "Any idea what time you wrap tonight? We could meet later for a little drinky poo? Been ages, we're long overdue." India's eyes suddenly lit up at the prospect, as she seemed to find a million more reasons why it was the best idea ever. India was infectious. Her lust for partying was almost as high as her lust for men. This was the common denominator between them. Man magnets the pair of them. One was dangerous, but two, dynamite. It was just what Jamie needed.

"Fabulous idea. We're shooting over a few days, so it shouldn't be too late. I'll text you when I'm done." Jamie was already figuring out which sensational outfit to wear.

"Great. Laters dolly." India had visibly given up on her fringe, which was now totally obscuring her fine features. She had more exciting things to worry about.

"Purrfect." Jamie smiled.

Rushing back to her dressing room, Jamie was relieved to have company that evening. Tabitha had offered to let her stay at one of the model apartments, but she felt a little too old for that and had checked into a hotel instead. Model apartments were usually reserved for younger, newer faces, often 'in town' from abroad. She'd been there and done that a million times, and besides, London was her city, even if she had left it for a Mediterranean island.

Entering the room, Jamie was greeted by a frenzy of preparation. The hair and makeup team were already setting up their products on the long counter, which was going to be her dressing table for the day. Matty, the hair stylist, announced himself with a wave in a magical puff of hairspray. He had short hair with a Cruella streak, but instead of white, it was purple. Very tall, very thin, his face perfectly made up with killer cheekbones highlighted to perfection, he could easily be a model.

"And I'm Poppy. I'll be doing your makeup today, darling." Poppy was laying out a battalion of products along the counter. It always amazed Jamie just how many products needed to be used, even to look natural. That 'barely there' look was anything but. Studio lights have a habit of washing you out. Jamie found it curious how so many makeup artists barely wore makeup themselves, and Poppy was no exception, although her naturally ruddy cheeks didn't need any added colour.

* * *

"Ahhh, divine." Matty was practically dancing as he admired his handiwork. Jamie examined her reflection in the mirror lit up by a hundred dazzling bulbs. Her hair looked, well, it kind of looked how it always looked, except without the frizz. A frizz-free twist on Mother Nature. Poppy was still pushing her way in as she swept what felt like five different brushes over Jamie's face. Three hours had passed and she'd only stepped onto set once to check the lighting. Still, it was only nine in the morning. Jamie heard her phone beep. Reaching into her deep leather bag, she fished out her phone. It was Kate. Jamie was excited to have a reply so soon. *Please don't be mad, please don't be mad.*

To:	fallen-angel@scoopmail.com
From:	katebuchanan@scoopmail.com
Subject:	Buggering off

Oh Jamie, what can I say? Yes, of course I'm totally gutted. But I understand. I know you've been feeling stressed about the lack of work in Mallorca and this is great news that you've got work lined up for you in London. We will make it work. We have to. You've been like a little light in my otherwise boring life. Now for being practical ... let me come and help you pack up. I'll bring supplies, rubber gloves and marker pens. Haha. I am the queen of packing. How about next Thursday? Let me know. And Jamie, I know you're going to miss the island and meeeeeeee but this is the right thing for you.

Huge hugs. Kate.

P.S. Thanks for the plastic surgeon's contact. I am going to look into it, but between you and me, I'm not sure I can go through with it. Surgery? Ufff I don't know. I'm processing it!

Jamie let out a big sigh. Maybe it was all going to work out after all.

* * *

Today's look was a posh take on plaid. Jamie amassed all the enthusiasm she could to pretend it was just fabulous as she tried on outfit after outfit. There was no changing room in today's designated 'wardrobe,' sometimes there was barely a towel. It was customary to strip down to your G-string in front of total strangers. No room for modesty, or cellulite in this business. Kendall and Jenna, the stylists, worked in tandem to achieve the look of their brief. Jamie couldn't figure out if they were sisters or just looked alike—bottle blondes, and not a day over thirty-five, both in those god awful low-crotch nappy-style pants that seemed to be so popular amongst the hardcore yoga crowd. Whilst Jamie loved to exercise, she was not the namaste-type. Kendall and Jenna barely spoke to Jamie, just mumbling between themselves as best as possible with pins in their mouths—the risk of being pricked was dangerously high today.

"We need her now." Beth rushed in frantically, swinging her arms about wildly. Kendall and Jenna—*'Kendall Jenner'*—Jamie thought jokingly to herself as the penny dropped—were putting on their finishing touches. "Quick quick!" Beth was on a mission to get Jamie out and ushered her out through the cold corridors and into Stage 6. Shoots never made any sense; she'd been waiting around for hours. Hair and Makeup took forever to make her look, well, not that much different than when she came in, but suddenly they were on the clock. She reminded herself that she was getting paid and just smiled.

The huge studio was a frenzy of preparation, and icy cold; goosebumps immediately sprung up all over her body. The sky-high ceiling was equipped with rigs and lights and pulleys. Jamie tried to remember what else had been filmed there just as Richard, the director, wandered across.

"Hi Jamie, okay so what we need you to do first is …" Richard was straight to it. There was no time for chit-chat. The star of the show was already lit up and ready for her close up. The new golden Volvo was positioned in the middle of the studio, flooded by lights from every angle. It was Jamie's job to demonstrate just how wonderful this new model was and why everyone should want to buy it—commercial modelling in a nutshell—selling a fake shiny happy lifestyle no one really has. Once she'd shown off the generous boot space and elegant lines, her next scene was to sit inside and pretend to drive off. Quite why she needed to pretend, she wasn't sure, but this was the land of make-believe where nothing was really real. Oh, and don't forget to smile, smile, smile. Her cheeks would be aching by the end of it. At least twenty takes of each shot, undeniably broken up by another two hours of waiting whilst they set up the next scene. Jamie flashed them one of her mega-watt smiles as she longed for those three little words: 'It's a wrap.' But she still had hours to go.

BOREDOM
Mallorca, Spain

"Hurry up, you're going to be late," Kate yelled down the stairs to David's basement office for the umpteenth time. The girls stood patiently by the front door. A beautiful, arched, double-fronted antique oak door with black iron studs, salvaged from a derelict church. A rare find that Kate and David stumbled across hidden in the back of one of the many antique shops they liked to frequent in the village. Kate turned to her girls and proceeded with their morning ritual.

"Homework?"

"Check." The girls grinned in unison. This was their little game. They called it the 'Check' game. Kate knew it would be easier if she arranged everything herself, but she wanted them to get into the habit of being self-sufficient, and this was her genius way of turning everyday chores into something fun.

"Lunch?"

"Check." Both girls held up their respective lunch boxes. A Barbie one for Tali and a black one for Emily, who'd insisted on trading in her matching Barbie one for something more mature. Recently, Kate noticed Emily gravitating with more frequency towards everything black and hoped this wasn't because she herself was in the habit of doing so.

Every night before they went to bed, they'd look at the spreadsheet with magnets on the huge chrome fridge. All colour-coordinated with different activities marked for different days: swimming, horse-riding, tennis, sailing, and most recently, piano. Yes, the girls' agendas were crammed full, but Kate wanted to expose them to everything possible. She remembered someone telling her, 'If you throw enough spaghetti at the wall, some of it might stick.'

"Emily, you don't have activities today, so I'll pick you up at five, and we can head down to the beach for an hour whilst Tali is swimming."

Emily smiled. She loved it when Tali had an activity and she didn't, as that meant one-on-one time with her mum.

David materialised from his office, looking at his watch before glancing back up at Kate.

"Why were you hurrying me? We've still got three minutes." David liked to live on the edge.

Kate liked everything organised. How they cohabited with such opposing characteristics was anyone's guess.

Kate turned back to resume her checking. "Rabbits fed?"

Emily looked at Tali. Tali looked at Emily. They both looked at Daddy.

"Why are you looking at me? I haven't fed them," said David rather defensively.

"Me no feed wabbits." Tali looked like she was about to cry, her bottom lip thrust out and quivering.

"Sorry, Mum"—Emily was quick to chime in—"I haven't either." A somewhat less remorseful response from her eldest.

David, realising an eruption was imminent, darted towards the girls. "Come on. We've got to go, don't want to be late." He ushered them out the door.

"David!" Kate's face grimaced in disbelief. But he was already strapping on Tali's seat belt.

"I'm not going on-site today; I'll do it when I get back," he said nonchalantly as he got into the car.

Kate watched them zoom down the gravel driveway, lined with red bougainvillea hedges, before disappearing into the distance. She wondered what to do next. Make the beds? Painfully boring. Tidy away the breakfast stuff? Excruciatingly boring. She might as well feed the rabbits. They must be starving, and it would be half an hour before David returned. It wasn't poor little Fluffy and Floppy's fault that she was the only one looking out for them.

Kate grabbed the bag of rabbit food and wandered into the garden toward the bunnies. She felt increasingly unsettled. She couldn't quite put her finger on what was wrong. Could it be that it irritated her having to take responsibility for the rabbits? Was she upset that Jamie was leaving after they'd had such an instant connection? Or did she feel that by living on the island, she was missing out on something? But what exactly was she missing? She wouldn't swap David and the girls for Jamie's fun-filled existence for anything, but sometimes she felt like they'd already retired.

By the time Kate reached the end of their garden, her mood had worsened. As she stood longingly, gazing at her fine sculpture of an embracing man and woman which stood proud in one corner of her little oasis, she contemplated the day ahead. She'd agreed to help Jamie pack up her flat. She was excited about seeing her, but equally sad that she was leaving. Despite being so different, there seemed to be this unconditional acceptance of one another that usually only comes after a lifetime of friendship.

Upon reaching the rabbit's hutch, a tsunami of anxiety washed over her as she spotted the hutch door open with no rabbits in sight.

Oh my god. The rabbits had escaped. *Oh my god. How? Where?* Her brain scrambled to make sense of how this was even possible. Perhaps the girls hadn't locked the hutch when they'd fed them last night? The significance of the absconded rabbits fully hitting Kate. It would devastate the girls. They could be anywhere.

Kate contemplated climbing through the hedge and into the fields beyond, with the daunting task of trying to locate two little fluffy bunnies amongst the long grass.

"Floppy, Fluffy, where are you?" As she scrambled through the hedge, twigs grazed the flesh not covered by her Marks & Spencer's pyjamas. This was ridiculous, like trying to find a needle in a haystack, and now her arm was bleeding.

"Floppy, Fluffy, where the bloody hell are you, you little fuckers?" What was she doing? Rabbits don't respond, rabbits aren't dogs.

"Nice juicy carrots. I have lovely, juicy carrots. FLOPPY, FLUFFY, get your fluffy little arses back here now." Kate's distress increased by the second as she envisioned Tali and Emily's crestfallen faces when she informed them of their disappearance.

Kate continued to search for the rabbits; it felt like she'd been scouring the back fields for an eternity, but then David finally materialised.

"Kate, where are you? I can hear you. In fact, the entire village can hear you, but I can't see you." David emerged from the front of the house.

"I'm over here," Kate yelled.

"Where's here?"

"Underneath the hedge at the back. I'm looking for the rabbits. Shit, David, I think they've gone forever."

Suddenly, David's head popped over the hedge. "They're in the hutch in the garage," he said sheepishly. "I thought I saw an owl looking suspicious in that tree over there last night." Pointing to the enormous palm tree that overhung the hutches. "I thought it would be better if they were inside until we finished their enclosure, at least."

Kate stopped and stared incredulously. "Why the bloody hell didn't you say anything then?"

"It's just that …" He looked perplexed, like he genuinely didn't understand that he'd done anything wrong. "I didn't think of it. I told you I was going to feed the rabbits when I was back. It didn't cross my mind."

"I can't believe YOU." Kate's rage had now reached an inferno-like fury. A small part of her brain recognised that perhaps she was being overly dramatic, but it felt fantastic to let it all out. "Do you think I've got nothing better to do with my time than crawl around the undergrowth in my pyjamas?" Kate shot up, dusting herself down as if to emphasise the point, before scrambling back through the hedge. Then, with a face of thunder, marched back to the kitchen and slumped herself down at the long antique pine table.

David sidled up to her and stood looking at his pretty, troubled wife. The harsh reality was there was nothing better to do than look for two rabbits that weren't even lost. In fact, she had nothing better to do at all.

"David." She sighed.

"Yes?"

"David."

"Yes, you're right, I'm sorry I should've told you." Moving behind Kate, David pulled her off the chair and onto his lap, cradling her in his arms and stroking her hair.

"I know. I'm not really angry about the rabbits," Kate whispered under her breath; now stroked and petted into submission.

"I think I've figured that out. So what's up?"

"I'm bored." Kate looked glum and felt guilty for yelling at him. "David, I'm really, really, extremely bored. We never go out, we have no social life, I'm not sure I can do this for too much longer. I feel like my brain's gone dead."

David initially felt relief. Not a clue this time, but the actual problem. He wouldn't have to play a game of charades with Kate's emotional state. However, the relief was short-lived when he considered the implications of her boredom.

"Do you want to go back to London?" he almost whispered, his face etched with disappointment.

"No, no, not at all." She knew he was better here. The kids were better here. How could she ask that of them? No, she'd never let him know how she sometimes yearned to be back in her fold. "No, honestly, I don't want to go back," Kate said, not being honest at all, "but I need something more. I need to go out. We need to have more of a life here. Can't we try to do something together?"

Kate leaned her head on his chest and felt warm and safe nestled against him, breathing in his familiar smell. She was happy that what might have been an unnecessary argument had dissipated quickly. Nothing was ever achieved when they argued; it was much better when it was like this.

"What do you want to do? Do you want to come to the tennis club with me this week?" David asked with all sincerity, having moved on from figuring out the problem mode directly into solution mode.

"No, not tennis. We need to find something new—something we're both either good at or both useless at. It doesn't really matter as long as we can have fun together."

"Why don't we get a babysitter and go out for a meal?" David was still trying to find solutions, and the best he could do involved tennis, which she was crap at, or eating, which she was marvellous at but that would only make her more depressed about her weight.

"Nah, don't want to go out to eat. Don't worry about it. I'm just premenstrual." Kate launched herself from his lap and was thankful, not for the first time, for being a woman and having the most wonderful excuse of being premenstrual or postmenstrual. Besides, there was no point in putting this on David. He wasn't responsible for making her happy. She had to figure out a solution by herself.

"I understand you're frustrated and you're right about finding something fun to do together. Have a think about options and I'll go along with it, I promise," David said with all sincerity as he got up from the table and walked towards the door leading down to his basement office.

Stacking the dirty dishes into the dishwasher, Kate wondered what they could possibly do together that might be fun? There had to be something that would take them out of the house. Perhaps a cookery class? No, that also involved shoving more food down her gob. This new activity had to be something that didn't involve food. Yoga maybe? She was sure that she'd seen an evening yoga class advertised in the local paper, so went in search of it, wondering whether David's promise to do anything would extend to something that involved contorting his body.

The paper was not where she'd left it, maybe David was right about moving to digital, but she liked having a physical paper other than when it went missing. Its absence irked Kate. Happy, sad, happy, sad; what the bloody hell was wrong with her?

"DAVID," she yelled down to his office. "Have you seen this week's local newspaper?"

"You mean the Daily Bulletin, the one you always ask me to buy but never read?" said David with the hint of dread that a person might experience having escaped the lion's den only to find themselves dragged back in.

"Yes, that would be the one; it's not in the rack."

"Oh."

Kate didn't like the sound of that 'Oh.' In one simple syllable, she ascertained that David not only knew of the newspaper's whereabouts, but that she wouldn't like what he'd done with it.

"Erm." Came next. She liked that even less.

"Where is it then? There's an ad I want to look at. I've got an idea for our new activity."

David groaned. "It's in the garage, inside the rabbits' hutch." No doubt in the absence of hay, the Daily Bulletin seemed a good enough alternative.

Too tired to have another moan, Kate went in search of the paper. With any luck, it would be retrievable. Wandering down to the garage, she felt quite excited at the prospect of learning something new, like yoga. But upon reaching the rabbits' hutch, Kate gasped. Floppy, the innocent little white fluffy thing—who Kate realised was far from innocent or floppy at this precise moment, was now perched on top of Fluffy—the poor innocent little black fluffy thing—humping away!

Kate ran back into the house to alert David to the new rabbit drama and shouted down to his basement office, "DAVID, DAVID, COME TO THE GARAGE, QUICKLY." He'd promised her that the rabbits were both male. It was one of the very first questions she'd asked, as she'd envisioned an army of bunnies bouncing all around her immaculate home, creating carnage and dropping their little bunny poos in their wake. Not waiting for a reply, she headed back to the garage and didn't have to wait long for David to join her.

"What's the matter?" David came scurrying up, alarmed by Kate's dramatic outburst.

"Our bunnies are HOMOSEXUAL."

David stood staring at the rabbits and laughed.

"Why is this funny?" Kate was clearly suffering a complete sense of humour bypass.

"You've got to stop them. I thought you said they were both males?"

"Well, technically, I said I thought they were both males. They're too young to tell, but I guess we know now," he said, stating the obvious.

"I'll have to take Floppy to the vet and get his bits chopped off, and I'll have to take Fluffy as well, in case she needs an abortion," Kate said, now with a note of purpose in her voice. "We need to separate them immediately. Can you take Floppy back to the hutch in the garden, and Fluffy can stay here until I can get them both to the vet, and let's pray Fluffy isn't pregnant already."

Kate watched David head back to the garden, holding Floppy in the palm of his hand. Maybe she was being ridiculous; they were still so tiny. Turning her attention back to the hutch, she spied the paper, and reached in to retrieve it. *Uff, disgusting.* It was soaking wet. Dropping it immediately, she resigned herself to abort her mission. But then she noticed another sheet of the paper, which appeared to be urine-free. Just a little perfectly round poo pellet. Could she? Her eagerness to search the classifieds for their 'new activity' overcame her disgust at the poo. It was only a little poo, and without thinking further, she just flicked it off and successfully retrieved the paper. Scanning it like a professional proofreader, her brow furrowed with concentration until she found what she was looking for. Grinning and feeling excited. This was it. She had it.

* * *

"David?" Kate tried to contain her excitement as she entered his office, his refuge.

"Yes, hun?" David didn't look up from his plans.

"Sweetie pie," she said, at which point he looked up. Now he was worried.

Minutes earlier, she'd been in a foul mood that the rabbits hadn't been lost and that the Daily Bulletin had been. Yet now she was calling him 'sweetie pie.' This was not a good sign. David knew she was coming to him with their proposed 'fun activity.' The likelihood of it being something he wanted to do was as remote as West Ham winning the league! It irritated David that he'd offered himself up like a sacrificial lamb, and now he was on his way to the slaughterhouse, faster than you could say chop chop.

Taking one look at David's disgruntled face, Kate decided timing was the key to broaching this request. "Just wanted to know if you wanted a cuppa, my darling?"

"Don't beat around the bush; go on, hit me with it. What's this new activity that you've found for us?"

"Well, I've given this some serious consideration," she said.

"I only just suggested you look for this supposed activity five minutes ago. Don't tell me you've given it serious consideration, just tell me what it is."

"Well, first I thought about a cookery class …"

David's face lit up. *Cookery classes, what a great idea.* That would involve food, and he loved food.

"And then … then I remembered I'd seen an ad for yoga classes," Kate said as David visibly slumped lower onto his desk.

"And then …"

A hint of relief swept across David's face.

"The rabbit peed on the yoga ad."

David's relief was now replaced with genuine confusion.

"But darling, guess what? They only did a tiny poo on another part of the ad section," she said, not waiting for him to actually guess. "They have Salsa classes on a Tuesday in Palma Nova." Kate finally concluded, looking very smug and extremely pleased with herself.

David gawked at her with total bewilderment.

"It was a sign," she clarified. Her face a picture of innocence.

The confusion showed no signs of ebbing.

"Salsa classes? A sign? What sign?" he spoke slowly, as if he'd misheard.

"Yup, and you said anything. Shall I make you that cuppa now darling?" Kate said, all sweetness and light, running up the stairs before David had time to voice his discontent.

"Better make it a bloody brandy."

LINGERIE & HARDWARE

Jamie taped the box shut and sighed. Wiping a bead of sweat from her brow, she surveyed the kitchen, a sea of boxes all neatly labelled 'kitchen.' How could there be so many boxes from one relatively small kitchen? She wondered if she was being stupid shipping it all back. Surely it would be cheaper just to buy new. But she recognised that as soon as she landed in London, she'd have to continue her gruelling schedule of shoots for the car campaign. There simply wouldn't be time to do anything else. No, she was definitely doing the right thing. Just pack it all and sort everything out once they are settled. But who, in their right mind, decides to move to another country and then only gives themselves a week to turn it around?

The doorbell rang and startled her. "I'm coming," she yelled out, rushing towards the door. Jamie imagined she must look a right sight, so briefly checked her reflection in the large bronze-framed mirror by the door—yet another thing to be packed. Her ensemble of cut-off denim shorts and a light blue halter neck top wasn't unlike something Madison might wear. Her curls were scraped up into a messy bun on top of her head, looking remarkably like a pineapple. A messy pineapple at that.

"Only me." She heard from beyond the door, blocked by an

army of more boxes. Deftly edging her way around them, she opened the large wooden door and felt awash with relief. There stood Kate with a huge grin on her face. Jamie smiled as she leaned in to hug her friend, who surprisingly had on white denim shorts with a not so surprising white baggy T-shirt. Jamie nearly commented that she'd never seen Kate in any other colour than black. Kate caught Jamie looking at her and as if she read her mind. "Black is only for the winter. I flip to white in the summer."

"Oh my god, you have no idea how happy I am to see you." Jamie took one of Kate's hands, attempting to help her navigate back through the boxes and into the clear. "This packing is doing my head in. I've spent hours and only finished the kitchen. Doesn't seem that long ago that I packed everything to come here."

"Fear not, your very efficient friend Kate is here. I'll have you know I'm a whizz at packing, and labelling. We'll get this done." Kate refrained from mentioning that she did, in fact, spend many a day organising the insides of her cupboards just to have something to do. She could do this with her eyes closed. "And besides, you're forgetting our secret weapon." Kate lifted the large Marks & Spencer's fabric tote she'd brought with her, clinking as she opened it, to reveal a bottle of vodka, Triple sec, cranberry juice, Perrier and two limes. Kate was now beaming, clearly very happy with herself.

"Amazing, I knew we became friends for a reason haha! But what's the Perrier for?" Jamie looked quizzically.

"Ah, now that would be for me. I have to collect Emily from school today. Tali has swimming, and it's our special time, so mine will have to be a virgin Cosmo, but nevertheless just as fabulous—almost."

"I'm not drinking alone; can't you ask David to pick up the girls?

Pretty pleeeease." Jamie pulled the cutest, most angelic face she could muster.

"Trust me, I can't. I want to. But I can't. Thursday is the only day I get to spend any one-on-one time with Emily. I can't let her down. We can both have virgin Cosmos if you like?" Kate said, trying to ignore Jamie's now bleak and disappointed expression. "Come on, Jamie, let's get cracking." Kate's attempt to distract her friend was thwarted as she became aware of her surroundings. Kate gazed around the open-concept living area, which had a small kitchen tucked away through an archway at the back. It was the perfect fusion of old Spanish charm with clean, modern lines. Kate took note of several large paintings that dominated the walls. One in particular caught her eye. It was a woman wearing a red dress, dancing almost Flamenco-style. The figure was slightly blurry, as if you could almost feel her every move. It was breathtakingly beautiful and undeniably passionate.

"Oh wow, Jamie. This duplex is amazing." Kate finally averted her eyes from the life-sized work of art. Noticing the French doors, cast wide open, leading out to the balcony beyond the lounge area, she made a beeline for it.

"Crikey, what a view." Kate leaned onto the wrought-iron railings, looking out to sea. The apartment was every beach lover's dream. The water looked almost cobalt as it glimmered under the sun, dotted with several white fishing boats, which only served to further accentuate its rich colour. Kate watched with fascination as the world walked, ran, and cycled along towards the beach below. Whilst it wasn't exactly city-living, there was far more life here than there was in her little village of Santa Maria. Irresistibly charming Mallorquin life. It wasn't hard to see the appeal. "This is just amazing Jamie." Turning now to face her friend, who was standing behind her. "Are you ready to go back to London? It's going to be a bit of a change after having this," Kate said with all sincerity, sweeping the air with her arms.

"I know. The view is incredible. But I don't have much of a choice at the moment. It's weird because for the last month or so I've been feeling restless here, but now that the reality of going back has finally hit me, I feel kinda sad."

"I know. But it's the right thing to do, you know it is." Kate understood. "Honestly, I think I'm a little jealous."

"Jealous? Of what?" Jamie couldn't imagine what Kate could possibly be jealous of. Her life seemed to be so idyllic and secure.

"Ufff, Let's not get into that now. I'm here on a mission." Kate grinned, promptly changing the subject. "So kitchen fully done? But how are you going to cook? You're not leaving for another week?"

"Haha, you obviously don't know me well enough. I don't cook. I don't even eat. But there are such things as restaurants, and I'm pretty sure we can get a takeaway for my mum and Maddy somewhere around here." Cooking was the least of her worries. She found it funny that it seemed to be Kate's primary concern.

Stepping away from the railing, Kate turned towards her friend. "So bedrooms next? Which one shall we start with?" Grabbing her marker pens from her bag.

"Let's do mine." Jamie decided as she led Kate back through the duplex, up the stairs and into her bedroom. "We can start here. It's where I have the most stuff, anyway." Jamie threw open the doors of her walk-in wardrobe and Kate's jaw dropped as she surveyed the contents. It was like a fireworks display of colour; a treasure chest of emeralds, rubies and sapphires all glistening. God, she was so boring, thinking of her own cupboards, which literally only had white or black, and she made a mental note to brighten up her own wardrobe.

"Have you separated what you need for the next few days?" Kate said, stepping into her uber-practical mode.

"Well, no, but good thinking. Hmmmm." Jamie glided her fingers across hanger upon hanger of exquisite clothing, stopping to touch a dress. Looking at the black and incredibly skimpy number, Kate started laughing.

"Jamie, you need that? Really? I was thinking more along the lines of knickers, a bra, jeans, and a couple of tops."

"Yeah, yeah, those too but I do have a few days left. You never know." Jamie winked, as thoughts of Tomás popped into her mind.

"Bloody hell girl. We are so so different. Have you done your charity pile yet?"

"What charity pile? I'm not giving any of this away. You never know when I might need them, especially back in London."

"You need all of this? Wow." But as she looked at the backless sequined dress with the plunging neckline, Kate realised that Jamie's clothes had a very different destiny than her own.

"Okay, fine. Let's move on. Why don't you do your bedside drawers? And I'll focus here. Do you want me to leave your lingerie drawer, or are you happy for me to do it?" Kate saw that the first drawer was filled with lingerie. She was going to say 'underwear' but recognised that whilst her own full-coverage bras and functional knickers could be called that, Jamie's definitely fell under the category of 'lingerie.'

Jamie, now engrossed in transferring the contents of her bedside drawers into a box, didn't even look at Kate. "Nah, I have nothing to hide. You can box all of that."

"Do you need a black bag for the rubbish?" Kate noticed Jamie was emptying the contents directly into a small box without sorting them out first.

"What rubbish? I haven't had a chance to accumulate any."

Whilst Jamie continued to put things straight from the drawers into boxes, Kate wanted to do things more methodically. Focusing on the opened drawer, she noticed that whilst the contents weren't arranged by colour—as hers were—they were certainly very organised.

"Aha!" Kate announced, like a detective finding an important clue.

"Aha what?"

"I've found rubbish. In your lingerie drawer. You do have rubbish, after all." As Kate pulled out an unidentifiable mass of flesh-coloured string.

"That's not rubbish." Jamie chuckled while Kate continued to twist and turn the item. "That's definitely lingerie."

"How is this lingerie?" Kate was mystified at how a ball of string could be underwear. "It looks like something from the ironmonger."

"The ironmonger? Kate, do you know you use words left over from a different century?"

"Okay, the *ferreteria* as they say in Spain." Kate was almost taken aback for remembering the word for hardware store. Brilliant, she couldn't remember normal useful things like 'where is the toilet?' but she knew what the hardware store was. *Bloody marvellous.* Jamie was near pissing herself laughing.

"You are mistaking my very useful underwear for a ball of string." Giggling, she went to retrieve the item from Kate.

"Look, this bit goes under here. That bit goes under the breasts." Jamie was demonstrating over her clothes. Kate was now in equal hysterics.

"*Voilà!* Lingerie. It's for when you are wearing a see-through dress." Jamie hoped to help Kate grasp the functionality of the item in question.

Kate could hardly breathe. She was laughing so much that tears actually started to fall. Whilst choking with laughter, she managed to spurt out, "See-through dress." She just couldn't stop laughing, especially as Jamie now looked ridiculous. "See-through dress." She was on a loop. She couldn't manage any other words, almost doubled over now. Like a see-through dress was the last thing she would ever own, and just the thought of what she would look like in one prolonged her hysterical fit of giggles.

"I think I've peed myself," Kate finally announced. "Okay, Jamie. So not string from the hardware store. Well, that's a relief."

Both girls returned to their respective tasks with the occasional murmurings of, "See-through dress," from Kate. Once Jamie had finished with the bedside drawers, she sat down next to the giggling Kate, and the two girls systematically finished all the contents of Jamie's cupboards. Once the last box was sealed, Kate couldn't resist labelling the lingerie box as 'Lingerie & Hardware.'

"Now what, bathroom?"

"Yes, I guess we could. Might as well get it sorted. How long have you got?"

"Emily's school is only five mins away. I've got a good hour. Can you separate what you need for the next few days, and then we can pack the rest?"

They walked into the bathroom and Jamie stopped. She needed all of this.

"I have never seen this amount of cosmetics—anywhere. This is like being in the Selfridges cosmetic floor. What's this for?" Kate grabbed a small silver bottle.

"It's a primer before you put on your foundation. It's wonderful. Gives such a smooth base," said Jamie.

"Primer?"

"Yes, it's a makeup must. Come here, let me show you."

Before Kate had a chance to object, Jamie pulled down the toilet seat and guided Kate to sit on it. Wiping Kate's hair back from her face, Jamie started applying the primer in circular motions with her fingers.

"Are you sure we've got time for this? Shouldn't we get started in Madison's room?" Kate felt a little embarrassed that she didn't know about basic beauty tips like primers.

"Stop avoiding Kate. Let me give you a makeover, please. Two main rooms are done. Let's have some fun. God knows when we'll see each other again."

"It will take more than a bit of cream to transform me," Kate said, still feeling a little uncomfortable. Jamie stopped what she was doing and crouched down so that she was eye level with Kate, speaking to her in the same way that Kate would often speak to her girls.

"Kate, you do know you're really beautiful? You don't need primer or any makeup, but sometimes it just helps a little, accentuates what you naturally have." Jamie, now reaching for another bottle, continued with a now compliant Kate.

"My god you're going to be amazed. It's not for every day, but wouldn't it be nice once in a while when you go out?" Jamie continued her makeover, not waiting for an answer.

"I'll look ridiculous. I never wear makeup; I don't want to look like a clown." As the last bit of her resistance withered away. Besides, she never really went out, but Kate didn't want to upset her enthusiastic friend with the full disclosure that she was a boring person. Jamie seemed to see something different in her, and Kate suddenly became aware of her own potential as seen through her friend's eyes.

"Kate, please trust me. I'm going to make it look so natural, I promise, and you're going to love it. David is going to love it too. Just give me half an hour. Oooohhhh and let's have a Cosmo, seeing that you've bought all the stuff. And for the record, we will be seeing each other again. You'll come to London, I'll come back to visit; and in the meantime, we can text and FaceTime and still email too. So please stop thinking this is the end. But first, it's Cosmo time." Jamie headed down to the kitchen.

"Shit," Jamie shouted up from the bottom of the stairs, loud enough for Kate to hear.

"What?"

"I packed the friggin' glasses." As she resumed rummaging around the kitchen, "Are you sure I can't tempt you to a proper one?" Jamie yelled up again.

"NO, you absolutely can't. I cannot be led astray." Kate was adamant whilst thinking that was exactly what was happening, letting Jamie give her a makeover. Jamie returned, grinning with two disposable *Frozen* cups leftover from Madison's party.

"Look what I found."

Kate sniffed her drink.

"What are you doing?" Jamie looked perplexed.

"Checking you didn't spike my Perrier!"

THE RABBITS

Kate sat, twiddling her thumbs. The vet's surgery was gloomy and small, the blinds drawn to prevent a potential furnace-like atmosphere manifesting from the sun's strong rays, even though it was only ten in the morning. The rabbits were now in two separate carry cases, each perched precariously on her knees. Wearing her usual ensemble of tracksuit bottoms with an oversized T-shirt, Kate had the added glamour of two fake Louis Vuitton pet carry cases—the local pet store having had a very minimal selection. It had been Louis Vuitton or a rather disgusting orange-coloured case decorated with fluorescent pink flowers. Fake Louis Vuitton winning hands down, Kate was just thankful that nobody she knew would bear witness to her looking such a fright.

Turning her attention dutifully back to her rabbits, Kate hoped the vet spoke English, as her grasp of the Spanish language left a lot to be desired. Having a minute to think about the situation, she realised she didn't have a clue what the Spanish word was for vasectomy or abortion. *Bloody hell.* When she didn't know a word, Kate would act it out; it was the only way she'd succeeded in getting by this long on her minimal Spanish. But given the delicate nature of this particular scenario, this could get embarrassing.

"*Buenos días.*" Kate glanced up in alarm as the gorgeous god of a vet strode into the small, minimalistic reception room. *Shit. I should have worn the white outfit.* Kate considered, not anticipating her local vet would be such a tall, dark, incredibly handsome specimen. Kate prayed he spoke English, not relishing the prospect of impersonating two humping rabbits and cutting off balls to this dreamy man. Feeling her cheeks flush scarlet, she blurted out her ever hopeful, "*¿Hablas Inglés?*" *Please, please, please let him speak English.*

"*Muy, muy poco. ¿Que les pasa a los conejos?*" said the gorgeous, smiling, clearly non-English speaking vet. He stood tall at around six feet, which was unusual, as Kate had noticed that in general, the Spanish men seemed to be shorter and leaner than your average British male. His brown eyes glistened, and his deep olive skin accentuated his penetrating eyes. He wore a white doctor's coat and his movements were so smooth it was as if he had glided in on skates.

"*Es mi conejos.*" Kate was thankful that she was able to at least recall the word for rabbits.

"*Yo tengo dos.*" Yes, she was doing well … she had two rabbits and what else did she want to say? This vet was very yummy. *I have two rabbits and one is a boy and one is a girl and they have been humping. Here goes.* "*Yo tengo dos conejos. Este blanco es un niño and el otra es niña.*" Now for the challenging part. How could she express humping without using the word and without doing the actions? The vet was smirking at her. *The bastard.* She wagered he knew exactly what she was going to say, but was obviously finding it all highly amusing and certainly not about to help her out.

"*Este conejo,*" she said, pointing to Floppy; now what was the word for on top? *Come on Kate, think, think.* Nope, the word eluded her.

"*Este conejo y este conejo,*" she said pointing to Fluffy and then hesitated. Surely he could work it out? Nope, he was still standing there with his arms crossed, looking amused. *Oh fuck it*, there was no alternative and who cared anyway if she embarrassed herself, as long as it accomplished the mission and she could cross one top priority action off her to-do list. Kate started gyrating her hips back and forward in a humping motion.

"Ahhhhhh!" The vet laughed out loud. "*¿No quieres más conejos?*"

That's bloody right, Kate thought. *I don't want any more flaming conejos.*

"Do you no want babies?" The vet god spoke. The thought crossed Kate's mind that she wouldn't mind trying to have babies with him, and then admonished herself. What the bloody hell was going on? Why was she thinking about sex? Maybe she was having some sort of hormonal imbalance? However, this was neither the time nor the place; she needed to stay focused on the task at hand.

"Yes, I no want baby rabbits, you help me?" Why had her command of the English language suddenly abandoned her?

"No problem," he said, taking the carry case with Floppy in it and heading off into the back room.

Kate dutifully followed him through a heavily frosted glass door into a cramped room that was monopolised by a large metal table where Floppy now was, placing Fluffy's case next to the other. Standing back to keep out of his way, she surveyed the small room. The walls were floor-to-ceiling, covered with locked glass cabinets hosting a vast amount of medication and creams. All neatly classified. *Not only gorgeous but organised too*. A man after her own heart.

"No worry," he said, directing her towards a grey plastic chair in the corner, which she presumed was an instruction for her to sit and get out of his way. Evidently, he spoke a little English. She was relieved she could ditch her rather dismal and clumsy attempt at communicating with him in his own language.

Kate plopped herself down on the chair, still speaking like a two-year-old trying to make polite conversation. "So what you do?"

"We take rabbit and cut off bollocks," said the vet matter-of-factly. At first, Kate thought that this was his attempt at being humorous until she looked at his face and saw that he was being deadly serious. She giggled nervously.

"*Señora*, 'bollocks' not good word?" he said, not quite liking that she was now laughing at him.

"No, no, 'bollocks' is just fine." And moving swiftly on. "*Y la otro conejo?* Possible baby?"

"No, *señora*, too young, *conejos solo* practise." *I'd like to practise with you*, she thought. *Arrrrggggghhhh.* She didn't even like sex. What was happening to her? Fabulous news: Fluffy didn't need an abortion, now she only had to deal with Floppy's bollock chopping. Could rabbits even have abortions? She wondered, relieved that she didn't have to attempt to have that embarrassing conversation as well.

"You come later, *dos horas, todo* ready," the vet said.

I wish I could come later, Kate thought to herself with a chuckle, thinking for the first time of a different sort of rabbit, 'The Rabbit.' The vibrator, which now having witnessed the interactions between Floppy and Fluffy, she knew was most aptly named.

David had bought it for her the previous Christmas and had stupidly placed it under the tree, unaware of the surprise visit from his parents. Kate shuddered at the recollection of opening up the gift. How could he have forgotten to remove it before the present-opening ceremony? Ooohhhh, the embarrassment, the shame.

The vibrator had remained in its box since its purchase, yet with visions of the dreamy vet now planted in her mind, it might be a good time to test it. Kate wondered whether David would play tennis that afternoon, then promptly felt guilty. David had bought the Rabbit for them to play with together, yet each time he'd suggested it, she'd made an excuse.

"Yes, I come back later and get rabbits. *Muchas gracias, señor.*" With that, Kate retrieved the carry case with Fluffy and left the surgery, already excited about the prospect of returning home and test driving her very own electrical rabbit.

* * *

Kate heard the front door slam, signifying David's departure to his tennis lesson and with enormous trepidation, went rummaging on the top of her wardrobe, where she'd thrust the offending vibrator thing. She wondered whether there would be a clear instruction manual or was she being dense? Perhaps an instruction manual would not be required. Perhaps it was as simple as shove it in, flick the switch and hey presto—orgasm. She hoped it was that simple. With trembling hands, she took the vibrator out of its red velvet-lined box. *Fancy packaging.* Kate thought, wondering whether David had invested in a deluxe version. She cocked her head to one side quizzically. *Bit large, isn't it? And why is it fluorescent purple?* Kate wondered if it might also glow in the dark. *Now that would be a great idea*, she thought, not relishing trying to find her orgasm in the stark daylight.

Kate kept looking at it with a grimace of disgust. In what way was a big purple penis supposed to turn her on? What did this big purple penis have that David's lovely soft flesh-coloured-with-a-freckle-on-the-top-penis not have? Why would this penis succeed where no other penis had succeeded before? Kate found herself humming the theme tune to *Star Trek*. *La la la la li la. These are the voyages of The Starship Rabbit. Its five-minute mission to explore strange new worlds. To boldly go where no man has gone before.*

She giggled, the humour not lost on her. A visit to the vets and a sudden emergence of a strange, unidentified tingling sensation in her groin had materialised. The next thing she knew she was pulling shut her long white, flowing linen curtains and locking her bedroom door in the middle of the day, whilst humming the theme tune to *Star Trek*. All while trying to have a rendezvous with a big, purple, plastic penis. *Stay focused, Kate, let's see if we really are dead down there or if there is life after all.*

Turning her concentration back to the big purple thing, Kate lay back on her bed, but the sun was now penetrating through the curtains. Getting up again, she decided an extra layer of obscurity would be appropriate and then closed the blackout blinds as well, so the room was pitch black. Shuffling back to the bed, arms waving in front of her to avoid bumping into anything, she again got into position, wiggling out of her tracksuit bottoms and knickers that had once been white but were now a dirty grey. She closed her eyes and positioned the offending item. On the count of three, she decided she'd switch both switches to maximum at the same time, hoping to optimise her chances of the elusive orgasm. She briefly wondered how far she should push it in and then rationalised that she'd had two babies, so she could probably manage to shove it in as far as it could go. With a shove and a count to three, Kate flicked the switches, scrunching her eyes tightly shut in anticipation of 'the orgasm.' One … two … three … go.

Nothing happened. Nothing happened at all. She opened one eye, then the other. What was wrong? Why didn't her Rabbit work? Could she have gotten a faulty Rabbit? Just her bloody luck. Destined to live a life less orgasmic, only to read about it in books and possibly vicariously through Jamie.

Sitting upright, she turned on the ornate bird-shaped bedside lamp reminiscent of origami paper cranes, and inspecting the vibrator further, discovered that underneath the switches was a battery compartment with, of course, no batteries inside. The moment had definitely passed. Chucking the odious object into her bedside drawer, Kate let out a resigned sigh and slipped back into her knickers. The quest for 'the orgasm' could be shelved for now, perhaps indefinitely. After all, she thought, there were plenty of other joys in life to explore and conquer. Kate decided to put the ordeal behind her, and abort her search for 'the orgasm' until another day, or possibly never.

Feeling utterly defeated, she slumped back onto the plush pillows, pulling the light duvet over her body, cocooning herself in a fortress of comfort. With a determined flick of her fingers, she started scrolling on her phone, ready to embark on a new pursuit of 'investigations' into the mysterious realm of tummy tucks and boob lifts. TikTok and Instagram were her usual go-to's, where recipes and dog videos often dominated her feed, but today, she was on a mission to find something more relevant—a path forward, perhaps, or a sign to guide her through this life-changing decision, to have surgery or not. Deep inside, she wrestled with a whirlwind of emotions. The part of her that loathed her body, yearned for the empowerment of doing something about it, dreaming of the day she could reclaim her confidence and revel in self-love.

She often shared with her daughters a particular passage from *The Serenity Prayer:* 'God grant me the serenity to accept the things I cannot change; courage to change the things I can; and wisdom to know the difference.' This was how she wanted to live her life, and the tummy and the boobs were definitely something she could change. But then there was another part of her that was so fearful of the surgery, and an equally dynamic voice kept nudging her in the direction that she should embrace her body and love herself exactly as she was. So what if she had a bit of sagging skin and a few stretch marks? It wasn't as if David cared. But then this wasn't about David; this was about her. She would never put herself through this for a man. The dilemma raged on, and social media didn't help. There were two camps online, and it was clear she wasn't going to make a decision based on others; she was going to have to dig deep and figure this one out on her own.

Kate lost track of time as she continued to scroll and flick through feed after feed, until an ad suddenly popped up that caught her attention, entitled: 'What Turns You On?'

Certainly not the odious purple Rabbit, Kate chuckled to herself.

Slinking lower down into her bed with the screen close to her face, Kate clicked on the 'Take quiz' button that would apparently determine her sexual compatibility with her partner, although she doubted there would be any surprises there:

Question 1: How often do you like to have sex? Pick the answer that most corresponds to you, and then do the same afterwards for your partner:

A) Anytime I can get it!

B) Twice a week.

C) On special occasions only.

They should have a D) Only when I have to so I can keep my husband happy. She clicked A for David, and in the absence of a D, selected C for herself.

Immersed in her quiz, Kate didn't hear the door open at first and jumped with a start when she realised David had entered the room and was standing at the end of the bed. Clutching the phone to her chest closer than a Cadbury Creme Egg, she asked, "Didn't you play tennis?" Trying to act nonchalant.

"Yes, but only one set; it started to rain," he answered, looking puzzled. "What are you doing in bed in the middle of the day? And why are you cuddling your phone?"

Kate was relieved that he hadn't walked in whilst she was fiddling with the Rabbit. "It's raining? That's so weird; it was so sunny before." *Deflect, deflect.* If David caught her doing a sex quiz he'd definitely see that as an invitation to rip off all his clothes and jump her.

"Well, that's Mallorca, isn't it. You'd have known if the curtains weren't shut. What are you doing by the way?" he asked, perching on the side of the bed and bent down to kiss her on the lips, taking a peek at her phone. He looked surprised. "You're doing a sex quiz?"

Busted! "I was just researching this tummy tuck and boob lift. I don't know what to do about it and then I actually came across a sexual compatibility test, and I just started."

His face transformed like a Halloween pumpkin, its grin stretching from ear to ear.

"And you need to do this with the curtains closed and in bed because …?" he chortled.

Not waiting for an answer, David manoeuvred himself into the bed next to Kate. Both fully clothed snuggled under the light duvet, as Kate read the next question to him:

"Question 2: What's your favourite place to have sex?

A) The bedroom obviously!
B) Anywhere and everywhere!
C) Public toilets!"

"I'm a definite B," David said without a smidgen of hesitation. Kate shuddered at the thought of anywhere public, let alone toilets, and once again thought that there should be a D) *Too tired to have any sex, would rather not.* But settled for A. David started to read the next question but Kate stopped him, placing her phone firmly down on the bedside table.

"This is a stupid quiz. We both know that we're not going to answer any of them the same."

David seemed disappointed, but he knew as much himself. "Did you get anywhere with the to do or not to do the tummy tuck dilemma then?"

"No, honestly. I didn't. I was hoping I would but now I'm even more confused than ever. Let's not talk about it. This cuddling is nice." She snuggled further into him so that his chin was resting on the top of her head.

"Kate, you are just so deliciously weird and wonderful. I love you. I truly do, and I just want you to be happy. I don't see what I think you see. I see a beautiful, sexy woman who is the mother of my children, who makes me laugh every day even when she doesn't mean to, who walks with me by my side to make life easier and … who I can't keep my hands off!"

David's word of reassurance fell on deaf ears. All Kate could focus on were those last few words: 'who I can't keep my hands off,' and visions of David initiating daytime sex popped into her mind. Whilst she recognised he might also just be enjoying a beautiful intimate moment, history had taught Kate that any moment had the potential to be a sexual one for David. Quicker than a wild hog escaping a lion, she leapt off the bed in record time, yelling, "Fluffy, Fluffy, I forgot to feed Fluffy. Sorry darling, laundry to do, lunches to make, rabbit to feed … "

"Maybe we can finish this quiz later then, together?" David called out to Kate's fast receding back, but Kate had escaped.

MAN MAGNETS
London, England
(Three Weeks Later)

"Don't look. They'll be over soon," announced Jamie. India looked. She wasn't the type to follow instructions. Luckily for Jamie, India didn't know who she wasn't supposed to be looking at.

"Look at me," said Jamie as she laughed loudly at nothing. She slowly ran her fingers through her smooth hair, which she'd taken great pains to tame with straighteners earlier that evening, in anticipation of their Saturday night out. "The guys that just sat two tables behind us. They'll be over soon."

"How do you know?" But India didn't need to ask. She knew better than to question Jamie's man-knowledge.

The girls had been in deep discussion over the female orgasm, and on their third round of Porn Star Martinis at Beach Blanket Babylon, or 'BBB,' as they liked to call it. Discerning enough to keep out the riff-raff but cool enough to lure a captivating audience. It had always been one of their favourite haunts, especially in its original gothic era. The candlelight offered just enough glow to filter the dark shadows of the late-night revellers, belying them as attractive as could be after a few drinks. Jamie had clocked the two guys from the moment they'd entered the bar; it would only be a matter of time before they made a move.

"Hi there, can we interest you girls in joining us for a drink?" The better looking of the two was the first to speak. Jamie and India feigned surprise at their impromptu intrusion. Ah, it was so easy. Men were predictable, and Jamie was rarely wrong.

"Hmmmm, okay, but just give us a moment; we're in the middle of something." Jamie liked to keep men waiting. In fact, she was professional at it. She played them like they played other women. Except Jamie played them better at their own game.

"Okay, maybe we can get you some drinks in the meantime?" The taller, cuter one seemed to be doing most of the talking, his eyes never leaving Jamie for even a second, as they both hovered, ever so hopefully, next to the girl's table.

"Sure, we'll have another round of Porn Star Martinis, thank you." India had zero interest in either, but wasn't about to turn down free drinks. The girls watched as the boys walked over to the busy bar, buying them enough time to figure out their next move.

"Ooh, he's so your type babe. You should totally go for him." India smiled at Jamie as she pushed her fringe, now long enough to tuck behind her ear.

"Oh, I fully intend to. Did you see those eyes? Damn, so sexy." Jamie hadn't met anyone she fancied in a while, and this was the type of distraction she could really go for. She made sure to keep up with the aimless laughter. Sure-fire man magnet. What man didn't like fun-loving girls? Much less those that weren't so easy to get.

It wasn't long before the boys were back and bearing drinks. Four perfect Martini glasses, with black straws and a dried passion fruit piece inside the middle of each.

"Hope you don't mind, but we added the Prosecco at the bar. Easier to carry. Is it okay to join you now?" This one had a cheekiness about him, and Jamie noticed a slight dimple on his right cheek as his smile broadened. His teeth were pretty nice, too. She looked away, not wanting to give away her interest too soon.

"Sure, take a seat." India made room as she shuffled her seat closer to Jamie's, taking one of the drinks and sucking the contents through the straw faster than you could shout, 'another round, please.'

Mark and Cameron were their names. It was obvious from the start that Cameron and Jamie had the strongest attraction. Cameron was exactly Jamie's type. Tall and boyishly good looking, with messy brown hair that she could run her fingers through and grab at an opportune moment. He had the deepest blue eyes—her favourite kind—shrouded in thick black lashes, and lips that were pink and full and just waiting to be kissed.

"So, what do you girls do?" Mark finally made small talk whilst making big eyes at India. Mark was from New Zealand. He loved to surf and had a particular liking for Diesel clothing, and now India. India, however, seemed distracted, more interested in fiddling with her outfit of the evening—a preloved silver baby doll dress she'd chanced upon in a thrift store in Paris, teamed with black Isabel Marant ankle boots she'd 'borrowed' from a shoot. Jamie knew the signs.

"Oh, we're models." Jamie smirked, as if it weren't obvious enough. She loved the way men's jaws predictably dropped when she said that. Somehow, their already evident interest would burst into orbit at the mere thought of being seen with cover girls. Men, so easy to impress.

Cameron was a graphic designer. At least, that's what he said he was. He'd been working on a rather large project for a new brand of beer. The mere mention of the word 'beer' had him drop a few levels in Jamie's estimation, but it wasn't his work talents she was after. In fact, Jamie wasn't listening too much to what he was saying. Mark said he worked in finance. Again, who knew and who really cared?

The boys had to be given credit for their efforts, as the girls weren't making it easy for them. Visibly uninterested, India suddenly piped up, with a trill in her voice, "Need to powder my nose, boys. Would you excuse me while I go to the little girls' room? Coming, Jamie?"

"What is it with you girls, always going to the bathroom together?" Mark was agitated that he wasn't able to secure an uninterrupted chat with the blonde bombshell. His face seemed to flush scarlet, in keeping with the strawberry blonde tone of his hair. Little did he know, India passionately disliked redheads. Mark had a snowball's chance in hell of getting anywhere with her.

Tinkering down the narrow stairs to the toilets, under the watchful glare of the washroom attendant, India feigned sickness and ran into one of the cubicles with Jamie closely behind.

"No, girls, No. Only one person in each toilet." The visibly despondent woman who had been sitting next to her little shop of perfume, gum, and all other manner of 'freshening up items' needed on a night out, stood up in panic.

"She's going to be sick. I need to look after her." Jamie barged her way into India's cubicle and quickly bolted the door closed behind them. Not totally convinced, the attendant succumbed, "Oh, okay, but no funny business," returning to her chair.

But funny business was exactly what India had in mind, as she pulled out an old rolled-up fifty pound note and a little bag of white powder that she'd stuffed into her padded bra.

Crouching down, she sprinkled some of the powder onto the

loo seat and, with precision, used her silver credit card to divide the happy dust into two perfect little lines.

Just before she took her first hit, India made the required retching sound, promptly followed by, "That's it sweetheart, get it all out," from Jamie, for the benefit of the attendant.

Nose powdered, India looked up at Jamie. "Want some?" Jamie declined. She wasn't into drugs. Vodka-based cocktails, yes, but so far, drugs hadn't really been her thing, despite many models doing it. Most did it to keep their weight down. But it was also just a part of the party scene, and no-one ever seemed to question it.

"No thanks, dolly. Maybe later." Jamie was leaning against the cubicle wall, her long legs struggling to find room. Thankfully, she was wearing jeans, so her skin didn't need to touch anything unsanitary. Her favourite black Rag & Bone skinny jeans, with a grey deconstructed T-shirt on top, and killer embellished Tom Ford heels for added statement factor.

"Oh come on babe. You need to chill. It's been a big month for you moving back to London. This is our night out. Let's have some fun." India wasn't wrong. It hadn't been easy leaving the island. There was so much she missed and she didn't want to focus on what she couldn't change.

"Go on then." Jamie gestured towards the one remaining line as anxiety started to creep in.

"That's my girl. You deserve some. Plus, we need to celebrate." India didn't need much of an excuse to celebrate. Waking up in the morning was reason enough.

As the metallic taste reached the back of Jamie's throat, a sudden surge of empowerment filled her. Yes, she was going to make London work for her again, and if she played the game properly, she was going to have sex with Cameron too.

* * *

"Hey, we thought you girls had done a runner," Mark announced as the girls returned to the table. Another round of cocktails seemed to have materialised in their absence.

"Well, we like to keep men waiting," Jamie purred, casting a sly glance in Cameron's direction. "Speaking of which, I'm afraid we're going to have to love you and leave you. My darling friend here isn't feeling too good, so I'm going to take her home." Jamie knew all too well that being difficult was only going to fuel Cameron's pursuit further, and she equally knew a foursome with India and Mark was not on the cards.

"Now? Really? Let's at least finish these drinks." Cameron's beautiful blue eyes widened. Bless, he was even sexy when he wasn't being cool.

"'Fraid so. Have to tuck her up safe and sound in bed." Jamie winked. "But okay. We'll have one for the road first." Jamie placed the straw in her mouth and ever so slowly sucked up the sweet liquid. Cameron watched, mesmerised. Inching in closer, he whispered in her ear, "You can't leave without giving me your number." His voice was deep and inviting and impossible to resist.

"Well I can." Although Jamie had every intention of giving her number, and the rest.

Cameron placed a hand on the back of her chair. It was taking all the restraint he could muster to not actually touch her. "I'd really like to see you again. How about dinner? Tomorrow night?" *Ooh, he smells as good as he looks too.*

Jamie smiled. "Well, tomorrow's another day. I'll see if I still remember you then." Grabbing Cameron's phone from his hand, stroking his fingers as he willingly released it, she held the screen to his face to unlock it. Deftly, she put her number into his contacts, naughtily adding, "You'd better be hungry."

Just as the girls were walking out of the building, Jamie's phone beeped, signalling a text. **Just checking.** It was Cameron. Sweet. Next time, she'd eat him alive.

* * *

Still groggy from the night's entertainment, Jamie snuggled under her luxe white silk bedding, hidden somewhere beneath her oversized duvet and the plump feather pillows. Their night on the tiles had ended up with the pair of them teetering legless into a car with Charles, another one of India's recent illustrious beaus. A forty-something banker from New York had his driver for the night and had called out India's name as they emerged from BBB. She must have messaged him from inside, or when she slipped out for a smoke. India was going through a phase of 'dating' older men. It was probably experimental; either that or they just had more money to spend on drugs.

Charles had managed to convince the girls to join him on an expedition of the seediest—correction—'sleaziest' joints that Mayfair had to offer. Every bar was overflowing with barely legal hookers or Eastern European titillators syphoning drinks from unsuspecting men. After India decided to carry on the party back at Charles' Belgravia pied-à-terre, Jamie decided her own bed was what she wanted most and snuck home.

It seemed no time had passed, and suddenly Madison had stormed into her room. "Mum, when did you get back?" Her small hands defiantly placed on her slim hips.

"Arrrrgggghhhh! I'm sleeping, I'm really tired. Let me sleep. Go back downstairs, sweetie, pleeease." That's all she needed, Madison on her case. Next, Maria would be up and interrogating her too, as was customary after each and every one of Jamie's nights out. That was more interrogation in her house than the local police constabulary probably got through in a week. Being so ridiculously puritanical in her views, Maria was never going to approve of Jamie's lifestyle. 'You should be a virgin until you're married,' was one of her first recommendations, but that fell on deaf ears as Jamie discovered the joy of sex—as well as every page in the *Kama Sutra*—by the age of sixteen.

Jamie pulled the covers over her head. Perhaps Madison would go away if she ignored her, but Madison just stood there, staring with despair at her slightly worse-for-wear mother.

"Locita. You're just like a child, Mum. I'm going downstairs."

The harsh reality was Jamie could not sleep in all day; she had a ten-year-old daughter to look after. Although with her head and room spinning and her heart doing ten to the dozen—one line had turned to three—she wasn't exactly perfect mother material. If she could just get some sleep, she could deal with the rest of the day. Glancing again at her phone to check the time, she contemplated texting Cameron, but quickly cast the ridiculous thought from her mind. She was wasted, but not so much as to do something that stupid. After all, she liked Cameron. No, she would wait. He'd call later, and that way she kept the power.

As the room spun faster, Jamie thought of Kate. She missed Kate. Responsible Kate, who would never allow her to get into such a state. What was it about being back in London that made her act so differently? Was it the city? India? Her friendship with India was nothing like her friendship with Kate. It was almost as if she wore a different persona with India. She wasn't so sure if she liked her

London-self as much as her Mallorca-self. Or more accurately, the person she was with India, compared to the one she was with Kate. *Ufffff, what was I thinking? Stupid drugs.* Jamie made a mental note never to take them again. The aftermath just wasn't worth it. Pulling her black satin mask over her eyes, the world started to blur again until she finally got back to sleep. Out cold.

* * *

"Mum, do we have to eat here? Why can't we go to McDonald's?" moaned Madison, as Jamie walked on ahead, following the young, French and rather tasty waiter as he showed them to their table at the High Road Brasserie. "But Mum, I really want to have chicken nuggets." Madison dragged her feet in protest.

Jamie ignored her and kept smiling through gritted teeth. She didn't want to create a scene or fuel the existing one further. Especially not with the gorgeous waiter hovering around, and especially not in the only place to be really seen in W4 since the Soho House chain had branched out to what was practically suburbia.

Madison reluctantly parked herself on the green leather banquette opposite her mother and huffed profusely. Her face was contorted into an unrecognisable demeanour, resembling someone who'd just swallowed a fly, or a slug or something equally distasteful. Jamie was not impressed. She had hoped for a lovely, relaxing afternoon, but it was clear she wasn't going to get one.

Looking back at Madison, who was momentarily quiet and fiddling with her hair—no doubt waiting for her mother to change her mind and offer lunch at McDonald's as she'd requested—Jamie smiled inwardly. Yes, Madison could be an annoying little brat at times, driving her to the brink of insanity, but she was still her daughter; her very pretty, manipulative, clever daughter, who she loved dearly.

"There's nothing I like on the menu," Madison announced loudly as she inspected the menu for McDonald's-style items. Lovely warm thoughts about daughter suddenly evaporated.

"Well, don't eat then." Anything to keep her daughter quiet; she didn't want a scene.

"But Mum, I'm hungry; do you want me to starve?" Madison's voice grew louder to match her now saucer-sized eyes.

"Shush." Jamie's patience was wearing thin as she glanced around to see if anyone was staring. Her head was pounding too. What was she thinking, taking Madison out to lunch today of all days?

"You like fish fingers, don't you? What about spaghetti or …" Jamie was still hopeful of finding a way to salvage the afternoon, and one that didn't involve McDonald's.

"I hate fish fingers. When did I say I liked fish fingers? God, you don't even know what your own daughter likes to eat. I like chicken nuggets. Why can't we just go to McDonald's? Daddy always takes me to McDonald's."

Jamie pulled a face, as if to say, 'ooh, Daddy this and Daddy that.' So what? Did taking one's child to a fast-food chain suddenly elevate one to Parent of the Year? What about all the times he wasn't around? Was he so great then? He certainly wasn't the one putting food on her plate, except for the occasional Happy Meal.

"I can't believe you, Mum. You're just going to let your own daughter starve?" Madison had now entered into her standard theatrical mode and fellow diners were beginning to stare, as was the cute waiter. Jamie grew tense. She glared across the table at her daughter, dressed in what felt like a statement outfit, not too dissimilar to her own. Low slung flared jeans, a white T-shirt with the words 'I'm not bossy I just have leadership skills' emblazoned on it, a purple cap, and graffiti print Converse trainers that Jamie had bought her in Berlin. As if it weren't embarrassing enough to have your own daughter dress like your twin—although Jamie's top was void of any wording—the last thing she needed was to attract the attention of normal civilised people trying to enjoy an uninterrupted lunch. As Jamie tried to look every which way but at her daughter, she noticed someone looking her way.

Several tables to the left of them sat a man who appeared to be sharing the same plight. His son—Jamie assumed it must be his son because why else would he choose to spend a Sunday lunchtime with someone else's child?—probably around the same age as Madison, she guessed, was also throwing a tantrum. Contrary to the flustered Miss King, the father appeared to be handling the situation remarkably well; he was cool and incredibly calm. Jamie was impressed; mesmerised by his patience. When he caught her looking back, he smiled a knowing smile, acknowledging their mutual predicament. Jamie smiled back; it was the first time her face had genuinely cracked since they'd arrived, and in that moment at least, no longer felt alone in her misery.

Jamie shook her head in dismay. It just wouldn't do. She decided it was best to get out of the restaurant as quickly as possible and make a swift exit before Madison really humiliated her. Besides, she was already sacrificing precious siesta-time. She rationalised it as a 'work' requirement, given she was booked for a shoot early the next morning. Dark, puffy eyes would not go down well at all. *Uhhh*, why had she stayed out so late, and why had she succumbed to the stupid drugs? The most fun she'd had was chatting with

Cameron, and then the night just went south. Speaking of Cameron, she still hadn't replied to the text he'd sent earlier whilst she was passed out. It read:

> La la la lala la la laaaa.
> I just can't get you
> out of my head. One
> minute we're talking
> and the next you've fled.
> Let me take you to dinner.
> Cameron - in case you've
> forgotten already.

Cute. Very cute. He was clearly paying homage to Kylie Minogue's classic, which she'd commented she liked, when it came on in the bar. Yes, she would reply. But later.

"Why aren't you ordering any food, Mummy?" Madison's tone had changed, and her face had taken on a worried expression, as Jamie was jolted out of her reverie. She was too tired for this.

"Because you don't want to eat. You don't like anything, remember?"

"B-b-but—" Madison tried to justify herself, but this time Jamie was the one doing the butting in.

"No buts, Maddy. You said you were starving, and you didn't like anything on the menu here, so we're going. You can eat something at home."

Madison went quiet. She pulled a sad face and painstakingly kept it that way as Jamie frog-marched her out of the restaurant. Passing the father and son, Jamie shrugged her shoulders as if to say, 'I give up.' The man shrugged back with a look that all but said, 'I know exactly what you're going through.'

En route home, Jamie realised she'd forgotten her cap, but she couldn't return now. That would be too embarrassing. She'd have to pop back the following day without Madison. She was a familiar face. She even had membership to High Road House now; for sure they'd keep it for her. Once home, Madison bolted upstairs to her room, slamming the door behind her. This alerted Maria, who went to investigate. Jamie knew Maria would only sympathise with Madison, but she really didn't have the energy to stop her. Frankly, she was grateful for the peace and quiet, and retreated to the sanctuary of her own bedroom. Sitting on the edge of her bed, Jamie took her laptop and decided to email Kate all about her woes. Kate would be sympathetic.

Laying back onto the warm, inviting covers, once she was done, Jamie was out cold. For the second time that day.

SALSA UNDER DURESS
Mallorca, Spain

Having run out of both credible and ridiculous excuses, David could no longer avoid the Salsa class. The night had arrived, and Kate was in her dressing room, standing in her underwear, trying to focus on getting ready. The class was in an hour and they needed a good half an hour to get there. Tali sat at the end of Kate's bed, her little hands cupping her face and watching her mother's movements with suspicious eyes.

"Why you go out?" she kept repeating over and over again like a mantra, yet with no soothing meditative effects. Tali's relentless whining was somewhat dampening Kate's excitement at the prospect of doing something fun. Kate appreciated that going out with David was a rarity; she couldn't even remember the last time someone else had put the girls to bed. But, on this occasion, their next door neighbour had agreed to babysit, and the girls knew her well, so it wasn't as if she was abandoning them with a complete stranger.

"I wanna go out." Came the next whine, having figured out that her mummy wasn't putting on her pyjamas, as she stood there in a semi-state of undress. When this also failed to achieve the desired response, Tali did what any other four-year-old who was being ignored would do; she sobbed. Her little chest heaving with her misery and imminent abandonment. *Oh, not the crying.* Kate was useless when the girls turned on the tears. You'd think she'd become immune to the sound by now, but she still couldn't bear it. She felt guilty. She knew it wasn't rational and that normal parents didn't stay in every night with their kids, but she also recognised that this was an unfamiliar experience for Emily and Tali. Desperate to comfort her little one and ease her own guilt, the words were out of her mouth before she'd processed them.

"If you're a good girl and have a happy smiley face when I go out tonight, then tomorrow, after school, we'll go to the pet shop and get you a goldfish." There she'd said it.

Yes, if Tali was going to play the 'guilt trip' crying card, then Kate would have no choice but to play her 'ace' bribery card. Besides, having now become a pet person, Kate saw no reason not to push the boat out a little further. Tali stopped the tears abruptly, as if someone had flicked a switch.

"I get fish, I get fish." Tali clapped her hands in excitement, jumping up and down on the bed, like it was a trampoline. Then her face went serious. "I get *dos* fish. Okay Mamá?"

Hmmmm, Kate thought, proud that her daughter had inherited her very own aptitude to negotiate and manipulate. Kate smiled. "Okay, okay, two fish, but no more tears." She watched Tali bounce off the bed. Mission accomplished. Now to finish getting dressed.

What, she wondered, did one wear to Salsa? Still in thought and undecided, the door to her bedroom burst open with such force that Kate jumped. An extremely angry Emily was approaching with a face like thunder. *Oh, what now?* Would she ever be allowed even five minutes to get ready? Emily charged at Kate, the force of which felt like a herd of wildebeest stampeding on the Serengeti plains. She was amazed that dust hadn't risen from the floorboards. The finger was out and being waggled in Kate's direction accusingly. Kate instinctively backed away and felt the urge to crouch in a ball, preparing for impact.

"I want a fish, how come you're getting Tali a fish and not me? You love her more," spewed Emily, her beautiful face contorted with rage.

Obviously, Emily had inherited her dramatic gene. Kate groaned. Was it too much to ask that just one of her children might've inherited David's lovely, placid nature? She was constantly being held to ransom by the 'you love her more than me' line. Kate decided that tonight the situation could be sorted out faster if she didn't brush off Emily's feelings of neglect. She grabbed her daughter by the hand and pulled her onto her lap. Emily, who just moments before had stood rigid and defiant in her declaration of loss and unloved status, quickly melted into her mother's arms.

Emily needed a lot of love. In fact, Emily needed copious amounts of love and reassurance, and Kate often wondered why her eldest daughter was so insecure when she was so loved. It was true that Tali had a knack for making Kate laugh, just the way she spoke with her funny little accent always tickled Kate's humour. Yet Emily was so kind, so loving and she knew deep in her heart that once Emily made it through childhood and they'd survived the teenage years; yes, she knew that once Emily had left home, then they would have a sensational relationship.

"Is this about the fish?" Kate kissed and stroked Emily's face, already knowing the answer and relieved that this time there would be a simple solution.

"Yes, I've been asking for a fish for months, and you keep on saying, 'no, we're not pet people' and then Tali gets one and she didn't even want one," Emily whined whilst doing a fairly good impersonation of Kate's, 'we're not pet people.'

Kate decided that perhaps now wasn't the best time to correct Emily by telling her that Tali was, in fact, getting two fish. Whilst Emily had stopped shouting, her tone had a definite moan to it, and Kate had to accept that she had made a bloody good point. Why had she been so quick to offer the fish to Tali? She probably should've just offered chocolate.

"I was going to tell you when I finished getting dressed that I was going to get you some fish," Kate lied—another great parenting tool.

Kate continued to kiss and stroke her daughter until Emily became all floppy in her arms. Once successfully placated, Emily eventually sauntered off. *Phew. World War five, thousand and eighty nicely diffused.* Perhaps indulging one's children was not the best long-term strategy, but Kate was happy to have a quick fix on this occasion. To not have her first evening out in ages marred by the ravaged faces of her two girls, standing at the door, waving goodbye as their mother deserted them to have, god forbid, a life of her own.

Should she wear black? Yes, black. Light linen trousers, black halter neck top, of which she had many, and black strappy sandals.

"Are you ready? Are you sure about this? Can't I tempt you to a night at Cocco's instead? We can have pizza," David almost implored entering the bedroom, dragging his feet like a slug on Valium. After nearly a month of every conceivable excuse, ranging from aching body parts to urgent work that needed his attention, which, surprise surprise, would always happen on a Tuesday night, they were finally going to Salsa. Before Kate had a chance to answer, a strange noise emanated through the house.

"What's that noise?" said Kate as they both stood in silence, listening to the unidentifiable noise. "That noise. That buzzing.

What is that?" Looking quizzically at David, who stared back at her with an equally mystified expression, shrugging his shoulders. "Tali, Emily, what's that noise?" Kate shouted out to the girls again. She needed to get dressed. She'd also planned to put on some makeup and she was running out of time.

Giggles and laughter echoed around the house.

"It's the back-massager thingy. We thought it was broken, but then we saw it didn't have any batteries, so we took them from the TV remote. It feels so great Mummy," Emily shouted back from the playroom at the end of the hallway.

Kate looked at David. David looked at Kate. Neither of them had a clue what Emily was talking about; they didn't own an electric back massager. Seeking further clarification, Kate yelled out, "What back massager?"

"Da big purple funny one wid da liddle rabbit on it," said Tali in all innocence, entering the bedroom, holding Kate's vibrator over her shoulder and moving it all around her neck. Kate wanted to die, her face turning strawberry red. Why was it that every time that Rabbit made an appearance, she ended up wanting the ground to swallow her whole? She turned to David blushing. David now had a huge grin on his face.

"Getting in the mood for Salsa, were we? This might not be so bad after all."

* * *

"So ...?" David took the slip road onto the main motorway that would take them through Palma to the Boomba Bar.

Kate was silent. *Uff, the bloody vibrator. Of course, he wouldn't let this go.* It was unusual for David to speak whilst they were in the car. She was used to sitting in silence, happy to watch the world go by. During the day, one could see the Tramuntana mountains. She loved driving in Mallorca. She'd hated driving in London, but here it gave her pleasure, 360 degrees of magnificent beauty. Those mountains hugging her little village and the route to the main city of Palma. She was never tired of the view; it was as if her own energetic frequency harmonised with her surroundings. Every journey, an exquisite moment of joy, a delectable feast for the senses. As they never went out at night, this was a relatively new visual experience for her. The sun was just beginning its descent to bed; shadows cast their long fingers across the mountains, as an orange glow seeped across the horizon. An invitation to gratitude. It was both spectacular and calming.

Kate could have purred, so great was her feeling of contentment at that precise moment. She wondered whether she'd be any good at Salsa? Would David? Maybe they wouldn't work together? After all, there was a height difference. *Damn, I should've worn heels.* What would the instructor be like? What would the other people be like? The questions whirled.

"So?" David interrupted her reverie. There was no avoiding it. Trying to delay the obvious conversation, Kate averted her eyes from the sky to David. A small smile played on his lips. Kate noticed he'd put some gel in his hair, so it was sticking up rather than flopping over his eyes as usual. *At least he's made some effort.*

"What?" Although Kate knew exactly why he was breaking his no-talking persona in the car; she attempted to veer the conversation elsewhere. "How's the project going? Are you going on site tomorrow?"

David started grinning. "Come on Kate, are you going to tell me about your vi-bra-tor experience?" He said the word slowly, each syllable accentuated, whilst his voice dropped an octave as if he were Tom Jones about to launch into a rendition of *Sex Bomb*. There was no avoiding it.

"I didn't really have an experience, to be fair. I tried, but there were no batteries." She twirled her hair around her index finger and simultaneously chewed on her bottom lip.

"But you got it out of the box at least. That's movement in the right direction." His eyes never left the road, even though he was tempted to steal a glance at her to gauge whether he was entering dangerous territory. Feeling brave, he decided to keep going. "And yet our ten-year-old and four-year-old managed to figure out getting batteries out of the remote?"

Kate started to laugh. "Yes, it's taken me six months to get it out of the box. I'm doing great"—she said with sarcasm—"and the batteries are far more useful in the remote than in my vibrator," Kate said, stating the bleating obvious. David was encouraged by her obvious good humour. He was jesting. Sort of.

"I thought we were going to have a play with it together," David said gingerly. His hair, despite being gelled, had now succumbed to gravity and made its way into his eyes. He stuck out his bottom lip, trying to blow the rogue strand before he allowed his hand to momentarily leave the wheel to swipe it to one side. He wanted to have this conversation, and he knew that Kate absolutely didn't, so he needed to tread carefully.

"I don't think it's an 'us' project. I think it's something that I need to explore on my own, to be honest."

"But you do want to explore?" David's voice flickered with excitement as he stole a quick glance over at her.

Avoiding eye contact, Kate turned her attention back to the sky without answering. The sun had now completely disappeared behind the mountain, and the orange glow morphed into a fuzz of magenta. The street lights blinked into action as if they'd received direct instructions from the sun to pick up the gauntlet and illuminate the world.

"When did this failed attempt occur?" David persisted.

There was no point in trying to change the subject or ignore his questions any more. They were having this conversation. The sooner it was done, the better, and then she could get back to thinking about Salsa.

"That day you came home from tennis early and caught me in bed, going down a rabbit hole on social media about my tummy tuck and boob lift, remember?" Kate murmured, still finding herself mesmerised by the sun's symphony.

"So, your moment with the Rabbit ended up with you going down the rabbit hole! Nice play on words."

She hadn't meant to be funny, but yes he was right and they both had a chuckle, when she saw them pass the exit to Palma Nova. "DAVID!"

"What?"

"You missed the turning—again." Kate didn't shout. This was such a normal occurrence.

It wasn't uncommon for Kate and David to turn a five-minute journey into half an hour. Even on a route they'd done a million times before, she could never presume that David was going to head there. She'd often been distracted looking at her phone, only to look up a moment later to find they were going in the complete opposite direction. It used to irritate her, but over the years, she'd come to accept this as one of David's not so endearing qualities.

"Whoops."

"No worries." Kate felt relieved she'd built in the extra ten minutes to their journey to allow for this precise scenario. "Just take the Magaluf exit and circle back."

"Anyway …" He was eager to return the conversation back to his favourite topic. "So, will you give it another go?"

"What?"

"The vibrator. Now it's got batteries. Will you give it another go?"

"Yessssssss, don't worry. It's on my list of things to do." She didn't mention that it was currently the very last thing on the famous list, ranking just below 'research new washing machine.'

"Because it's important."

"The vibrator is important?"

"No, you finding your elusive orgasm is important"—he hesitated—"to me. Please don't give up, Kate. It can be better. I love you. Honestly, you are the most amazing mother. You run our house and make our lives all so enriched. You are my best friend. It's just that …" He couldn't find the right words, but he needed to tell her, "It upsets me that you won't experiment and try to find a way to enjoy sex as I do. I don't want to feel like you're doing me a favour. It's important for us." He concluded as he stole a glimpse at her.

"No, sex is important for you. I'm not you. It's not that important to me. Our love, our children, our health, our connection, those things are important. The sex would be a bonus, but I'm just not wired like you." Seeing the sign for Palma Nova again. "The Salsa class is important. David, the turning."

This time, he successfully managed to exit the motorway.

She felt guilty. Again. Defensive. Again.

"At the roundabout, take the first exit and then, at the next roundabout, take the first exit and the Boomba Bar should be there."

David was quiet as the change in mood cloaked the car. This was not how this evening was supposed to go down.

"I will. I promise I will continue to explore, but I need to do it on my own first. Can you just please give me the space to do that and stop talking about it all the time? It's just too much pressure."

"Okay," he said as he reached the next roundabout and the bright neon sign of The Boomba Bar came into view. "Whatever you need to do, Kate, just do it. Please."

She wasn't sure what he meant by that, exactly. Buy more vibrators? Go see a therapist? But they were entering the car park.

"And," he said.

Oh my fucking god. STOP. Kate dropped her head into her hands.

"If you need help, then obviously I'm happy to try new things. You know that." David was relentless. Thankfully they'd reached their destination. If the Boomba Bar had been as far as Andratx, she'd probably have jumped out of the moving car by now.

"Happy to try new things? What about handcuffs?" she said, desperate to lighten the mood whilst thinking that if she could restrain him, she could run away and get on with more important things.

"Handcuffs?" His face lit up. "Yes, yes, that's exactly what I'm talking about. I could cuff you, no problem." Not realising that she'd been joking.

"Actually, I would cuff you." Kate was quick to correct him but happy that they were now parked and the dreaded conversation would have to reach a conclusion.

"No chance," he said, turning off the ignition and opening the car door. "You'd probably cuff me to the bed and go watch telly."

"Ha ha, you're right. Although difficult—no batteries in the remote!"

THE LESSON

The building was dark. As they opened the door, they hesitated, allowing a moment for their eyes to adjust. The stairs in the foyer were lit with neon lights, and arrows indicated the Boomba Bar was downstairs. Slowly, they descended, David dragging his feet behind Kate. As they reached the bottom, she turned to face him, "You don't want to do this, do you?"

"Think I would've preferred a cookery class, but I'm prepared to try it, if it makes you happy." He seemed genuine enough. Kate felt warm and happy. Such a lovely, kind, sensible man.

"It's pretty amazing that you found an English-speaking Salsa teacher. Well done."

Kate stopped short. Warm, happy feelings vanished faster than a pizza at a party full of starving teenagers. Stupid, annoying man. Why did it have to be an English Salsa teacher? Why did David presume it was going to be in English? She'd never told him that. She didn't have a clue whether the teacher was Spanish, English, or Japanese. Why was it important, anyway? It was a dance class, not a book club. Kate felt worried. David wouldn't do it if it was in Spanish; he'd use that as a convenient excuse to wiggle his way out of it. *Shit. Shit. Shit. Please let the teacher speak English. Pleeeease.*

As they pushed open the double-frosted glass doors at the bottom of the stairs, they entered an empty bar. Things obviously didn't get going here until much later. The inside of the bar wasn't any better lit than the foyer, yet it seemed like a fitting ambience to dance Salsa. Plus, it conformed exactly to the image Kate had conjured up.

A large dancefloor dominated the room and a disco ball, a throwback from the seventies, twirled, casting its mesmerising light show over the empty dance floor. In the background, acoustic Latin American music reverberated as if in harmony with the disco ball light show. Hugging the outskirts of the room were low-level couches; the sort that were no doubt very comfortable, but hell to get up from. To the far left was a long bar, which stretched the width of the room, and floor-to-ceiling mirrors, which gave a sense of grandeur far greater than the reality. Blue fluorescent lighting surrounded this palace of mirrors, lighting up the corners of the darkened room. Kate made a mental note that white bras should be avoided at all costs on Salsa nights.

Looking around, Kate noticed a couple standing at the far end of the room. The woman was shuffling her feet and staring down at the floor, whilst the man was looking around and appeared to be more enthusiastic than his partner. The woman was stunning; long blonde hair and elegant clothes. Totally out of place in this seedy environment; far better suited lounging on the front of a luxury yacht. The man seemed perfectly at ease, but as Kate observed him, she noticed the confident manner in which he carried himself. Tall, sun-streaked blonde hair and an athletic build; she guessed he was in his late thirties. An air of arrogance surrounded him. On closer inspection, Kate noted that the woman looked more miserable than anxious, with a pained expression furrowed on her face. Kate imagined that perhaps, like David, she was also here under duress. The man was now stroking her back; there was something so sensual about the way he glided his hands up and down that a shiver ran down Kate's spine. Next to them stood a group of three women, clearly friends, giggling and whispering to one another, no doubt about the two young men standing on the opposite side of the room. Kate wondered with amusement if the men, like the girls, were discussing who would get to dance with whom.

In the corner stood a woman shuffling papers. Kate surmised she must be the teacher and walked across to her, dragging a reluctant David behind her.

"Hello, we're here for the beginner's Salsa class," Kate said, with more confidence than she felt. David extricated his hand from her vice-like grip, and she instinctively reached back to grab it. Partly to give her the confidence she wasn't feeling, but mostly to stop him from doing a runner.

"*¿Perdona?*" came the reply. *Shit. Spanish.*

Ignoring David, who was now pulling at her hand, Kate tried again in her best Spanish, "*Nosotros estamos aquí por la nueva clase de Salsa.*"

"*Si, apunte su nombre aquí. La clase empieza en cinco minutos.*"

Kate wrote their names down on the list as instructed, whilst David started tugging with increased frequency as he hissed into her ear, "No way. There's no way I'm doing this in Spanish. You lied to me. I'm here under false pretences. Let's go."

"I didn't lie to you. I honestly didn't know." Kate stalled while trying not to rise to the bait. Taking a deep breath, she said calmly—well, more calmly than she felt—"Look, we're here now. Just give it a go. You only need to watch the steps; it doesn't matter what language it's in."

The teacher, Isabel, introduced herself. She looked almost exactly how Kate had imagined—long dark hair twirled into a bun like a ballerina, with a glowing olive complexion. Kate was grateful for the interruption. Isabel clapped her hands and signalled to the motley group to approach the dance floor. A look of relief flooded over the singletons. No partner choosing tonight. Obviously, they were going to learn the steps first, and the whole partner thing would come later.

"*¡Mira!*" Isabel said. "Watch!" Kate translated for David in a whisper so as not to disturb the other students.

"I'm not a complete imbecile," David growled under his breath.

Isabel, very slowly and with precision, placed her left foot forward to the count of '*uno.*'

Kate didn't bother to translate, '*uno*' into 'one,' hoping that years of Spanish lessons might at least have enabled David to count from one to ten. Now '*dos,*' the weight shifts back to the right foot and then '*tres,*' the weight transferred again to the left foot.

Isabel clapped and David, who'd begun to sweat, his hair sticking to the nape of his neck, whispered into Kate's ear, "I feel like a complete and utter prat."

Kate squeezed his hand in an attempt to soothe him and whispered back, "You're doing great. We're all in the same boat." She was exhausted. They'd only done three steps, but it was the energy consumed by David's misery that was draining her.

Something like a "Humph," left his lips.

Reaching '*cinco,*' Isabel continued with her instructions, but Kate was confused; what had happened to '*cuatro,*' the number four? David didn't seem to question the disappearing number. His face just screwed up trying to work out which foot was going where.

This is great, thought Kate.

This is a nightmare. David's thoughts were far removed from his wife's.

Confident that the class had mastered the first few steps, Isabel decided to try it to music. Turning up the volume, the Latin beats that had been playing inconspicuously in the background suddenly filled the room.

"*Uno, dos, tres … cinco, seis, siete. Uno, dos, tres … cinco, seis, siete.*" Isabel called out repeatedly.

Kate still felt confused about the missing number four and wanted to put up her hand, but as nobody else seemed concerned, she tried to let it go and found herself focusing on Isabel instead. She noticed how her hips seemed to gyrate to the rhythm of the music and attempted a similar movement of her own. David was just sort of bobbing up and down, his movements bearing no relevance to the beat whatsoever. In fact, his whole body seemed rigid with tension.

Kate looked around. The two boys were also doing similar bobbing movements but at least had the grace to be smiling, whilst the girls seemed to have grasped the hang of it, adding a little wiggle of the bottom here and a swing of the hips there, just like Isabel. The other couple were behind them so Kate couldn't see how they were faring, but she smiled and was satisfied with her efforts.

"Isn't this fabulous?" she whispered to David.

"Yes, just fabulous." David's eyes rolled.

"*Uno, dos, tres … cinco, seis, siete.*" They continued to practise until Isabel clapped her hands together, signalling a break. David made a run for the bar, where water bottles had been conveniently laid out, and seemed relieved to be off the dance floor.

"So you go forward first, and then you come back to the same place, and then you go forward again?" David attempted to show a modicum of enthusiasm. At least he'd get points for effort, as there'd be none awarded for style.

"Yup, nothing to it," Kate said confidently.

The boys had mustered up the courage to speak to the girls as they all congregated at the far end of the bar, seemingly relaxed. Kate looked around for the other couple and spotted them outside the door. The woman seemed upset. She was trying to go up the stairs. The man was trying to mollify her, pulling her from behind. Kate watched mesmerised, as he stroked her cheek and whispered in her ear. David was still next to her, mouthing "*uno, dos, tres ... cinco, seis, siete,*" as he continued to bob up and down.

Isabel called the group back to the dance floor. Kate couldn't take her eyes off the couple. She watched with fascination as the man drew the beautiful woman into his arms. He picked up a strand of her hair and ran it through his fingers, looking at his partner with such intensity that it made Kate shiver. The woman still appeared to want to leave, but his powers of persuasion were working. Just a few more strokes of her face and whisperings in her ear, and she finally came around, allowing herself to be led back through the doors and onto the dance floor; this time with a smile on her face.

Kate wondered what he could've whispered to have caused such a dramatic change of attitude. As they entered the dance floor, the man spotted Kate looking at him and winked. Caught as a voyeur, the blood rushed to her cheeks. Kate tried hard to pretend that she hadn't been watching them by keeping her eyes fixed to the point just beyond his head and a blank expression on her face. Thank goodness the room was so dark.

During the second half of the class, they concentrated on learning the next steps. It seemed inconceivable that in one hour, they'd only mastered two steps. As hopeful as Kate was, she couldn't imagine they'd be dancing Salsa in the clubs anytime soon, if this was their rate of progress. Perhaps they might have to do an intermediate class before they went public.

"I'm not coming again," David stated matter-of-factly when Isabel announced that the class was over.

"But you promised me." Kate looked down at her feet, exhausted. If only she had the same persuasion skills as the blonde man had with his partner. She reached up to grab a strand of David's hair and tried to mirror the actions of the man. David manoeuvred himself away from her, swiping her hand as if she were an irritating mosquito. "No, I'm sorry. I can't do this in Spanish. We have to do an activity that I can understand. I didn't get a thing she was saying."

"But she didn't say anything, only one, two, three, five, six, seven." Kate's face pulled into a grimace.

"Ha bloody ha. That was today. What happens when the steps get more complicated, and she says things like twirl, or swirl or kick or flick? No, sorry, I can't do it in Spanish."

Kate didn't want to get into it there, but she found it amusing that David's understanding of Salsa would be that they would be kicking, flicking, twirling and swirling. Determined not to give up so soon, she went to speak to Isabel. Perhaps she knew of an English Salsa teacher in the area. *Fat chance.*

David watched Kate gesticulating with her hands and started praying. *Please don't let her know of an English-speaking teacher.* Minutes later, Kate rushed back to him with a huge grin on her face. *This isn't good. This is bad.* David groaned.

"You'll never guess what?" she said.

"What?" He sounded distinctly disinterested, having already presumed he'd extricated himself.

"You'll never guess."

"What?"

"Fabulous news. She's doing the next class in English because most of this group doesn't even speak Spanish. Guess she's going to do a crash course and learn the few relevant words that she needs to know, no doubt including twirl, flick and swirl," Kate said cheekily.

There was very little David could say and, he wondered, as they walked out of the club, what body part he might have to break in order to get out of this? Ten weeks seemed like a life sentence to him. Perhaps he could buy her something to get out of this predicament.

As they walked towards the stairs, Kate heard the tail end of the conversation between the man and the stunning woman, "Robert, I no come next week"—she was saying to him in a strong accent—"I no like it. I really no come at all." Kate couldn't pinpoint where she was from exactly; clearly somewhere exotic with those looks.

The man seemed to ignore his distressed partner and turned back towards Kate. Their eyes locked. This time, Kate didn't avert her eyes. She found herself hypnotised and inexplicably drawn to him. She shuddered involuntarily but still held his gaze.

WILD ABANDON
London, England

"You see this part here … God spent a whole extra day creating this part," announced Cameron as he brushed his finger along the inside of Jamie's arm.

Unsure whether to cringe or smile sweetly at this obvious 'line,' Jamie settled for keeping quiet. After all, he was unbelievably hot, and she didn't give two hoots what he was saying.

Jamie's restraint had clearly done the trick in whetting Cameron's appetite. They had met a few times previously, always at night, always with alcohol, but never enjoyed more than a kiss—or however many kisses go into a kissathon. Kissing was fine. Sex was fine too. But on this occasion, recognising the potential player in Cameron, Jamie decided to make him wait. As much as he tried to keep his cool after their dinner, he simply couldn't keep his hands to himself any longer. Wanting to draw out the inevitable as long as possible, Jamie suggested a round of vodka shots would be rather fun, but this only served to set their temperatures rocketing further.

Tucked behind the curtain in The Parlour at Sketch, a long-time haunt of Jamie's, cosied up in the corner seat, the kissing frenzy started up again. Gently nibbling at first, sucking, and then more intensely. Jamie was actually quite taken aback by Cameron's technique; this boy was rather good. It wasn't often that a man fared well by her impossibly high standards.

Cameron took his index finger and softly drew it across Jamie's lips. Trembling a little, she couldn't resist grabbing a bite. Not too hard, but enough to make him jump a little. Taking his now wet finger, Cameron slid it across her face and behind her ear, before slowly but surely sliding it down her neck and then along her spine, through the opening in the back of her slinky and ever so skimpy golden dress. Jamie shivered. She liked that.

Jamie considered leading Cameron into one of the 'pod' loos, but that would be too obvious. No, it was time to take this party elsewhere. Within minutes, they were headed out of the bar and into the nearest cab.

* * *

As the black cab pulled up outside Cameron's apartment building, Jamie slid her hand inside his black dress coat and grabbed his T-shirt, aggressively yanking him towards her. She placed the other hand at the back of his head and, tugging on his hair, pulled his face to hers. Her lips attacked his with such force that he almost lost his breath. Cameron's heart was beating so fast now that Jamie could feel it pounding against her chest. Then she drew away—but only for a moment—before finally going back in and softly but firmly biting his upper lip. Jamie smiled. A knowing, come-hither smile that would guarantee her the night they'd been building up to. She knew what she was doing. She needed him to be worked up into a sexual frenzy in order to ensure wild abandon. Wild abandon was what she lived for. It was the only time she allowed herself to focus purely on the moment–the deliriously delicious moment.

The time it took between leaving the cab and getting inside the apartment was a total blur. No sooner had the couple entered the hallway—barely remembering to shut the door behind them and quickly casting aside their jackets—Cameron had Jamie pinned up against the wall. He took one hand and lifted her already short dress, exposing even more smooth flesh. Jamie wrapped one thigh-high booted leg around his waist, yanking him in closer still. Their mouths ravenous, licking, sucking and biting with such vigour that Jamie knew a red rash would be inevitable the following day. She had a feeling the rash might be worth it and allowed him to continue. Cameron moved down from her mouth and onto her neck, his hands exploring her body, feeling her every inch, every curve.

Jamie felt an urge to take control. She pushed him away with all her force and onto the floor. Straddling him to keep him down, squeezing his torso with her thighs, she lunged forward and licked his lips, then slid her tongue down towards his neck. T-shirt in the way, she grabbed the bottom of the fabric and hauled it upwards. Cameron instinctively raised his arms, allowing the cotton garment to slide off effortlessly, before Jamie cast it aside and threw it to the floor. Faced with this delicious boy's bare chest, she took a moment to savour the view, as she gently ran her fingers ever so softly from his Adam's apple down to his navel, over the tanned, toned torso, before making a beeline for his nipples. She licked her finger provocatively before touching, teasing them into erection. Cameron's eyes closed, and then he looked up, narrowing his stare. "Fuck, you're hot."

Jamie smiled slyly. Before she could think further, he grabbed her and, in an almost fireman's lift-style movement, carried her into the kitchen, placing her onto the work surface. So far, Jamie had barely taken note of her surroundings, but the kitchen was brighter than the entrance, as the window was large and uncovered, allowing the orange glow of the street lamp to filter through. The white melamine units glistened in the rich golden hue. They deceived one into believing the appearance was more beautiful than they really were, in contrast with the stark industrial harshness of the aluminium-effect flooring. Everything was clean and tidy. Jamie almost felt disappointed. As much of a neat-freak as she was, it would've been much more dramatic and sexy to knock things off the work surface in the heat of the moment. Jamie visualised everything; she lived her life as if she were in a movie. It must have been all those years spent on set.

"So, what are you going to do with me now?" Jamie coyly twisted her hair around her little finger.

"I'm going to make you scream." And she believed him, although she did feel a slight urge to giggle, but now was not the time for humour.

Jamie watched intently as Cameron ran his hands up and down her black leather boots, each time reaching further and further north until he was playing just outside her knickers, sliding a finger gently under the edge, and then back out again. Jamie trembled with anticipation.

"Take your dress off." Cameron was more forceful now. She suspected he would be a confident lover, and all signs were clearly pointing that way now.

Jamie began to lift up her flimsy mini-dress, slow enough for him to relish each new exposed part of her body, one inch at a time.

"You can keep your boots on though," he said with a half wink.

Jamie knew the boots would be a good choice. She had this whole evening planned, right down to every item in her 'you never know' bag, which contained compulsory oversized dark sunglasses, essential for the next morning. And the boots? Her one-way ticket to 'pleasuredome.'

With Jamie now sitting on the kitchen counter in nothing but her panties and the boots, Cameron wasted no time in exploring her further. He was licking her breasts, her waist, her fingers. This boy was biding his time. Making her wait. Making her hot. Very hot. In fact, she couldn't stand the anticipation any longer. She reached for his belt and swiftly, adeptly, unbuckled it, snatching it from the loops, discarding it to the floor. "Fuck, just come here will you!" she said as she pulled him in close, launching her tongue deep into his mouth and savouring each and every sensation. Her groin now pressed hard against his.

"Not so fast," Cameron protested as he prized her away and started his descent. His tongue didn't leave a spot of skin untouched. Jamie knew where this was going, and yet she still felt excited, as if she were experiencing it for the first time. His fingers had already delved inside her knickers and were now gently testing how wet she'd become. By the time his mouth had reached her navel, she was more or less tearing his hair out. How could he be so strong? How could he hold out this long? But before she could think any further, Cameron pulled her knickers to one side and buried his mouth deep within her. She stopped whatever it was that she was doing. It was futile. She had melted. Melted into the moment. Melted into his tongue, into his lips, into him. This boy had obviously done this before and plenty of times.

Jamie's heart was beating so fast now she could hardly breathe. She grabbed a mop of his hair and wrenched him upward, digging her nails into his back as she pulled him towards her. His Calvin Kleins had now been pulled down to his upper thighs when she quickly thought and blurted out simultaneously, "Condom." She was a safety girl, and besides, she didn't need any more grumbling kids begging her to take them to McDonald's. Gathering her thoughts, which was hard to do in the moment, Jamie insisted, "We need a condom." With the words finally registering, Cameron slid his hand into his pocket and adeptly proceeded to pull one out, unwrap it and have it on quicker than you could say, 'ta-da!' Wasting no more time, Cameron finally thrust deep inside.

Jamie moaned, "Oh my god."

Then again, he forged forwards, knocking her slightly backwards into the cupboard door, but she held tight, holding onto anything she could grab hold of. On this occasion, the kitchen tap and a cupboard handle. Then, unexpectedly, Cameron slowed down. Jamie looked perplexed. *What's he doing?* His thrusts became slower and more provocative until he came out of her, teasing her, toying with her, making her beg him to re-enter.

"Come back here," she ordered, but Cameron, a master at endurance, was making her wait, waiting for her desperation to peak, to be on the brink of eruption. Then he literally grabbed her again, off the work surface and into the living room, this time onto the small charcoal grey leather sofa.

Clearly this is Cameron's idea of a guided tour, thought Jamie amusingly to herself. Stepping out of his jeans and boxers in one professional swoop, Cameron climbed on top of the eager Jamie, who had arranged herself in a most tantalising manner, ensuring her body was looking its best. After all, he wasn't after her brains.

Launching in on her lips first, Cameron kissed her with such passion that when he did re-enter her, she shook uncontrollably. Jamie did her best to gyrate with the flow, moving with him, clinging to him like a finely tuned machine. She wanted him to go faster, harder, deeper and so she coaxed him into it by speeding up her own movements. She also wanted to burn as many calories as she could. Before long, the couple were so in sync that Jamie thought she was about to climax any moment, but suddenly Cameron lifted her up and turned her around.

Arrrrgggghhhh. Now on her hands and knees, Cameron had Jamie right where he wanted her. Jamie glanced back at him and watched as he bulldozed into her tiny frame. Despite enjoying it, Jamie abruptly moved away, pushing him onto his back. He wasn't running the whole show. She climbed on top of him, dominantly. She knew what she had to do. Now it was her turn to drive him wild. Drawing upon years of experience, Jamie worked the poor boy so hard he was gasping for air. She paused to look at him. His eyes were hazy, his mouth blood red and ajar.

"Oh my god," he yelled, his body trembling. She felt him gasp, then again. Finally, when Jamie could see Cameron was in that heightened state of euphoria, she pushed it just that bit further. He tried to pull away. She didn't let him. Eventually she had to, or risk game over.

Cameron lifted Jamie up to standing and turned her to face the wall. She held one hand out to stop herself from crashing into it, whilst the other hand continued to try to feel him, touch him, anything, but he pushed her arm away.

"You're one horny bitch, you know that?" he hissed.

Jamie narrowed her gaze and smiled.

He thrust and thrust until Jamie could take it no more. Panting slightly, slippery in their sea of sweet sweat, their bodies had become one, and like a bottle of Coca-Cola that had been shaken vigorously, eventually the lid was removed and they both burst into pure ecstasy.

Cameron gently turned Jamie around to face him. His demeanour now soft, he carefully cupped her face in his hands and tilted her head upward toward his, "You're incredible, you know that?"

Jamie didn't respond, she just stared, quizzically. She often lost interest in men once they'd had sex. She'd even been known to leave and go home once the guy had fallen asleep, only to receive a poor, sorry text hours later, asking 'Where's Jamie? Did I dream her?' It was more about the chase. She enjoyed the time leading up to the main event. On this occasion, she wasn't sure what she felt. But she sure as hell wasn't about to reciprocate the compliment.

* * *

A few hours later, Jamie woke up in Cameron's bed, enveloped in his strong athletic arms, and still wearing the boots. She must have fallen asleep, and now the daylight was peeking through the thin curtains. She'd stayed long enough. She had to get out of there. The evening had been wonderful, but she had to leave. Gently, she stroked his back and whispered, "I'm going now."

Cameron opened his eyes. "Why? No. Come back here."

But she had to leave.

ALTER EGO
Mallorca, Spain

Kate didn't want to go to the Boomba Bar. Kate didn't want to go anywhere; especially not to the third Salsa class that was taking place that evening. She paced up and down the length of her bedroom, ransacking the far depths of her imagination for a plausible excuse. This was no easy feat, particularly after all the nagging and cajoling it had taken to get David there in the first place. Headache perhaps? No, that wouldn't work, she never had headaches. Something more serious than that. Period pain? Nope, that wouldn't work either. David knew exactly when she had her period. She needed to be more innovative. Brain tumour? Yes, that was it, a brain tumour, she thought rather dramatically. Or death? Perhaps she could just drop dead, and then all her troubles would be over?

Back and forth she paced, inwardly groaning. In what seemed like a most unlikely and ironic turn of events, David actually wanted to go to Salsa and all she wanted to do was dive under the covers of her big, crisp, white linen duvet and stay there, forever. Shaking her head in despair, Kate continued to pace. How could this have happened? How could she, of all people, prim n' proper Kate, have gotten herself into this situation? Out of nowhere, a voice—her alter ego's voice, a presence that had materialised in the last class—

suddenly invaded her thoughts, taunting her. *Go to Salsa ... go to Salsa ... go to him.* Kate inwardly screamed back. *No. No. No.*

The battle had been raging ever since she'd returned from the previous Tuesday's class. She could not give into this evilness. Oh, why had she suggested they take up Salsa? Why did the rabbit have to pee on the yoga ad? Why hadn't it peed on the Salsa ad and done a poo on the yoga one instead? Yes, it was the rabbits' fault, and who'd bought the rabbits? David. So he'd brought this on himself. Kate continued to rationalise. This was all David's fault; she was blameless, innocent even.

Suddenly, David popped his head around the door. "Are you getting ready?"

Kate glared at him, her eyes squinting accusingly, and said nothing.

"What?" David asked in all innocence, confusion sweeping through him—not for the first time that week. Something was strange. Something was different. Kate was acting strange and different, and he knew he needed to tread carefully. Extremely carefully.

"Problem?" David spoke in his usual gentle manner, which seemed to snap her out of her peculiar trance.

Kate shook her head as she plonked herself dramatically onto the super king-size bed that dominated their bedroom. A pained expression took over her face. "Um, not sure I can be bothered to go tonight. It looks like it's going to rain." She glanced nervously out of the large window at the big, dark grey cloud that hovered ominously over the orange groves beyond.

Weird, thought David, acknowledging that it did look somewhat overcast, but it rarely rained in July, and it was not like Kate to miss out on Salsa. He'd even caught her putting on a CD and practising the steps around the kitchen table a number of times; her face at first scrunched up in concentration and then delight as she perfected what they'd learnt. After the first class, he'd resigned himself that escape was impossible and total compliance a forgone conclusion. To be perfectly honest, David wasn't really thinking about the class itself, but what had happened after the class. There appeared to be some sort of peculiar correlation between Salsa and Kate actually wanting, no, more than that, liking and participating in their love-making.

Images filled his mind of the way she'd been after the previous class. Her skin soft like satin, her smell sweet like banoffee pie. Yes, definitely worth an hour of misery if it meant he'd get a repeat performance. He had to get her up and out to Salsa so they could have the 'après Salsa.'

"Come on, sweetheart, you love Salsa. It's not that bad out, and I promise not to step on your toes." David waited to see some movement from Kate, but no action ensued. "I promise I'll dance with you tonight. You won't have to dance with any strange men this time." He attempted with renewed vigour.

Kate groaned as guilt coursed through her. David thought she didn't want to go because he'd all but crippled her toes last time. She was a bad, evil woman, and she was suddenly conscious that it was imperative he must never guess the real reason she didn't want to go. She didn't care about the rain; she didn't even care if David stepped on her toes. She didn't want to go because of him. The sexy man. Robert. The man with the astonishing hazel eyes and floppy blonde hair. Robert, who she'd ascertained during a polite conversation, actually lived on a yacht. How amazing, and free, and liberating to live in that way. A red flush crept over Kate, as she thought about him.

In an attempt to tame what was now a furiously beating heart, she jumped off the bed and grinned, masking the ravaging turmoil that was raging inside. "Yes, of course, just being silly and lazy. I'll hop in the shower now." *A cold one*, Kate thought, as she turned on the taps and stepped into the shower, ready to take the punishment that she so clearly deserved; evil vixen that she was.

Even as she braved the freezing cold droplets pelting down onto her warm flesh, she couldn't get him out of her mind. *Robert.* She sighed. *Robert.* Then sighed again. It wasn't David's fault nor the rabbits'. Desperate to apportion blame anywhere but on herself, she thought about the girl Robert had brought to the first class. It was her fault. If she'd come to the last class, then nothing would have happened. Silly bitch with her size zero body. It was all her fault. If she'd come, then Kate wouldn't have been forced—well perhaps too strong of a word—to dance with Robert and the tingle would never have materialised.

The bloody stupid tingle. The ache, the little throbbing sensation that had appeared in her lower abdomen. Lust? The tingle must be lust. She barely recognised the feeling. It was only because of its surprise guest appearance the other month at the vets that she could identify it at all. Kate felt confused. If the tingle was lust, and therefore she was in fact capable of lust, then why didn't she feel it towards David? The man she adored, worshipped, loved and cherished, the father of her children. *Shit. Shit. Shit.*

Kate cast her mind back to the last class …

* * *

She'd wondered at the time why Robert's girlfriend hadn't shown up. Was it because she'd found the strength to assert her own will and resist him? It had been obvious that she hadn't enjoyed the first class, but even so, it surprised Kate that she hadn't come. A more plausible explanation could be that Robert had dumped her and hadn't yet hunted down his next unsuspecting victim. She recognised Robert was probably one of those people commonly referred to as a 'player.' Not that Kate had ever met a player before, and David certainly was not of this ilk, but she'd read about this strange breed of emotionally dysfunctional people whose sole purpose was to hunt down unsuspecting prey.

On Tuesday night Robert hadn't remained partnerless, as Isabel had stepped in, with a tad more enthusiasm than was perhaps professionally appropriate. Had it not been for David and the whole toe-crushing incident, then Kate would never have partnered with Robert. The tingle would never have emerged and she could've quite happily continued with the classes. It just wasn't fair.

After a short period of practising the steps they'd learnt the previous week, Isabel instructed everyone to take partners. Kate turned her face full of fear and horror and looked up at David; she knew he still hadn't even mastered the first steps properly. David looked meekly down as if to apologise in advance for the damage he would no doubt imminently administer on her feet. Meanwhile Isabel, in her limited English, instructed the class to begin, "Now the men, one *paso* forward, walk left. Woman, walk back, the right foot. Basic step, *por favor*," she trilled, despite the vacuous faces of the group staring back at her.

Very slowly, Kate and David did as instructed. Kate, who'd perfected not only the step but had implemented a wiggle and gyrating of her hips, found herself unable to do either with David. With his eyes rooted to the floor and body frozen rigid, David began to sweat profusely through sheer concentration, holding onto

Kate for dear life.

"Can't you look at me?" she whispered with irritation, not being able to move in the way she wanted.

He looked up in surprise and immediately trod on her toes. "No, I bloody well can't."

"Why do you have to look at your feet? What's wrong with you? Look into my eyes, this is the dance of passion," she snarled at him through gritted teeth, freeing herself from his grip just in time to prevent any further assault on her toes.

"Shut it Kate, just shut it," he growled straight back, whilst lunging forward with the wrong leg and colliding into her with such force that she howled in pain. The other students laughed, but neither Kate nor David saw the funny side. Isabel rushed over, clearly wearing her marriage guidance hat to see if she could fix the problem.

Realising the root of the problem was that David hadn't yet mastered the basic steps. Isabel motioned for Robert to come and practise with Kate, whilst sweeping David to the back of the class to go over the first lesson.

Kate stood awkwardly in front of Robert, although he seemed delighted to be standing in front of her. "You saved me," he whispered into her ear; his voice like milk chocolate dripping down her throat, immediately sending a shiver down her spine. *Stop it, Kate. Stop it. What a ridiculous reaction. He's just a man.*

But a gorgeous, sexy, stunning man, said another voice quietly from deep within.

"Saved you from what?" she said as casually as possible, whilst trying to ignore her internal utterances.

"Isabel. Very scary to be dancing with the teacher. Are you enjoying yourself?"

"Yes." Monosyllables were suddenly all Kate could manage, aware of the awkwardness that shrouded the moment. She couldn't remember the last time she'd ever danced with a man who wasn't David. There had been no other men. She was in extremely unchartered territory.

"I'm Kate," she finally uttered as she held out her hand formally to shake his. Robert looked down at it with surprise, then slowly picked it up, bringing his lips gently to rest on it. Kate wriggled with embarrassment. Now she felt even more uncomfortable, if that were possible. "Do you live here in Palma?" It was the first thing that popped into her mind as she extricated her hand from his lips, desperate to normalise the incredibly abnormal moment.

"Sort of. I live on a yacht and travel around Europe." His gaze held hers, and it was incredibly unnerving.

"Shall we dance?" she eventually managed to squawk, conscious of the fact that the rest of the class were dancing whilst they were standing still like a couple of awkward teenagers. Besides, dancing had to be easier than talking. If they could dance, then she wouldn't have to speak, and speech was especially hard when your heart was bouncing around inside your body and small vibrations were coursing through your veins.

Glancing at David, Kate was relieved to see that he was oblivious to what she was doing. *Interesting.* If it had been the other way round and David was dancing with a gorgeous specimen, she definitely would've kept an eye on him. However, as David's head bobbed up and down with no correlation to the beat of the music, Kate noted that he was too engrossed with his private lesson to be aware of her, and slowly she relaxed into Robert's arms.

It's strange how there are some defining moments in life, how you know when you hit one. How you feel it in the core of your being. This was one for Kate. Robert reached out as if in slow motion, taking her hand in his and squeezing it, or perhaps he didn't. Perhaps she only imagined the squeeze, but it felt like an electric current charging through her body. Even slower, he circled her waist with his other arm, resting his palm on her hip and it felt like he brushed her back in the process. She was conscious of the music, conscious of the room getting darker, and conscious that he seemed to pull her closer towards him so that her hips brushed against his groin. Was it possible that her imagination was running away with her? She was so caught up in the moment that it really did feel like they were being held together by some invisible force.

His movements were so subtle that she felt genuine confusion about whether they were deliberate or a figment of her overactive imagination. The sensation was so alien to her that she swallowed deeply, and resting her left hand below his shoulder, looked up into his eyes. For a moment, neither of them talked. It must have only been seconds, but to Kate in that moment, right there in the middle of the dance floor, with her husband just a stone's throw away, she felt something shift within her. So great was this shift that it terrified her. The way he looked and the way his smell entered and consumed her was overwhelming.

And then Robert spoke, as if it were the most natural thing to do in the middle of a tornado. For it was a tornado that Kate felt she was in. Everything inside her body had turned upside down, whizzing around faster and faster, higher and higher.

"Shall we dance?" Robert repeated Kate's earlier question, his hazel eyes, with flecks of gold and a stunning blue rim the likes of which she'd never seen, boring down into hers, deeper and deeper into her mind, into her soul. It no longer mattered that David was there. It didn't matter that anyone was there. There were only the two of them in the room, with the music washing over them, surrounding them, stroking them as if they were entwined in a piece of silk. He moved forward as she moved back. He pulled her in closer and their hips grazed once again. Kate felt as if she were on fire. Was he feeling the same? Could a reaction to a person as intense as this, make you forget everything? A reaction that could suspend time and space, possibly just be one-way? Kate was too inexperienced to know, too naïve to understand, and by that point, too consumed by the moment to even care.

Attempting to regain some control, Kate looked at her feet, anything but gaze into his eyes. She could not, would not, continue to stare into those deep hypnotising pools that reminded her of liquid gold. A man like Robert wouldn't be attracted to a woman like her. Robert was attracted to gorgeous slim model lookalikes, not small plumpish housewives. The more she thought about it, the more she relaxed. It was all in her head. But then the music began again, the imaginary silk binding them, pulling them closer and closer together as their bodies moved as one, '*Uno, dos, tres … cinco, seis, siete.*' He didn't take his eyes off her, not even for a second. She wasn't sure if he was even blinking; so intense was his gaze. Then, as if by magic, she didn't feel scared or threatened anymore and smiled and gazed right back at him with equal intensity. The smile was not one of innocence, and nor was it one that Kate Buchanan had ever made before; this was a different smile, as if she'd morphed into someone else in that moment.

Kate suddenly felt confident. She felt beautiful. She felt sexy. That's what being in Robert's arms made her feel. All the things that she wanted to be and none of the things she felt she was. The way Robert looked at her made her feel more like a woman than she'd ever felt before. No longer just a wife or mother or daughter or friend; she was Kate. Glorious, beautiful, sexy Kate in all her grandeur, in all her magnificence and the euphoria swept through her body and she smiled; the smile of a seductress.

The music stopped abruptly, and Robert released his hold on her. The spell was broken. Then came the embarrassment, cascading through her body like a tsunami. Gazing up at Robert, he looked almost smug. *Oh my god*, had he known that she'd responded to him? She quickly stepped back from him, just in time to see a smiling David approaching. "I've got it, darling. I think I've mastered it." Oblivious to Kate's emotional turmoil.

Robert backed away, muttering, "Thanks, you dance really well."

Kate morphed back from 'The Seductress' into the dutiful wife and almost threw herself at her unsuspecting husband. "Have you? Really? That's great, fantastic." She was gushing, and she knew it, so toned it down a little. "Really great, sweetheart, pleased for you." *He mustn't suspect anything.* Oh god, if he were to suspect anything she would die. Nothing happened, she told herself, yet a voice from within that she presumed belonged to her now alter ego, The Seductress, mockingly taunted her. *Yes, it did.*

Nothing happened, she argued back to herself. The voices raged, and all the time she clung to David, desperate to leave the hall and never return; she never wanted to feel that way again.

On their way home, Kate had been uncharacteristically quiet. David had seemed more jovial than usual. Obviously the private lesson with Isabel had paid off and he was feeling more confident. "Sorry I trod on your feet," David said apologetically.

"You can tread on my feet anytime you like." She smiled innocently up at him. Looking at his profile as he drove the car home with that silly little grin on his face. She'd been ridiculous. Nothing untoward had occurred; oh dear, she really was very dramatic sometimes. She reached for David's hand as they drove back in silence and their fingers locked and Kate's equilibrium was once again restored.

Except that night, when they lay in bed, and when she closed her eyes. She reached out for David, but it wasn't David she felt stroking her back.

* * *

Kate felt numb. No longer feeling the ice water, she turned off the tap and stepped out of the shower, grabbing a towel. Heading into her dressing room on autopilot, she got dressed. In the absence of a brain tumour and with no apparent death on the cards, it looked like she was going to Salsa that night. Dressed with twenty minutes to spare, she decided to email Jamie. It had been on her mind for days, but with much of the last week spent obsessing about Robert, there hadn't been room left in her head for much else. As she opened up the laptop, she paused for a moment, contemplating the wisdom in sharing her confusion down on paper. Potentially stupid. But then heading up the subject in a very 007 manner, 'Delete after reading' she quickly bashed out her dilemma.

"Kate, Juanita is here. Come on let's go," David yelled, just as she'd finished purging.

Great, Kate thought. Their neighbour, Juanita, must be the only Spanish person who was actually punctual. Once Kate had sent the email, she deleted the original herself. Kate grabbed her coat and lunged out the door. Vodka, yes, that would help the embarrassment. If they left now and didn't get lost, then she could have a quick vodka before the class. It would no doubt create carnage on the footwork, but it would take the edge off seeing Robert again.

STRANGE MYSTERY MAN
London, England

Lost in thought and too preoccupied with avoiding any awkward chit-chat with fellow parents, Jamie hadn't even heard the school bell ring. Suddenly the floodgates opened and a flurry of hyperactivity was coming her way—fast. Did she hear someone shout, 'Brace! Brace!'? Instinct told her to run and hide but it wasn't an option. One of the flurry was her very own daughter, who appeared to be dragging alongside another overexcited offspring.

"Muuuum. Mummmmy." Madison and the other child were approaching at a speed of knots. The owner of the child appeared to be approaching too. Jamie felt a surge of panic at the thought of a potential playdate situation about to unfold; slowly she felt herself shrinking backwards towards the wall, to the safety of the colourful shrubs that flourished within the confines of the school driveway.

"Mum, Mum, this is my friend Abigail."

Too late.

"Nice to meet you, Abigail," Jamie lied as she smiled through gritted teeth. Although the girl, who was quite a bit smaller than Madison, seemed harmless enough. *Please don't ask me to invite her over. Please. Oh no, too late, her mother's here too.*

"Hi, I'm Felicity, Abigail's mum. You must be Madison's …

mum?" Felicity asked, almost questioningly, eyeing Jamie up and down. Having just come from her Pilates class, Jamie was still dressed in leggings and a vest top, with a denim jacket thrown on top, looking younger than her years.

Felicity didn't wait for an answer. "Abigail keeps talking about Madison. I think they'd like to have a little playdate?"

There it was. Jamie froze. "Ah yes, that would be lovely. We must arrange something ... soon." *Please, please let's just leave now.*

"But Mum, I wanted Abigail to come over today." Madison had adopted her usual pout.

Dammit. "We haven't organised anything sweetie. Why don't we make a plan for, say, next week?" Jamie hoped by then she'd have to work and it would become a non-issue, or Maria could look after them.

Now both girls were big-eyed and pouty-lipped, expectantly waiting for a different response. Felicity remained silent. Clearly, she was hoping for a child-free afternoon herself.

"Why can't she just come today? Pleeeease." Madison was a master of persuasion. Persistent demands more like.

Flushed, Jamie felt all eyes upon her. She had to think fast. Yes, Maria happened to be visiting her niece that evening, but they were only two small girls. Kate had two girls. Kate had two girls every day. No, it would be fine. They weren't puppies, for goodness sake. They even looked rather sweet in their little grey and red uniforms. She could handle this. It might even make for an easier afternoon. After all, entertaining Madison alone was often rather challenging.

"Alright then. As long as you promise to behave?"

"We promise." Two angelic faces with ever widening cartoon eyes. If only that were true.

Driving back in the black Mini Cooper Jamie had rented since returning to the UK, the girls appeared to be settled already, singing along to *Shake It Off* by Taylor Swift, blaring out from the radio. Jamie smiled to herself. What had she been so worried about? Car journeys with Madison normally involved some sort of theatrics or demands. This drive, by contrast, had been … dare she say it, enjoyable.

Pulling up outside their home, which was now a small three-bedroom mews on the outskirts of Chiswick, the girls giggled amongst themselves as she led them both through the front door, which had been painted a calming shade of duck egg blue.

"Madison, why don't you take Abigail to play in your room?" Attempting to contain any mess to just one location, "Show her that new game Nonna bought you. If you need me, I'll be in my room. Just knock." Jamie hoped they wouldn't need her. Wow, this was actually easy. In fact, this was better than easy. This was perfect. Madison should have playdates more often. It certainly took the pressure off her.

Back in her bedroom, her hideaway, Jamie flopped herself onto her bed. She felt drained of energy. She'd been working a lot recently, and the early mornings were getting to her. Plus, she was always running on empty, which didn't help. Even though the house was a rental, Jamie had tried her best to decorate it as much to their taste as she could in the short time they'd been there. It was hard to compete with their beachside duplex in Mallorca, but West London it would have to be right now. Sprawling over the mountain of pillows and throws, Jamie felt like a mermaid swimming in a sea of plush fabric. Suddenly, she remembered her phone had beeped a few times during the drive home. Extending out one long arm like a human Stretch Armstrong toy, Jamie attempted to grab her bag from the floor without actually having to get up. Finally, her fingers succeeded in hoisting the handbag up to her, and diving one hand into the soft cream leather, she fished out her phone. A smile washed across her face as she saw the name on the screen. There appeared to be two messages from him.

Cameron:	Can't stop thinking about the other night. Think I need another Jamie fix very soon
Cameron:	Also pretty sure I have a boot fetish now!! ;)

Damn, he was cute. Jamie had continued sleeping with him. The attraction between them was so irresistible that she wasn't ready to give it up just yet. And besides, one night with Cameron was probably equal to three spin classes. It was a 'win win, hell yes baby, win' situation.

Looking at her phone, Jamie suddenly remembered Kate. She'd seemed uncharacteristically out of sorts in her email yesterday. She had to reply to her immediately before she forgot. Feeling too lazy to get off the bed, she decided to email from her phone.

To:	katebuchanan@scoopmail.com
From:	fallen-angel@scoopmail.com
Subject:	Stop it already

My dear dear silly Kate. First of all, STOP IT ALREADY. You are absolutely allowed to find another human being attractive. Everyone does, it's human nature. Goodness knows I see men I fancy all the time. Actually, that's not true, but when I do, I really enjoy it. Don't tell me you don't get all hot when you see Chris Hemsworth in a movie, or David doesn't gawk over Zoë Kravitz. Yes, it is totally

NORMAL. So stop chastising yourself over nothing. But I for one am glad about something ... you finally found your fire. You see, it was there all along. And if Salsa Man—I'm intrigued—was the one responsible, then that's a good thing. I think these classes are doing you a world of good. Getting you out, injecting a little excitement. Really, nothing to feel guilty about at all. Oh and what I wouldn't do to be on a beach with you right now sipping Cosmo's ... sigh. Always here for you,

Jamie Xxx

Lost in her email, Jamie didn't hear the door at first. Then another knock came louder.

"Mum, why aren't you answering?" It was Madison.

So soon? Still unwilling to get up from the bed, Jamie yelled back, "What is it?"

The door flung open. Standing at the threshold were the girls. "Mum, we're hungry," announced Madison, as Abigail stood beside her in solidarity.

"What do you mean, you're hungry? Didn't you eat at school?" Jamie was pretty sure that Madison's food consumption that day had probably been more than hers. "Just help yourself to anything in the fridge."

"But, Mum"—Madison's whining had returned, like an uninvited guest—"there isn't anything in the fridge."

Jamie huffed out loud as she reluctantly removed herself off the bed. What was she talking about? Maria always had food in. Flouncing downstairs to the kitchen barefoot, with the two Hungry Hippos in tow, Jamie opened the doors of her American-style fridge freezer and ... gasped. It was true. Her mother had clearly not had time to fit in a visit to Sainsbury's that day—nor the previous day by the looks of things—and all that sat in the fridge were: some eggs, a carton of milk, a whole uncooked chicken, some salad leaves and a few pots of yogurt. Nothing that was ready. Nothing that could be placed in the microwave for two minutes and then 'ping' dinner would be served. *Arrrrgggghhhh*. Jamie turned to the slate-grey cabinets and one by one started to open them, hoping to find something edible inside other than cereal. The contents revealed: pasta, rice, many tins and jars of unidentifiable herbs and spices … and of course, cereal. But, all except the latter required actual cooking, something she wasn't sure she could successfully manage.

Turning back to the fridge. "How about a yogurt? Oooh, look, strawberries and cream flavour … yummy." Jamie tried her best to sound enthusiastic, but the girl's faces revealed otherwise.

"Mum, we don't want yogurt, we want food."

Dammit. If she could survive off a yogurt, surely these two could last a few more hours.

Abigail was silent. Jamie peered back into the fridge, hoping something else would miraculously appear … and then, as if by magic, behind the pots of yogurt, Jamie spied a block of gruyère cheese. Hallelujah, there was a god. "Ooh," she squealed with delight and relief, as she took out the half-opened packet. "Cheese." Jamie looked pleased with herself. She liked cheese. She'd often have a piece of cheese when she felt hungry. Dairy, high in calories, good for their growing bones. What more did they need?

Madison pulled her mouth downwards. "Cheese? You want us to eat … cheese?"

Jamie looked perplexed. What was wrong with cheese?

Abigail broke her silence. "Actually, Miss King, I'm lactose intolerant."

What? Lactose what? She's ten. How could she be anything intolerant? Bloody hell. What is the world coming to? Frowning profusely, she racked her brain for something, some solution. Suddenly a brainwave. Sushi. She supposed she needed to eat something herself, having starved all day already, and what better than sushi? Light, nourishing and most certainly lactose-free. Jamie momentarily toyed with the idea of leaving the girls as she dashed out. It would certainly be faster, but could she really leave them alone? Moreover, should she? One wasn't even hers. Dammit, she had no choice but to take them.

"Okay girls, come with me. Let's go grab some food." She figured if she could find a parking space outside, she could at least leave them in the car whilst she ordered. She didn't want a repeat of her disastrous lunch with Madison. Which reminded her—her cap. She'd forgotten all about it. Perhaps she could pick that up too.

* * *

Leaving the girls in the car, just about visible, Jamie popped into Yoshi Sushi to place their order, before jumping back in and driving to The Brasserie whilst their food was being prepared. Parking spaces and Jamie were a strange phenomenon. She always expected to find one just outside, and she always did. At least she had the gods to thank for that small mercy.

The atmosphere in The Brasserie was markedly different from the last time she was there—less chaotic, less children. If only the girls weren't in the car, she would've had a drink.

"Hi there, I was in here a couple of Sundays ago and left my cap behind. You haven't found it by any chance? It's grey and by Pinko. I was sitting just over there." Jamie pointed over to one of the back tables.

"I don't do the weekend shift but I'll go and take a look in the lost property," said the youngish blonde girl who sadly must've been doing tasty French waiter's shift that day.

Hovering near the window to keep an eye on the car, Jamie suddenly became aware of someone looking at her. Glancing up, she noticed a man in a suit sitting in the far corner smiling at her. She squinted her eyes. Did she know him? He certainly was very well dressed in his all black suit, subtle pinstripe pants with black shirt and blue-black pullover. It looked very Ozwald Boateng, but then again it could easily have been Gucci? Jamie wasn't as au fait with menswear, but she knew good tailoring when she saw it.

Now he was practically beckoning her to go over. *Shit, who is he?* He obviously knew her. Just as she was about to walk over to get to the bottom of it, another man, also wearing a suit—although not nearly as stylish—arrived and they shook hands. Mystery Man shrugged as if to say, 'Sorry, busy now' but then the penny dropped. *Oh my gosh.* It was the man with the young boy from lunch that day with Madison. Blimey, he looked different. Not exactly a babe as clearly over twenty-five, so couldn't possibly fit into that category, but striking, nonetheless. He hadn't looked so sharp previously.

Quickly running out to check on the girls, Jamie was happy to see them giggling away as she peered through the car window. As she re-entered The Brasserie, she saw Henri, the head waiter, looking around. "One cap for you, Miss King." Henri had clearly been looking for her.

"Ooh thank you Henri," purred Jamie as she took the cap, but her eyes were drawn back to Mystery Man. She couldn't help but wonder what he did for a living? And what he was doing at The Brasserie on a Monday just before 5:00 p.m.? Meeting? Early dinner? *Dinner. Shit. Dinner. The girls. She had to go.*

"Miss King? One more thing. This is for you." Henri slipped Jamie a napkin with what appeared to be writing on it. What was that? A message for her? *Oh no.* Henri wasn't making a move on her, was he? She daren't look. She popped it into her bag.

"See ya," she said, dashing out before he could say anything else.

Driving back to Yoshi Sushi, Jamie collected dinner before making their way back home. Thankfully, the girls seemed to be whine-free for the journey. Hot-footing it into the kitchen, Jamie emptied the contents of the boxes onto plates and placed them onto the wooden counter of the small island where they usually sat to eat.

"What's this?" grimaced Madison as she inspected the contents of her plate. Her face even more contorted than the 'I hate The Brasserie' face but before Jamie could answer, Abigail piped up, "It's sushi."

"Sushi? You mean raw fish?" Madison looked horrified as she poked at the California rolls with her fork, almost expecting to see signs of life. Jamie had decided against chopsticks. Sushi and chopsticks might have been a tad too ambitious.

"Yes. I love sushi. We had a lot of it when we went to Japan. My Uncle lives there. Thank you, Miss King." Abigail, at least, was smiling.

Jamie was impressed, and, not wanting to look ignorant in front of her friend, Madison decided it was best to keep quiet and tucked in as well. Rather, she pushed the contents masterfully around the plate—a skill she'd probably learnt from her mother.

Jamie took a plate for herself and perched on a stool at the end of the island to read Henri's note: 'Sorry 4 intrusion but couldn't help notice you with your daughter last time. Had many moments like that with my son. I'm a single parent, how about you? Not always easy. Perhaps we could join forces one day? Strength in numbers. Karl.' He'd left his mobile number.

Oh gosh. Not Henri then. Karl. Who was this Karl? The man in the suit? Yes, it was the man with the son. Why had he sent her this note? Did he want a date? She wasn't looking for another plaything just yet. Cameron was doing just nicely and besides; this man was far too old for her. Yes, he was stylish and probably successful. The suit looked expensive enough, but he must've been in his mid-thirties, at least. That and he had a son; at least Cameron gave her an escape from parenting duties. Screwing up the napkin, Jamie tossed it into the bin and resumed picking at her sushi. Midway through her second bite, it suddenly crossed her mind that perhaps this Karl was a member of the High Road Brasserie. After all, she had seen him there twice already. What would happen if she were to bump into him again? There would be embarrassment, and Jamie hated awkward situations. She couldn't be rude and not respond, could she? No, she ought to say something, if only a 'thanks, but no thanks.' Scrambling over to the bin to retrieve the note, Jamie decided to send a polite text later.

* * *

With the girls now sitting watching *Big Hero 6* on Netflix until Abigail's mother came to collect her, Jamie continued to ponder the dilemma at hand. To respond or not to respond? Clearly, she had no physical interest in this man, but it had been a rather sweet note, harmless even. She shouldn't assume that he was suggesting anything sexual, or should she? *Oh shut up girl; all men want something sexual. Why else would he write you a note? To be chess buddies?* But it wasn't as if he'd made any suggestive remarks. Either way, she had to respond and get things clear and the sooner the better. It wasn't as if she actually had to organise to meet him. With that reassuring thought, Jamie pulled out her phone and began composing her text.

> Jamie: Hi Karl. Thanks for the note. Very sweet. Must've seemed like a total novice with my daughter! Yes, I am a single parent. And yes not always easy as she can be rather a handful! Very busy with work right now but no doubt bump into you soon at The Brasserie. Bye for now. Jamie

Jamie pressed send, not expecting to hear back at all. She was startled to receive a beep so soon after she'd sent it. Surely it wasn't him? None of the guys she ever engaged with would dream of sending a text back immediately. Opening her new message, the text read.

> Karl: No problem, don't get to meet many people in the same situation as myself and sometimes it would just be nice to talk to someone else who really understands. Most of my friends are single with no kids or happily married. Was a leap of faith, most unlike me to do that. Sorry again for the intrusion. Karl

Hmmmm. That was unexpected. Strange man, this Karl was. Honest and pretty much totally in sync with her own thought processes. Perhaps he was just a nice guy? Huh, that was an oxymoron if she ever heard one. But who knew? In a most uncharacteristic manner, it suddenly crossed her mind that maybe, just maybe, his motives really were honourable, and the thought of having a friend that could genuinely appreciate what single parenting was like, was extremely appealing. What's more, if he were a 'friend' then she wouldn't have to play the 'game.' The more Jamie thought about it, the more keeping the door open with this Karl guy appealed to her; she could always disengage herself from him later. In fact, she could always make it clear that she was only interested in a platonic friendship from the onset. With this thought in mind, Jamie, for the first time ever, replied immediately.

Jamie: No intrusion. Very lovely note. If you have any advice on how to handle loud moody almost-teenagers, I'd be sooo grateful!!

'Beep. Beep.'

Karl: Ear plugs!

Ha ha, he was a funny guy, and Jamie let the little smile play on her lips for just a fraction longer than usual.

WAKE UP CALL

FUCK. SHIT. FUUUUCK. Jamie checked her phone, which of course had been switched to silent. '10 missed calls' and all from 'Home.' It was eight in the morning, and on a school day. What had she been thinking?

Scrambling to her feet and quickly amassing her clothing, which seemed to be scattered all over Cameron's tiny one-bedroom apartment, Jamie went into overdrive. She hadn't even told her mother she was staying out. Maria would be out of her mind by now. If the police hadn't been called and she wasn't already registered as a Missing Person, it would be nothing short of miraculous. *FUCK*. She had to get out of there. Also, Maria didn't drive, which meant she'd have to take Madison to school in a cab, something she was only happy to do if Jamie had work. And Jamie had most certainly not been working.

Cameron still appeared to be sleeping. No need to wake him. She'd message him later … or rather, wait for him to message her. Jamie had been playing with Cameron for over a month now and that was getting seriously close to relationship territory. The sex was still pretty amazing, yes, but she always felt nervous about getting serious with a man. They always let you down. In any case, what did she really need from one? Great sex was more than enough.

Must get dressed. Now. Fast. Faster. Where the hell did I leave my flippin' top?

Top, along with oddly enough, a fuchsia feather boa was found decorating the bare hallway. *Ooh, the hallway. Such a great hallway. Stop your daydreaming you stupid girl and get the hell out of there before you find your face on the BBC news.*

"Are you leaving me already?" Cameron was awake.

Shit. She didn't want to get into anything now. Cameron didn't even know she had a child. Besides, he didn't need to know and she didn't have time to explain.

"Yeah, totally forgot. I have a casting. I need to go home and sort myself out," Jamie lied. She fumbled with the buttons on her denim miniskirt, which she'd successfully retrieved from the cold checkerboard bathroom tiles.

"I had an amazing time," Cameron enthused from the bed, the sheet only partially covering his naked body whilst half of his toned chest and firm, athletic legs remained exposed.

He's in such great shape for a 'graphic designer.' Not that they ever discussed work. In fact, they rarely discussed anything. Jamie tried to avert her eyes. She had to leave.

"Me too. Gotta dash. See ya." Grabbing her boots on her way out.

"Missing you already," came from the bedroom. But Cameron's words were left unheard as Jamie was already out of the apartment and halfway down the communal stairs to the front door. The communal area was dark and in desperate need of a paint job—and deep cleaning. Somehow, it just seemed to add to the sordidness of the situation.

Checking her reflection in the dusty, small black-framed mirror beside the front door of the building, Jamie was horrified to find the wild woman of Borneo looking back at her. *Arrrrggggghhhh.* What would her agent say if she saw her now? *Memo to self, next time 'you never know' bag must contain a cap or hat. Very large hat even better. Balaclava perhaps?*

Jamie's fingers frantically reached into the depths of her 'you never know' bag for her phone and immediately dialled home.

"Jamie, Jamie. Where you are? I been so worried. Why you no call me? Where you been?" Maria's voice was trembling. She was scared. Jamie had made her scared. It was all her fault. What kind of daughter doesn't inform home that she won't actually be coming home?

"I'm so sorry … " Jamie's mind scrambled to think of an excuse.

Upon realising her daughter wasn't in an imagined ditch somewhere, Maria's tone changed, and she began her usual interrogation instead, "And Madison? School? Where you were? Out with that India? No, don't tell me. Out with some horrible boy? *Sei pazzo?* Oh, you know what, I don't even wanna know. I take Madison to school myself, otherwise she be late. How you be so irresponsible? When Madison wake up, she ask where you were. I no idea you no home, so told her you must be working. What else I say?"

Maria went from being scared to relieved to finally ablaze with inferno-like fury. This was not good. Not good at all. Jamie was going to have hell to pay. Maria was going to crucify her, and then, when she was dead, she was going to feed her to the ducks at Chiswick Park. Jamie was not looking forward to getting home. Having a feisty Mediterranean mother could be brutal at times.

* * *

Ever so quietly, Jamie snuck into the house and quickly ran upstairs to her room. There appeared to be no sign of either Maria or Madison, so it was safe to surmise they'd already left. She would freshen herself up and think of an excuse. India? *Hmmmm. India got sick? Yeah, really sick. No, not alcohol poisoning, that would only antagonise Mamma further. Just sick. Food poisoning perhaps? Or worse? Perhaps a terrible stomach ache?* Something so bad that she had to stay by her side all night. Yes. A get out of jail free card whilst getting to look like the caring friend all at the same time. Sounded good, except for one thing—India. Best call and check she hadn't called home at some point during the night. No good creating an alibi if the alibi wasn't 'alibi-able.' But realising it was still morning, Jamie recognised it was way too early to call the lady of the night. India never woke up before noon unless she had to. And, Jamie was pretty sure she didn't have anything booked until Monday. Never mind; she'd understand. This was an emergency, for Christ's sake.

As fast as she could dial, fearing Maria's imminent arrival, Jamie called India's number from her ensuite. Ringing, ringing. *Please answer goddammit. Ringing, ringing. Oh, for crying out loud India, just answer the fucking phone.*

"Hello?" India's gravelly tones, clearly still half asleep, were like music to Jamie's ears.

"Babe, wake up. Wake up. This is an emergency." Jamie tried her quietest shout as she sat precariously on the side of the bath.

India, suddenly much more lucid and alarmed. "What? What is it? What happened?"

"Oh hun, please tell me you didn't call my house at any point last night?"

"No, why? What happened?"

"Well, I went out with Cameron again and let's just say I didn't come home."

Silence. India was clearly not amused by the not entirely catastrophic event in Jamie's world. "Yes, and? Is that why you're calling me? Now? At six o'clock in the morning. It's practically the middle of the night."

"Actually, it's nine thirty and I'm sorry about that. I need your help. I really need you to be an alibi for me. I've got to make up a good enough story as to why I didn't get back home in time to take Madison to school this morning. And also, why I bloody well forgot to call last night."

"Hmmmm, so how does this involve me then?" India didn't like the sound of this.

"Well … I thought maybe … maybe you could be sick? Like really sick. Vomiting all over the place, maybe even coming in and out of consciousness?"

"Dying? You want me to be dying?"

"No, of course not, hun. Of course I don't want you to be dying … but, almost? Sorry, I'm joking. Really. Of course I'm joking. I just need to pretend that I was with you last night and that, inexplicably and unexpectedly, you just got sick. So sick that I had to take you home, lost track of time. Next thing you know; I've fallen asleep next to you … from exhaustion. Are you okay with that? What else can I tell my mother? She'd kill me if she knew the truth." Voice sweetening a touch, "And you wouldn't want that now, would you, angel? Wouldn't want your dear friend Jamie to be murdered by her mother. Then who would you have to go and play with?"

"Sure babe, anything so I can go back to sleep."

"Thank you, thank you. I'll make it up to you, I promise."

Jamie hung up. Phew. Close call. Now she just had to get Maria to believe it. Splashing cold water over her face, followed by a concoction of brightening serums and concealer, Jamie managed to successfully resemble herself again. Hearing the front door close, she knew Maria was back. Renewed with hope, and cosmetics, Jamie sprinted back downstairs, full of the joys of spring. Hearing sounds emanating from the kitchen, she went to make her peace. "Hi, Mamma. You're back? Look, I'm really sor—"

"*Basta!* I don't wanna hear it," Maria's tone was abrupt, and she was avoiding making eye contact. Suddenly, making tea had become as ceremonious as a Hindu wedding, as she painstakingly went through what appeared to be an extended ritual just to brew a cuppa.

"But, Mamma, you don't understand. I couldn't come home … India was sick. Really sick. I had to look after her."

"Until this morning?" Maria's arched brow suggested she wasn't buying any of it, as she took a spoon to deliberately crush the tea bag before discarding it into the tall pedal bin.

"But Mamma. She was ill. What did you want me to do? Leave her?"

"*Non ne posso più Jamie*, I have enough of you and you lying. Even if India sick, which I no believe for second, she can look after herself. Who here look after your daughter?"

Jamie stood speechless. This was not going well. Not going at all as planned.

"But, she was ill, Mamma, Madison wasn't ill. India lives alone. She only had me to look after her. I think she had food poisoning or something because she was vomiting all over the place. I didn't even realise the time." Jamie winced at the whine in her voice, but it was too late; she'd set her path and had to stick to it.

"So why you no call me, tell me this terrible situation?" Maria had more than a hint of sarcasm in her voice.

"I ... er ... I ... was too busy looking after her. I mean ..." Jamie began to struggle. This was going from bad to worse.

"*Che nervi*, Jamie. If you wanna go out and act like some kind of *prostituta* with India, then that you business but you need think about others. All you think about is ME! ME! ME! You selfish and irresponsible girl. I have enough. From now on I no look after Madison, so you be here every morning or *scuola* will be calling to ask where she is."

Jamie's mouth opened to speak, but what could she say? Clearly, she wasn't a very good actress and her mother seemed adamant not to hear her out. Damn, she shouldn't have mentioned India. She should've pretended she was with another friend. Someone her mother actually liked. Someone like ... like ... there was no one.

With that, Maria took herself and her cup of Earl Grey and defiantly, victoriously, marched into the living room.

Shit. What now? Was she for real? Did she mean everything she'd just said? And what did she mean, I'm 'selfish'? Jamie looked after all of them. She was the breadwinner. If Maria wasn't prepared to look after Madison, she'd have to get a nanny. And how would she be able to afford that?

* * *

The room was dark, other than the light that illuminated Jamie's favourite painting, which hung above her mirrored desk-come-vanity table. It was home to her laptop as well as an extensive collection of makeup and beautifying products. The canvas perfectly depicted a deserted tropical beach with pure white sands and crystal clear waters. Gazing up at it from her desk, Jamie visualised herself there; immersed in its refreshing waters, with the sun's warm embrace enveloping her all but naked skin. Staring and staring, as if by staring hard enough, she could literally dive into the painting and transport herself—far away from her current existence. Anywhere would be better than where she was at that moment. Bloody hell. Why hadn't her mother believed her? Turning towards her laptop, Jamie decided to email Kate. Yes, Kate would commiserate with her.

Suddenly, her phone beeped.

Karl: Just finished an excellent book and thought you might be interested. *Raising Good Humans*. Offers practical strategies to make your life easier. Really great. Regards

Wow. How weird. Was this guy psychic? Perhaps it was a sign? Perhaps this book would hold the answer to her current dilemma? She wondered if it could be applied to hot-blooded Italian mothers too?

Jamie: Hey Karl, thanks, great timing! My life could really do with being easier. Will read the book and hope therein lies inspiration. I'll let you know how it goes. Thanx for thinking of me. J

The message went off, but as Jamie stared at the phone screen, she was startled when it started to ring ... *Karl?* No, it was India calling.

"Hi, babe."

"Hi, sweetie. What you up to? You at home?" India's voice was upbeat.

"Yup, where else? Feel like I'm grounded. My mum didn't fall for it. So don't worry, you don't have to pretend anything next time you come over. And guess what? Now she thinks I'm the worst mother and daughter in the world." Jamie's words spluttered out at a million miles per hour.

"No, seriously? I can't believe it."

"Believe it. I'm going to have to do something about it. I'm hoping she'll calm down."

"She will. Don't stress about it. Anyway, it's Friday night, if you hadn't noticed. Was calling to arrange where we'd go and by the sounds of it, you, my dear, are in desperate need of a drink."

"You have got to be joking. I'd be shot dead on the spot. My mum hates me right now, so I'm staying out of her way and have been holed up in my room all day. Actually, it hasn't been all that bad. Because she hasn't wanted to speak to me, she also hasn't bothered to try and get me to eat either. Bloody marvellous. Not even Madison's come up. I've actually had a break. But as for going out—impossible."

"Hmmmm, what if I come over then? Keep you company? I can sneak in a little bottle of something to cheer you up? Then when they're all asleep, we can sneak out. They won't even notice."

"Are you completely mad? She'd have you too. Guilty by association. As attractive as it sounds, I'm going to have to give it a miss tonight. Think I had enough of a biggie last night."

"You sure babe?"

"Sure. Go ahead and have fun without me."

"Well, if you change your mind, I'll probably be at The Arts Club and then onto Koko. I'll keep my phone on just in case." With that, India disappeared into the night again.

What now? It was Friday night. In fact, it was Friday the thirteenth. What was it with her favourite day recently? Friday the thirteenth always used to be such an awesome day. Not anymore. Strange forces were at work here. She was home, alone and with nothing but her horrible thoughts to keep her occupied. Staring at the half-empty bottle of Baileys on her desk, Jamie removed the lid and glugged several sips. Enough alcohol might just help her forget and fall asleep, and she could wake up to find the whole thing was just one long, nasty dream.

'Beep. Beep.' *A text. Cameron? That would be nice.* He hadn't actually texted her yet, which was odd. Although it was because of that little shit that she was in this mess. Beautiful little shit though.

Jamie picked up her phone and opened up the message:

Karl:	Chp 6. They title it Never Give Away the Ice Cream. In layman's terms, I think it should be called The Art of Bribery. Good luck. Am here if you need to offload and moan. K.
Jamie:	Actually you don't happen to know of a book called Raising Good Humans

	(Whilst Making Your Mother Believe You Are One Too), so she finally stops giving you grief? It's a long title I know lol.
Karl:	You live with your mother too? Oh boy. Think you're going to need a whole library!

Jamie couldn't help but crack a smile.

SEDUCTRESS BE GONE
Mallorca, Spain

It transpired that vodka didn't help. It didn't help at all. In fact, if the mission had been to sail through Salsa with integrity, dignity and an air of casual aloofness towards Robert, then using vodka as a tool to achieve this was a gross misjudgement on Kate's part.

It had been fourteen days since the last class. After fourteen long agonising days spent in disbelief and confusion, there was no way Kate was ever going to go back. Thankfully, she'd come on her period last Tuesday—for real this time—and by somewhat dramatising the pain and agony, successfully managed to extricate herself from going. But now it was Tuesday again and she needed to come clean. Well, not clean, clean. She just needed to tell him she didn't want to go anymore. Yet the thought of bringing up the subject left Kate troubled and in desperate need of a distraction. Besides, she had hours to kill before they'd have to leave for class.

She decided to reorganise the books in the playroom. The bookshelf was simple. The grain was dark red, carved from reclaimed railway tracks, then polished to enhance its natural beauty. Whilst not ornate, it had been specially commissioned so that it hugged the entire left-hand side of the playroom and gave the room a rustic yet homely feel. Pulling off all the books and the occasional cuddly toy that resided there, Kate dumped everything onto the floor. Taking a seat at the girls' arts and crafts table, she suddenly felt daunted by the task at hand. What had seemed like a good idea at first, now felt overwhelming, as she surveyed the piles of books spewed all over the floor. However, experience had taught her that when her mind was whirling and life felt out of control, focusing on colour coding proved to be a calming exercise. Having spent the last two weeks doing all the other cupboards in the house, the only room left was the playroom. Looking at all the books, Kate couldn't decide whether it was better to put them in order of height, which would be aesthetically pleasing, or go with her usual colour coding. *Perhaps*, she thought, with a sudden flash of inspiration, she could organise them by both? Ooh, it had never been done before; a challenge with the potential to divert her current obsessive thoughts to safe, practical, yet still obsessive thoughts. Absorbed in processing the dilemma at hand, whilst recognising her OCD had officially taken over, she didn't hear David enter … until he gasped.

She watched as his mouth dropped open, his eyes grew wide, and then a look of acceptance washed over him. There was no comment. This was not an unfamiliar scene. Kate seemed to be on a mission these days, and it felt like every time he walked into a room, she was emptying cupboards or rearranging something. Perhaps it was some sort of nesting mode? *Maybe she wants another baby?* He thought, as a flicker of excitement shot through him. *A little boy, perhaps?* He adored his two girls, but a little boy? Yes, he could go for a third. Definitely a discussion he might bring up, but maybe not in the midst of her OCD madness.

"I'm going to go pick up the girls. Do you need anything from the shops?" David gingerly stepped around the books, trying to make his way through the room. Getting up from the table, Kate too began to navigate through the books until they met in the middle. Rising up onto her tiptoes, she planted a kiss on his cheek.

"Thank you. Yup, can you get some salad stuff please? I've made a nice roast chicken for dinner tonight."

"Isn't Juanita coming? It's Salsa tonight."

Kate let out a dramatic sigh and plonked herself onto a small, book-free section of the floor. Crossing her legs, she reached for any that were in the 'blue' family. She couldn't look him in the eye when she was about to lie so blatantly.

"I cancelled Juanita," she said, whilst impersonating a person fully focused on the blue book search. In reality, her heart was pounding. Could she get away with this?

"To be honest"—*I'm going to hell*—"the Salsa classes aren't working, David." There, she'd said it.

"Okay," he said, partly relieved, but mostly confused, "Why?" He lent down to sit next to her, pushing the books to one side to make space for the two of them, passing his wife some blue books, which she slowly built into a tower.

"Honestly"—*definitely going to hell*—"it's just not working. We said we needed to try something fun and you've been amazing, but I know you don't really enjoy it." Not pausing for breath. "Plus, we don't work well together. I'm too small, you're too tall. You move up and down. I want to go side to side. It's not exactly the fun activity I thought it would be." Still focusing on her now-growing blue tower, she stole a glance at him. He didn't seem upset. He passed her one more book before standing up.

"I guess. We did kinda look sort of ridiculous. You're not wrong." David chuckled at the memory.

"Plus, it's boiling now, and the Boomba Bar is so gloomy. It just seems a pity to be inside when we should be enjoying the outside; it's such a beautiful time when the sun goes down." Kate added ammunition to her arsenal of excuses.

"Yup, you have a valid point." David dusted down his shorts and hopped his way back to the door as if he were a soldier on a rope obstacle training course. "Okay, I've got to get the girls. Salad stuff it is." He paused. "Maybe we can try something else after the summer? It was fun going out like grown-ups." Not waiting for a reply, he disappeared, closing the door behind him and relief flooded through Kate. She never had to go to the Boomba Bar again.

A column of blue books now loomed in the centre of the room, wobbling precariously. *What next? The red books? Or just get the blue books back on the shelf?* However, having extricated herself from Salsa, the OCD suddenly seemed to dissipate, and she couldn't be bothered to continue with the ridiculous project anymore. She had a good hour before David and the girls returned. She could just put all the books back, in no particular order, but first, she needed to catch up on some emails. Jamie had sent her one last Friday, and it had been weighing on her mind, plus she really wanted to share what had happened in the class. She knew she could trust Jamie. There was no part of her that felt Jamie would ever betray her confidence, and she could hardly speak to any of her other friends who knew David. But maybe she shouldn't put it in writing, maybe just share it when they next saw each other. Jamie would think her a ridiculous queen prude and they'd laugh about it. Hopping over the obstacle course of books, in a similar fashion to David, Kate returned to the table and flipped open her laptop. Bloody stupid spinning ball of annoyance flared up, and she made a mental note that on her next birthday a new laptop would be a perfect gift.

To: fallen-angel@scoopmail.com
From: katebuchanan@scoopmail.com
Subject:

The cursor blinked, and she hesitated. She wanted to call the subject, 'Selfish and irresponsible,' as that seemed to be the topic at hand, but Jamie seemed upset and she wasn't that insensitive, so she opted to leave it blank.

Hey Jamie. Bloody hell you poor thing …

Again, she stopped and watched the cursor flash again. Pressing the delete button, she removed 'you poor thing.' She thought Maria had a bloody good point. From all accounts, Jamie appeared to be swerving somewhat off the rails since her return to London. *Ufff*, how to address this? Delete, delete.

Jamie

I love you tons … don't be mad at me. I know how much pressure you're under and that you're financially responsible for both your mum and Madison. But … the thing is, Jamie, Madison is your daughter and your mum is getting on a bit now. I totally get that you're working and supporting them and obviously if you were working, that's when your mum needs to be there for you. And she has. But in this instance, you weren't. I'm not saying that you don't deserve to have some fun and downtime (I love that you have fun and lots of juicy stories to share with me) but on this particular occasion can you put aside your feelings of indignation and just look at it from your mum's perspective? I think this is a long conversation that we can process together. We need to get together. I have stuff I need to talk to you about too. We also need COSMOPOLITANS. Lol. So if you're not mad at me for speaking my mind, I have an idea. David's going back to London, the first week of August. Fancy coming to stay with me for a few days? Even a week if your work permits? The girls get on great. Will you think about it?

Love ya. Me.

P.S. I stopped Salsa classes. TBD
P.P.S. Mystery Man ... tell me more. How old is old? I'd put money on him not being old at all, just not your usual twenty-year-old.
P.P.P.S. No idea who Chris Hemsworth or Zoë Kravitz is, but if you'd said Matthew McConaughey, that's another story!

Kate pressed send and then started scrambling around, thrusting the books in no particular order back onto the shelf. For sure, she'd have another mental breakdown at some point and could do the books then. Now she just needed to clear the floor and be ready for her girls. Writing to Jamie about being more present for Madison made her realise the last couple of weeks she'd not been that present herself. Her fingers touched her lips as her mind wandered off again. Closing her eyes, she recalled the moments from the last Salsa class.

* * *

After knocking back not one but two vodkas, which were equivalent to perhaps four English vodkas, Kate felt confident and relaxed.

Robert wasn't with the same girl this time, but a new lookalike: blonde, five foot ten and very skinny; obviously his type. Kate spent the class trying to ignore him like a fifteen-year-old schoolgirl with her first crush, but at one point they brushed arms, turning her beetroot red. Damn, the physical reactions just wouldn't let up, and the vodka made her horny. It wasn't helping.

The class breezed through relatively quickly as David, true to his word, having now mastered the basic step, did not inflict serious harm on her toes, so there was no need for any partner swapping this time. If only it hadn't rained.

As soon as the class was over, Kate made a dash to get out. David, gallant as ever, went to get the car, leaving her propped up against a wall outside. Best place for her seeing that the vodka had now soaked into her system, making standing upright an arduous task. The weather irritated Kate. She hated it when it rained in Mallorca. It made her feel like she might as well be back in England with her friends and family. She sighed deeply for a moment, feeling a pang of homesickness.

"Big sigh for such a little woman!" Robert exclaimed, creeping up behind her with no sign of his dance partner anywhere.

Oh shit, thought Kate, as the hairs on the back of her neck bristled, as if standing to attention at his command. *Breathe. Just breathe. Say nothing. Do nothing. Do not make a prat of yourself. And more importantly, do not throw up.* All this negotiating with herself, however, seemed to be swept to one side as she was so taken aback at being addressed as a 'little woman.' Robert continued to speak politely even though she was looking at him with a glazed expression, mouth open. Well, vodka does that.

"Where's Darren?" Robert ignored the fact that she still hadn't spoken a word.

"Car ... rain, and it's David," she said slowly, conscious that she could be slurring her words—hardly the coolest thing to do. "And the new girlfriend, who looks exactly the same as the old girlfriend, have you lost her already?" Kate found a burst of lucidity, which appeared to amuse him.

"Not a girlfriend." He held her gaze intently.

"Blonde, five foot ten and twelve-years-old, your type then?" she inquired sarcastically, totally ignoring the fact that he'd said she was not a girlfriend.

"Usually, but sometimes I like to break out of my comfort zone and go for petite brunettes with piercing blue eyes."

"Ahhh. Versatile then," Kate bantered back, the vodka giving her confidence. *Who am I?*

Kate was enjoying the attention; in fact, she was flirting with him and it was fun.

Robert edged closer towards her whilst she, to retain some semblance of composure, edged further away until she'd left the security of the wall and the awning. Wobbling somewhat and shuffling awkwardly, she found herself standing in the rain, getting extremely wet.

"I like what you're wearing." His eyes travelled the length of her body.

She felt naked, even though her black sundress wasn't particularly revealing. He took a step closer to her, but still remained under the awning. She felt like purring, as if she was being stroked and petted. She wanted to hear more, but the small part of her brain that was not jumbled with vodka shouted, *Extricate yourself. Now. Don't flirt. David could be back any second.*

"Robert ..." But no words. "Robert ..." *Fuck* still no words. He seemed to be conscious of her rising distress.

"Sorry, Kate, I know I shouldn't be flirting with you ... I've just been thinking about the dance."

"Robert ..." *Goddammit. Come on Kate, say something else, you twit.*

"It's okay Kate, don't panic, it was a great dance, but just a dance."

Now she was the one feeling like a twelve-year-old. She'd wanted to be cool and sophisticated, but all witty repartees seemed to have disappeared, and she didn't know what to say because he was wrong, so very wrong. It had been more than just a dance—so much more. In typical Kate-style, her thoughts somehow manifested into words and then fell out of her mouth in large globules.

She gazed up at him, flashing her eyes in warning as if to say, don't come any closer. Yet the words that came out of her mouth were far more inviting, "It was more than a dance, much more, and you know it, but I guess for you it was just a bit of fun." Then indignantly, she added, "I'm married."

For a moment, Robert almost looked remorseful, but then he smiled. His eyes creased up and Kate followed the curves of his mouth to his jawline, finally resting on his lips. He took another step towards her so that he too was now in the rain, just an arm's length away from her, and she melted.

"Kate," he said, and then paused, "that's a great shame." His tone was apologetic, but there was a dangerous twinkle in his eyes.

"Yes. Shame," she echoed as she returned his gaze, this time without squirming or embarrassment.

At long last, The Seductress came to the rescue. Her eyes glinted with the excitement and the danger of their interaction. She raised her head defiantly as the rain came pelting down onto her face and then, as if by magic, as if once again they were dancing, time stopped. Sounds faded as he moved in closer towards her, rain droplets falling in slow motion; falling onto her cheeks and onto her lips. He reached out and caught a drop of rain in his fingertips, brushing his fingers across her cheek and down towards her mouth. Before she had any idea what was happening, he bent his head forward and touched his lips onto hers. It was not a kiss as such, just a connection; an incredible, powerful, bonding of two people, and though it lasted but a second, to Kate, it felt like an eternity. Her eyes closed as she succumbed completely to the power of his lips resting on hers.

At the sounds of high heels, clip-clopping on the stairs, Robert disengaged his lips from Kate's. He took a step back, his eyes never leaving hers for a second. "Shame." His voice was husky, and she shivered.

Taking hold of his non-girlfriend's arm, Robert walked off, leaving Kate standing in the rain, totally and utterly speechless. Her mind couldn't process what had happened. As she watched him walk away with his arm around the gorgeous blonde, she felt a longing for something that was so alien to her that she staggered backwards to the wall for support again. *What the hell just happened?*

Suddenly, David pulled up in the car. "Why are you so wet? Hop in."

And she did. But during the car ride home, she replayed it over and over in her mind and found herself touching her lips delicately with her fingers, trying to recapture the sensation that had shot through her.

LOST

Sitting in the departures lounge at London Gatwick, a Bloody Mary in one hand and her phone in the other, Jamie started to email Kate but then the message alert tone rang out from the phone, prompting Jamie to stop writing and she quickly pressed open.

> Cameron: Hey, gorgeous! Just wanted to wish you a fun trip and let you know I'll be thinking about you … and your return!! xx

A half smile crept onto Jamie's lips. She was still seeing Cameron, although that had become more challenging since the day she'd overslept at his. Nevertheless, she was beginning to tire of the relationship, if you could even call it that. The sex was still very good, there was no denying that. But what more was there? Ennui had started to set in. She decided to reply later and resumed emailing Kate:

> Anyway, I'd better go now, I left Madison checking out the shoes

for me whilst I try to calm my nerves before the flight. Y'know how it is. See you when we land.
CANNOT WAIT. J xxx

As Jamie put away her phone, she cast her eyes back into Dune to look for Madison, but she couldn't see her. Quickly dialling Madison's number, she heard ringing coming from her daughter's white carry-on, her favourite, emblazoned with fluorescent pink flowers. Jamie groaned, grabbing both of their cases and darted into the store, but Madison was nowhere to be seen. Where had she gone? She'd told her to stay in the store. She went up to the sales girl at the cash desk who was on the phone and interrupted, "Excuse me, my daughter was just in here. She's ten-years-old but looks about twelve; have you seen her?"

"Sorry, could you hold a moment?" the sales assistant spoke to her caller, "There was a girl in here, I think? But … we have so many people coming in and out. I really can't be sure." The pretty, but overly made up assistant paused before asking, "Who was she with?"

"She was with me. I was just sitting there." Jamie pointed over to the row of seats in front of the shop, somewhat irritated to have to deal with some young assistant who likely didn't give two hoots about anything.

The sales girl stared blankly around the tiny, virtually empty store, still holding the phone in her hand. "I'm sorry, I vaguely remember a girl like that, but I can't be sure."

"She was literally just in here. You must remember her. She's got long brown hair, and she was wearing khaki combat pants with a pink T-shirt and trainers. I just want to know where she went."

"I'm sorry. We have so many people coming in and out. I really don't remember …" her voice trailed off as she turned back to her caller.

Goddammit. They hadn't even left, and Madison was already causing trouble. Storming out of Dune, Jamie started to frantically pace up and down the stores, trying to guess where Madison may have wandered off to … then she saw it—Hamleys. *YES.* That was it. She'd be in there for sure, cooing over some new toy, no doubt. With a sense of relief, Jamie marched over to the store, but once inside, there was no Madison in sight. Certain that's where she would have gone, Jamie searched every inch of the interior, like a hungry dog sniffing for food, expecting to find her hiding behind a toy display or something. But Madison was nowhere to be found. *Of course she isn't; she's not five anymore, what was I thinking?* Jamie's heart started to race. She'd been convinced that she would find her there. She glanced at the departures board. Their flight would be boarding soon and she didn't have a clue where her daughter was. Heart now galloping, Jamie scurried around the terminal like someone who'd misplaced their phone, let alone their child. Her eyes darted so fast she could barely focus.

"Madison, Madison!" Her voice grew louder as she tried to be heard above the din of the crowds. Running this way and that, bumping into several travellers with their cases as she attempted to weave her way through. *Damn it, where is she?* She rushed across to Accessorize, hoping to find her looking at hair clips, but once again, she wasn't there. Over to LEGO—a possibility, although Madison hadn't played with LEGO for years. No Madison. *Shit. SHIT.* What if she wasn't playing at all? What if something had happened to her? What if someone had … gulp, kidnapped her, and she was on the next flight out to Guatemala? *FUCK.*

"MADISON, MADISON! Excuse me, have you seen a little girl?

Not so little actually." Jamie began to randomly stop passers-by, but her frenzy and the Bloody Mary left her hazy, unable to focus or even hear clearly. The terminal was one large blur of colours and motion. She felt dizzy. Any second now, she was likely to faint. Or throw up.

"Are you alright?" Jamie heard a voice come out of nowhere. "Are you alright, dear?" The question came again. A smartly dressed older woman appeared to be talking to her, but Jamie's mind, along with her rapidly beating heart, was in overdrive; nothing was registering. "Excuse me, dear? Have you lost someone?" The woman's eyes were kind and concerned.

Jamie snapped out of her stupor long enough to realise the woman was talking to her. "Yes, my daughter. I can't find my daughter and our flight is leaving soon and I can't find her." Jamie's voice had taken on a slightly hysterical quality.

"Why don't we go over to the Information Desk? They might be able to help there. They're bound to have a tannoy or something." The woman pointed across the crowds towards the arc-shaped booth.

"Tannoy?" Jamie's eyes widened at the mere thought of it, but the woman had already taken hold of her arm and was gently but firmly leading her in that direction.

"Hello, I wonder if you could help? This lady appears to have lost her daughter." The kind woman informed one of the women at the desk, before turning to Jamie. "What's her name, my dear?"

Stunned, Jamie stood gawking. Words escaped her. Just like Madison. Oh my god, what had she done? She couldn't even look after her own daughter for five minutes. Just five minutes emailing Kate and she'd lost her daughter. What would Maria say? *SHIT*. Maria would absolutely lose it. Why hadn't she just made Madison stick next to her? Like any normal mother would do? In an airport of all places. One doesn't leave baggage unattended, let alone children. *SHIT SHIT SHIT.*

"Excuse me, dear"—the kind lady interrupted Jamie's muddled thoughts—"what's your daughter's name? Can you describe her to us?" Now the lady at Information was also looking directly at Jamie, both waiting for a reply.

Like a robot that had just been unpaused, Jamie broke out of her daze. "Uh, sorry. Yes, my daughter … Madison. Her name's Madison. She was just with me. She was looking at the shoes in Dune. She was just with me."

"Yes Miss, could you describe her to me please?" said the dark-haired lady at Information, her thick-rimmed glasses obscuring her pretty features; contacts would be far more flattering. Distracted again, Jamie had to be reeled back in.

"Sorry, yes, of course. She's ten-years-old but tall for her age so she looks more like twelve, thirteen even. She's got long honey brown hair and hazel eyes, and she was wearing baggy khaki coloured combat pants, with a pink T-shirt on top and white trainers. A really cute outfit actually. Oh and she's also got her own bag—a lilac O'Neil rucksack with her Nintendo and snacks for the plane. No idea why she hasn't got her phone too!"

Jamie was frightened. What if she really had lost Madison? What if, heaven forbid, she never saw her again? Her stomach sank, and then it sank again, so low that it would soon be joining the Titanic. Suddenly, a two-tone signal sounded across the terminal. "This is a public announcement. If anyone has seen a little girl on her own, please could you bring her to information point B. She's ten-years-old, with long brown hair, and was last seen wearing Khaki trousers and a pink T-shirt." The voice rang out across the sea of travellers.

Oh my god, I can't believe this is happening. Not only have I lost my daughter, but now the whole world knows I have too. The whole world knows what a crap mother I am. The reality of the situation hit Jamie, whose mind was now beyond whirling. Why had she let Madison out of her sight? For even a second? What was she going to do if they didn't find her? *WHAT?*

"Excuse me. Is this who you're looking for?" The kind lady tapped Jamie on the back.

Suddenly, Madison materialised right before her very eyes. She appeared more beautiful and more precious in that instance than ever before.

"Madison!" Jamie leapt towards her daughter and hugged her with such force that Madison all but stumbled.

"Sorry, Mummy, I really had to go to the loo," Madison said sheepishly, clearly worried that she might be reprimanded for the obvious chaos she'd caused.

"Wonderful, she's here. That's so great. Just keep an eye on her next time. This is a busy airport, you know," said the customer service adviser, with warmth but still judgmentally.

"Happy that you found each other again," echoed the kind lady as she left.

"Don't ever, ever, ever, leave me again! Do you hear?" Jamie grabbed Madison's shoulders to face her.

"Yes, Mum. I just needed the loo so desperately and you were busy. I didn't want to disturb you."

"Never mind. Next time, I don't care what I'm doing, just interrupt me and we'll go together. Airports are dangerous places. Anything could've happened to you. Anything. Promise me, Madison, okay?" Jamie, relieved to have her daughter back, was still trembling from fear.

Once on board, Jamie's fears over Madison were quickly replaced by her fear of flying. She desperately wanted another drink to calm her down properly, but if she hadn't been drinking, and on her stupid phone, she would never have lost sight of her daughter. No, a drink would have to wait. She grabbed one of Madison's hands and held on just a little too tightly.

"I'm sorry, Mum ... about today. I didn't mean it. I promise I won't do it next time."

Madison gazed up at her mother, her huge eyes resembling one of those kitty cats that turn the cuteness up to the max so no one can resist. It was funny really. One minute she could have this feisty almost-teen attitude, and the next she was her little girl again.

"No Maddy. It wasn't your fault. There won't be a next time. I'll make sure I'm right here next to you."

As the plane began its taxi up to the runway, Jamie's anxiety levels started to rise again, palms becoming sweaty. For such a frequent flyer, she really shouldn't be this nervous. Eying up the aisle, she reconsidered another drink. Although only two hours, flights to the island were notoriously bumpy. But she would refrain. The terror of the last hour had still left her shaken. Suddenly, the roaring sound of the engines suggested they were about to take off. Yes, she would absolutely try to refrain.

* * *

"This is your captain here. Just to let you know, we will soon be starting our descent to Palma airport. You'll be happy to know it's a very warm thirty-two degrees." Some passengers let out a cheer, mostly the British ones. "On behalf of myself and the team, we would like to wish you a very enjoyable trip. Thank you for flying with EasyJet."

Jamie and Madison both peered out of the little oval window. The sky was clear and blue, with not a single cloud in sight. Ahead in the distance, their little island was coming into view, surrounded by a sparkling sea of turquoise. Jamie exhaled. This was the part of the flight she actually enjoyed. Landing. It had been bumpy, and she had ended up ordering a drink, rationalising that Madison could hardly get lost on a plane, and besides, she didn't want to pass on her fear of flying to her daughter. No, it was the sensible thing to do. Gazing through the window, Jamie was reminded of how leaving the UK to fly to Spain was like being in a black and white movie and suddenly finding yourself in full glorious Technicolour. Her heart skipped. She hadn't wanted to admit it to herself, but she'd missed the island. A lot. It was as if she'd left a little piece of herself there. She felt free there. Life seemed much less complicated. And lovely Kate was there, too.

"Mum look." Madison was excitedly pointing out of the window. "Look at all those boats. It looks so pretty."

Jamie took her daughter's hand, a little more gently this time. "Yes, it is sweetie. Soooo pretty. We're going to have an amazing time." And perhaps, for the first time ever, Jamie believed that was possible.

TRUE CONFESSIONS
Mallorca, Spain

"MADISON!" Jamie shrieked so loudly that not only did Kate jump, but so did others near them on the beach. Several eyes turned in Jamie's direction, investigating what could possibly elicit such distress. Kate, who'd been busy dragging her sunbed out from under the umbrella where they'd plonked their belongings, immediately stopped what she was doing.

"What? What?" Kate presumed she'd missed some imminent catastrophe whilst following Jamie's gaze towards Emily and Madison. The girls seemed perfectly happy, skipping hand in hand towards the sea; there didn't seem to be any obvious emergency unfolding. After scouring the beach for any potential shooters who might be threatening their children and checking the sea line for a tsunami, Kate returned her gaze towards Jamie.

"What's wrong? They're fine, Jamie. Why the panic?"

"Erm …" Jamie, now slightly embarrassed by her exaggerated public display of neurosis, looked sheepishly towards Kate. "Erm … nothing. I just panicked. I don't want to lose her."

Kate was completely mystified, not that they'd ever spent any real time together with their kids, but they'd had enough emails, calls and texts for Kate to have a pretty good sense of her friend.

And Jamie had never struck her as being an overprotective parent.

"They're fine Jamie. Emily knows she has to stay in my eye view and besides, she's so terrified of jellyfish she'll only go up to her ankles. Don't worry." With that, Kate returned her attention back to the sunbed, dragging the part that was still in the shade so that it was fully in the sun. As she began to lay out her towel, the thought of being in a bikini next to Jamie filled her with horror; she wondered how she could get into a lying position without having to remove her cover-up. Quickly, she started to drag the sunbed back under the umbrella. She could keep the cover-up on if she stayed in the shade.

"Why are you worried about losing her?" Kate was now safely back under the umbrella. "I lose keys, my phone, but I've never lost a child on my watch—yet," she said jokingly, unaware of Jamie's airport drama. As Jamie and Madison had arrived late the previous night, and with Emily and Tali already asleep, they'd decided to head straight to bed and pause their mammoth catch-up for this precise moment.

"It's a long story," sighed Jamie as she peeled off her cream crochet dress and relaxed onto the sunbed. Kate nearly gasped out loud. Not that she'd ever seen Jamie in a bikini before, but bloody hell, she was just skin and bone. She'd thought as much when she'd given Jamie a big hug the night before, but seeing her now in nothing but a tiny string bikini confirmed her fears. Images of how glorious Jamie had looked in her gym gear the first time they met compared to how skeletal she was now worried Kate. She never thought there was such a thing as 'too thin,' but looking at her friend now, she surmised that indeed there was.

Not questioning Jamie any further on the possible 'long story,'

Kate made a mental note to add whatever it may be to their ever-growing list of subjects to be discussed.

Jamie, on the other hand, seemed a little confused by Kate's sunbed dragging debacle, asking, "Kate, what are you doing with your sunbed?"

"I forgot how sunburned I am. Better to stay in the shade." Kate was quick to think of a good enough excuse and pleased with herself for providing a valid reason why she wasn't going to take off her cover-up. "Better stay covered today I think." Yes, there would be no need to strip off next to Jamie today.

Thankfully, Jamie didn't seem to question Kate and started to smother her pale skin with factor fifty, regardless of being in the shade. The sun was very damaging, and ageing, and Jamie King was going to do everything in her power to protect what she felt was her primary asset. With both girls lying in the shade, there was a moment of quiet as they both contemplated the beautiful vista before them. The sun bounced like glitter across the calm turquoise waters, framed at the side by rugged rocks, sprinkled with sunbathers. The sound of the tide lapping in and out was hypnotic, accented only by the sounds of chatter and laughter. This very moment, was pure magic. Where to start?

Kate looked around the beach and, spying a bar next to the massage booth, smiled cheekily. "We've got a lot to catch up on. I want to know all about this Cameron and life back in London. How's your mum? And how's work? And ooh, ooh"—forgetting what she felt to be a priority on the agenda—"the 'older' guy? The single parent. Now this is a story I want to hear. But before we start … shall we?" Kate's eyes were fully focused on the bar at the far end of the beach. Jamie followed the direction of her gaze and grinned. She knew exactly what Kate was thinking.

"Darling, it's past twelve o'clock somewhere in the world."

"I'll go." Kate was quick to volunteer. "First round's on me. I asked Juanita to pick Tali up from summer school today, so we have no rush at all. Today is our day."

With that, Kate launched off her sunbed and made her way towards the bar. Reaching halfway, she severely regretted not putting on her flip-flops. The sand was scorching. Not just hot, but burning to the point that it was unbearable. She needed to get to a cool patch immediately. Running on the spot for a split second to help ease the pain, she spotted an umbrella not far to her left. In a rare moment of athleticism, Kate crouched down quicker than a prostitute could drop her knickers, and launched herself long jump-style to the nearest bit of shade; landing not quite so athletically in a heap at the foot of two sunbeds. Overwhelmed with relief to no longer be standing on the blistering sand, she gathered herself together and looked up to see two blonde adonises staring at her from their sunbeds with great amusement.

"Sand. Hot!" she exclaimed, as if it weren't bleating obvious. A smidgen embarrassed, Kate grinned at them cheekily. They both laughed. Standing up, she pointed to the bar. "I forgot my shoes. Don't worry, I'll be out of your way soon. I just need to recover my feet for a moment," she continued in English; after all, they didn't exactly look Spanish.

"That's okay, anytime," one commented, whilst laughing, in perfect English with what appeared to be a Scandinavian accent, "Anytime." He was clearly trying to be flirtatious. "If you want to make a pit stop on your way back, and join us for a drink, you're more than welcome," the hot Scandinavian suggested, pointing to a large pitcher of Sangria. Kate laughed, partly with nervousness, unfamiliar with this sort of attention. But mostly because she felt happy and more relaxed than normal. Having Jamie there made her feel different. It was nice.

"I would"—Kate was quick to reply—"but I'm with my friend over there. Thank you though." Both boys followed Kate's pointing finger to Jamie, who unbelievably, at that precise moment, was taking off her bikini top and sensually rubbing sunscreen into her breasts. There was a moment of complete silence as both boys' jaws dropped. Kate sniggered, vicariously enjoying the adoration floating Jamie's way. "It's a girls' day." She was determined to thwart their now escalated desire to join them. There was no way she was going to share Jamie today, and especially not in front of their kids. Before they had a chance to try to persuade her, she all but catapulted herself in the direction of the bar, this time running. She had no idea how she was going to make it back with two glasses and decided that the boys might be onto a good idea—maybe she would get a pitcher of Cosmopolitan. Yes, that should keep them going.

Mission accomplished, Kate returned to Jamie with a pitcher of their favourite cocktail and two plastic glasses. Jamie looked up in surprise. "A pitcher. Really?"

"It's only a half-litre, and mostly ice. Trust me, you don't want to be making that journey. It's hazardous—in more ways than one." Kate was pretty sure that if Jamie clocked the two guys, she'd probably be keener than she was to have them join them. Returning to her sunbed and perching the pitcher and glasses onto the little round table that circled the umbrella, Kate poured them each a glass. Passing one to Jamie, they both smiled clinking their glasses together.

"So"—Jamie cut to the chase—"are you going to tell me why you stopped going to Salsa then?"

Kate proceeded to explain. It burst out of her like projectile vomit, so desperate was she to confess in the hope of receiving the absolution that she knew Jamie would award her with.

"Let me get this straight"—Jamie spoke slowly, sipping her second glass—"you gave up Salsa because you got a tingle?"

"Yup." Kate smiled sheepishly, trying to work out how Jamie wasn't slurring her words while she, on the other hand, was hardly able to talk? The Cosmopolitans were delicious but ever so potent.

"What sort of tingle?" Jamie was confused.

"You know?" Kate giggled. "The tingle."

Now Jamie was really confused.

"Hun, I'm sorry I'm just not getting it, one minute you're full of the joys of spring and about to become the latest shit-hot Salsa dancer down the Paseo and the next minute you're being evasive and talking about some sort of tingle. What tingle? Where was the tingle?"

"I got the tingle in my ..." Kate searched frantically for the word which might shed some light on the situation. "In my ... loins."

"In your what?"

"Loins. In my loins."

"In your what?" Jamie nearly bent over double laughing. Kate clocked that even sitting down, she didn't seem to have any rolls on her stomach.

"Loins, LOINS." Kate, also giggling so hard it almost hurt, shouted back at her.

"Kate, again! You're using words from the last century!"

"Rubbish, I do not."

"You absolutely do. Ironmongers!"

"Oh fair point, well, I don't know how else to put it."

"Try using modern day language. You're confusing me."

"I got horny."

"Ahhhhhh, now I understand. You got horny, and the tingle was in your loins?"

"Yup." Kate slurped the last bit of the cocktail out of the straw and started sucking on the sweet glacé cherry to access any alcohol that might've seeped into it. They were only on the first topic of their packed agenda, and they'd already gone through the entire pitcher. "Shall we order another? These are wonderful."

Jamie nodded her head enthusiastically, still trying to understand the correlation between feeling horny and giving up Salsa. "I'll go, but first, can you please just explain more?"

Looking out to sea Kate noticed Emily and Madison lying flat on their stomachs—partly in the sand and partly in the sea—kicking their legs in unison, engrossed in their own private catchup. "I got horny, but not towards David." There, she'd said it. She waited to be struck down by a bolt of lightning, the evil hussy that she was.

"Ahhh."

"Yup, ahhhh. Now, do you understand why I couldn't go anymore?"

"Well … ummm, no. Not really. Who was it, the instructor?"

"No. It was one of the other students, it was horrible. I had to dance with him because David kept treading on my toes and oh my god, he was gorgeous, and something really strange happened." Kate suddenly went bright red at the mere thought of Robert.

"Did you have an affair with him?" Blunt as ever, Jamie didn't mince her words.

"NO. Oh my god, of course not."

"Then what's the problem?"

"I'm married."

"Okay, so let me get this straight. You're married, so you can't have lustful thoughts towards anyone else?" Jamie started to laugh.

"This isn't funny." Kate's head dropped, and her shoulders

hunched up as the memories of her feelings towards Robert resurfaced.

"I'm sorry." Jamie tried to pull herself together, but the effort of trying not to laugh was insurmountable. Rolling onto her side, Jamie peered quizzically into the eyes of her mad friend.

"So, Kate. Please explain to me why you felt the need to give up something you love because of a feeling that you had that you didn't even act upon? I'm missing something here."

"It just felt wrong, that's all. And then there was the non-kiss."

"Ahhhhhhh, now we're getting there. You snogged him?"

"Well, not exactly. It was more a grazing of the lips."

"I see. And because you didn't sleep with him and because you didn't kiss him, you feel that you should punish yourself by stopping Salsa? Makes perfect sense." Jamie's huge green eyes rolled around in the back of her head.

"I can't explain it. It seems silly when I say it out loud, but you have to trust me, this man was dangerous, and I changed when I was with him. It was like I became someone else, and I didn't like who I became."

Kate suddenly felt forlorn, and it must have shown on her face because Jamie suddenly reached across the sunbeds and took hold of her hand. Softly speaking, her tone became more serious, "Listen to me hun, and listen carefully. You did nothing wrong. Nothing. So you had lustful thoughts, so what? Every man and woman walking the face of this earth has lustful thoughts. So what if you're married? Does that mean you're suddenly blind? Does that mean you no longer have the right to find anyone else attractive? You wouldn't be human if that were the case. I mean, consider yourself unusual to have survived this long without feeling it before. God knows I have lustful thoughts every day—in fact several times a day. I can't imagine I'd ever change just because I had a ring on my finger. Please, Kate, stop tormenting yourself over nothing."

"So if I've done nothing wrong, why the bloody hell do I feel like shit?"

"Why do you feel like shit?" Jamie repeated the question back to Kate like a therapist.

"Because it wasn't me. I love David. I'd never cheat on him. Never."

"And you didn't cheat on David. You didn't even kiss this man, so you don't have anything to feel guilty about. Look, it would be like me seeing an amazing pair of shoes in a shop window when I shouldn't be buying shoes, knowing I couldn't afford them. But imagine they're just so gorgeous that I can't resist walking into the shop; maybe even trying them on, but I still walk out empty handed. You know?"

Kate also rolled onto her side to face Jamie, grateful that she'd kept her coverup on and didn't have to breathe in.

"How can you possibly compare my lustful thoughts towards a stranger with wanting to buy shoes you can't afford?"

Jamie could see this analogy wasn't working and tried to explain things in terms Kate might understand better.

"Okay, let me put it another way. Let's imagine you're on a diet and you walk past a bakery and see this amazingly decadent death by chocolate cake in the window. Are you imagining it?"

"I am, I am." Kate returned to lying on her back and closed her eyes as she sank further into the sunbed. A wave of contentment washed over her at the mere thought of tasting something delicious. Eager to fully enjoy this imaginary game, she opened her eyes and winked at Jamie. "But better if I can imagine pizza? I prefer savoury." Closing her eyes again, she resumed the exercise that was going to release her from her guilt. Maybe this was like hypnosis?

Jamie laughed. "Okay, pizza it is. So, this pizza is there. The cheese is oozing, the mushrooms are glistening, and perhaps it even has onions. Your mouth begins to water. You know you want it. It's calling out to you, but you know you shouldn't have it but that doesn't stop you wishing you could, even just a little bite, does it? Do you see what I mean now? It's just human nature. Throughout our lives, we're going to be tempted by things we shouldn't have, but it won't stop us wanting them. All you had was a whiff."

"A bloody big whiff, though."

"Yes, but still only a whiff. You didn't even take a bite."

"No I didn't. I suppose I see what you mean. I just don't ever want to hurt David. I love David more than anything, but this man; this man was the king of all pizzas, you know, the sort with extra cheese. And I really, really, really felt like taking a huge bite and feeling that cheese oozing down my skin and dripping and …"

Jamie reached across the little umbrella table and play-slapped Kate. "Steady on hun. Just a little whiff, okay? Nothing more."

Jamie knew her friend was an honourable person, and she equally knew she'd done nothing wrong, so there was absolutely no way she was going to sit back and let her shred herself to pieces over a mere fantasy. As Jamie smiled, Kate began to smile too, realising that she was possibly the only person that would consider a whiff of pizza as grounds for breaking a diet.

"You know what, Jamie? You're so right. Honestly, I've really beaten myself up over this." She paused as if she wanted to add something else, but didn't know if she should. Jamie looked at Kate instinctively knowing there was something else she needed to share before she could put the matter to bed.

Staring back out to sea, Kate finally confessed, "I've been making love to David but thinking about Salsa Man."

"Good Lord, Kate. That's normal too. Honestly, sweetie. You've done nothing wrong."

"And …" Kate said, as Jamie covered her eyes with her hands in despair.

"No, no, Jamie. Please just let me tell you this last thing and then we can talk about you."

"Darling, you can talk about it all you like. I'm not frustrated with you sharing. I'm frustrated that you're always so hard on yourself. Get it all out," she said encouragingly.

"So … the thing is. I've been having all these sexual thoughts about Salsa Man and sure the fantasy was about having sex with him, but …" She stopped, wondering whether she could really share this part of her guilt with Jamie.

"Proceed." Jamie leaned in towards Kate.

"Well, the thing is … of course the main reason I gave up Salsa was because I'm married but also …"

"Yes, come on," Jamie said gently, sensing that this was hard for Kate.

"I didn't only not want sex with Salsa Man because I'm married. I didn't want sex because I feel disgusted with my droopy tits and my tummy looks so bad after the kids. Not like yours at all," she blurted out, enviously eyeing Jamie's taut, almost concave stomach.

"Oh, sweetie. You're so beautiful. You know this is all in your head. You've got something special with David, I know that. But you should think about going to see Malcolm Barnes, the surgeon I mentioned. If it will make you feel beautiful and better about yourself, then you should do it for yourself. Maybe this whole incident was all about you realising this and giving yourself the confidence to make that appointment. We discussed it months ago. If you're not having more kids, then this is the time. I'm telling you,

you'll feel like a whole new woman and forget all about this Salsa Man. In fact, you won't need any man to give you validation because you'll give it to yourself."

Kate felt calmer than she'd felt for weeks. Jamie was right. She was going to at least have a consultation.

"Let's call on Monday," Jamie said decisively. "There's no commitment. We'll just make an appointment and I'll come with you. Deal?"

"Okay, deal," Kate said with conviction. Then feeling like she'd monopolised the whole conversation, she flipped it back to Jamie. "So, come on then, it's your turn. Tell me first about Cameron. I want to know everything and please, spare no details." As she smiled, mischievously.

NOT SO FUNNY FUN BAGS
London, England

Kate sat fidgeting in her seat in the reception area of Malcolm Barnes' office. Where the bloody hell was Jamie? It was nearly noon, and she hadn't arrived. Kate groaned inwardly and started twisting her hair; a nervous habit she'd developed during her student years. What would happen if Jamie didn't come? Kate felt sick. Just being there for the consultation made her want to do an about turn and run. She tried to focus on her surroundings; the offices were stark, taking the word minimalistic to a whole new dimension. The walls were white and the only furniture, apart from a few chrome chairs, was a small glass reception desk, which stood at one end. The receptionist sitting at the desk looked about a hundred-years-old; permanent wrinkles etched her face and Kate couldn't help but think that she must be bloody good at her job because she certainly wasn't there as an advertisement for the miracles that Malcolm Barnes could perform.

Suddenly, the door opened and Kate bolted upright with anticipation; that was until a sixty-something-year-old lady walked in with bandages wrapped around her face. *Hmmmm, not a tummy tuck then.* The woman glanced in Kate's direction, and Kate was sure that at that moment a flicker of disgruntlement crossed her face.

Just as the door closed it lurched open again, and this time in walked Jamie, like a gust of warm summer air. Glorious, stunning, but extremely skinny. Kate had been shocked on the beach, but put it down to never having seen her in a bikini before. But Kate didn't ever recall seeing Jamie look this skeletal in clothes. Today she was wearing white jeans with a white vest, and a light cream and very chic cardigan—if you could call something so stylish a cardigan—on top. But the loosely woven fabric hung lifeless, as if it were three sizes too big. Jamie looked like a scarecrow, albeit a very chic and glorious one, and Kate knew she'd need to address this with her. Just not now. Now, she was close to hyperventilating with her own drama.

Whilst relief flooded through Kate at Jamie's arrival, she couldn't help but laugh at the reaction of the other woman whose jaw—had it not been restricted by bandages—would certainly have dropped to the floor. If the woman had been confused at seeing Kate, then she was completely flabbergasted at seeing the vision that was Jamie King.

"Darling, I'm so sorry. Am I late? Have you been waiting long? Are you okay? Oh gosh, it's soooo good to see you," Jamie gushed without taking a single breath, as she rushed over to hug Kate, oblivious to both the secretary and the other woman who were both glowering at her.

Hugging her so tightly that she could feel her bones through her clothes, Kate was awash with relief. "Oh, Jamie. I was just beginning to panic. I think I'm going to be sick. I'm so nervous."

"Don't worry hun, you'll be fine. It's only a consultation. Look, if you don't feel comfortable, then you just won't go through with it. Okay?" Jamie reached over and grabbed Kate's hand and Kate relaxed, a smidgen.

"How's it been since you got back?" Kate tried to take her mind off the impending appointment.

Jamie groaned and slumped her shoulders. "Okay." She didn't elaborate.

Without waiting for Jamie to reply, Kate probed further. "Go on. Are you still seeing Cameron? Did you meet Karl?"

"Let's not discuss me now … and anyway, I never said I was interested in Karl, that was your idea, remember?" Jamie flicked her hair as she made some sort of huffing sound.

"Mrs Buchanan, Mr Barnes will see you now," the receptionist called out.

Jamie grinned as she jumped up from her seat a little too eagerly. Dragging Kate by the hand she whispered, "Let's focus on you now."

Reluctantly, Kate found herself being hauled into Mr Barnes's office. What had seemed like a good idea on the beach after a pitcher of Cosmopolitan was rapidly disintegrating into an extremely bad one. The consultant's room was large, warm and inviting; a stark contrast to the reception area. With its smattering of antiques and large, sage green Chesterfield sofa, it resembled the foyer of an old country house estate. An Edwardian mahogany desk with a green leather surface dominated one corner of the room, with Mr Barnes seated behind it, who immediately stood up to greet them. In his late fifties, Mr Barnes seemed calm and approachable, and Kate felt slightly less nervous.

Taking his outstretched hand, Kate shook it. "Hi, I'm Kate, and this is my friend Jamie."

"Pleasure to meet you both. Please take a seat." Mr Barnes pointed towards the two cream bucket chairs on the other side of his desk. Jamie perched on the edge of her seat, keen to get started, whilst Kate sat as far back as she could.

"So tell me, Mrs Buchanan, how can I help you?"

"Well ..." Kate hesitated, searching for the words. It felt strange to be talking about one's breasts and tummy to a stranger; and a male stranger at that. Jamie kicked her, spurring her into action. "I've had two children and put on huge amounts of weight with each but I know I'm definitely not having any more now. I've exercised and dieted, but my breasts are just so loose and floppy and my tummy looks even worse; like some sort of Sponge Bob Square Pants inflatable toy." Kate was pleased with herself, feeling that for once in her life she'd been witty and concise.

Mr Barnes seemed to miss the humour of her analogy and merely smiled and nodded his head as he made some notes. Kate opened her eyes wide and looked at Jamie, who was finding it hard not to laugh out loud. They both exchanged a look that said, 'nice man, no sense of humour.'

After taking a brief medical history, Mr Barnes stood up. "Come this way please Mrs Buchanan. Let's have a look at you."

Kate was panic stricken. What? Look? Look at her ravaged body? Oh, this was horrible. But of course he had to look; he was hardly going to perform the surgery blindfolded. However, the reality of having to undress and let this man scrutinise her in all her glory felt more horrifying than her memories of sitting down for her Chemistry A-Level exam.

Mr Barnes walked towards the far end of the room and pulled back a black curtain, revealing a huge screen that took up most of the back wall of his office. Kate sat rigid in her chair, her body numb, her stomach churning. For the second time that morning, Jamie gave Kate a perfunctory kick and pulled her out of the chair, simultaneously pushing her towards the black curtain. Surely this was some kind of bad dream? Why was there a big screen? When she spotted the camera, Kate started to hyperventilate. Surely not? Surely it couldn't be? Surely he wasn't going to take a picture of her and … project it onto the screen? *Arrrrgggghhhh*. Kate, the woman who'd avoided looking in full-length mirrors for the last five years, was now about to be photographed in all her glory and displayed in Technicolour on a giant cinematic screen. Not just displayed but projected five times larger than life. *Oh my god, this is a nightmare. No, worse than a nightmare, as there's no waking up from it.* Jamie was now tugging at her sleeve and propelling her towards the black curtain; the black curtain of truth and horrific reality.

The walk towards the curtain seemed to take forever as Kate dragged her feet, feeling reluctance consume her with every step. She felt like a prisoner on death row taking her final steps; she could almost hear the plaintive wails of 'dead man walking.' Finally reaching their destination, Kate held up her hand to stop Jamie.

"What's wrong?" Jamie stared in disbelief.

"You. Stay. Here," Kate said, turning on Jamie like a Rottweiler; so great was her distress at this point.

"You've got to be kidding?" Jamie was no doubt expecting to follow her inside.

"Do I look like I'm kidding? No bloody way you're coming in here to witness this. You stay exactly where you are." Good friends or not, it was one thing having to face your own demons, but who needed spectators to one's shame? No, the fewer people who beheld the naked image of Kate Buchanan, the fewer people that would be psychologically scarred by its unveiling.

In a slightly softer, Rottweiler-turned-bunny manner, Kate turned to Jamie. "No, really, I'm fine." Jamie hung her head and dramatically hauled herself back to the chair, slumped in rejection as if she'd regressed to the age of five and been sent to her room.

The black curtain now pulled closed, Kate slowly began to undress. Over and over, she told herself how Mr Barnes did this every day; he would have seen tons of women's tits and she was sure he must've seen many tummies worse than hers, too. Kate felt the blood rush to her head and as if from some faraway place, she heard Jamie's lament.

"Can I come in, please?"

"NO!" snapped Kate.

"Pleeeease?"

Ignoring her as best she could, Kate stood in her knickers and with more trepidation than having to do a twenty-mile hike in a pair of seven inch heels, waited still to have her picture taken. Almost immediately, her image was projected onto the screen and it was official; the only thing worse than looking at oneself in a full-length mirror was looking at oneself blown up to giant proportions.

"PLEEEEASE?" Jamie was still going at it.

Kate just stood in shock at the image she was faced with. So much so that she was no longer aware of Jamie's pleas. Jamie took her silence as some sort of secret sign that entry through the black curtain was now admissible and came in. Kate was so speechless and horrified at the repugnant image that her ability to speak was rendered useless.

Jamie took one glance at her mortified friend whilst taking in the image on the screen and, conscious of Kate's rising distress, showed no signs whatsoever of being psychologically scarred for life. Calmly taking control of the situation, Jamie directed her attention away from the screen and towards Mr Barnes. "So, what do you think?"

Mr Barnes leapt into action and, taking a black marker pen started to indicate problem areas on the screen. Kate thought, perhaps it would be easier just to get a great big pot of black paint and chuck the whole thing onto the image. "I can't make you look like her," he exclaimed, pointing at Jamie, his face quickly registering the inappropriateness of his comment, and mumbled something indistinct under his breath.

Duh. Kate resisted the urge to retort, 'If I wanted to look like her, I'd have gone directly to God.'

As Malcolm Barnes started to talk, Jamie took out a notepad and pen, much to Kate's horror. This wasn't a university lecture. What the bloody hell was Jamie doing? Yet as Mr Barnes started to draw on the screen, he simultaneously began spouting out strange medical terms, which Jamie scribbled down furiously.

"For the stomach area, we can perform abdominoplasty; this will involve the removal of all that excess skin and the repositioning of the belly button."

Jamie continued scribbling notes. Kate remained silent, still in shock.

"Well, there are two other possibilities. We can do what we refer to as a lower body lift, which will deal with these problem areas over here"—Mr Barnes pointed at Kate's hips on the screen—"but that does mean there will be a scar going all the way around the body."

Arrrrgggghhhh. What was going on? Yes, she had hips, she knew she had hips, but she liked to think of them as womanly, and besides she was still under the delusion that possibly, with diet and exercise, there was a chance to shift the hips and hence avoid the aforementioned 360-degree scar.

"And these"—he continued, now directing his full attention towards Jamie whilst concurrently marking the screen where her breasts were exhibited hanging limply—"we can lift these up. Plenty of tissue here so we wouldn't need an implant, just a lift back to where they were pre-children. This is called a mastopexy."

Kate woke up at this point, but the power of speech still eluded her. Somewhere inside she wanted to tell him that she didn't want them where they'd been pre-children, as they'd already been droopy.

As Mr Barnes reached for a ruler, placing the ruler under her chin, he measured the distance from her chin to the current nipple position. "Hmmmm, just as I suspected. They're about eight centimetres away from where they should be."

Oh Lord, eight centimetres? Holy shit. There was no doubt about it; they were an awfully long way away from where they should be. The thought of having breasts in the correct position for the first time in her life gave rise to an unfamiliar burst of excitement, and taking one last look at the screen, Kate realised that she had to go through with it. She wanted to go through with it. She wanted her breasts eight centimetres higher and nothing was going to stop her. Miraculously, Kate found her voice again. "How long's the operation?" Directing the question to Mr Barnes.

"Well, obviously it will depend on which procedure you have; the mastopexy can take anywhere between two to three hours and the abdominoplasty is around three and a half hours. However, should you decide to have the lower body sculpture and the mastopexy at the same time, then that will take even longer."

Kate began to feel like she was in a Chinese restaurant. *That will be one portion of upright tits to start with, followed by ... hmmmm, let me see what I fancy? Ooh, I think I'll go for the full lower body sculpture. Excuse me? What? Oh, that comes with a scar all the way round your body? Well no, I don't fancy that after all thank you, I think I'll just settle for the abdominoplasty.* Kate's thoughts had now turned to side portions of Botox to erase the wrinkles that were fast-appearing on her brow.

Whilst Kate got dressed, Jamie continued questioning Mr Barnes, "If she did decide to go through with the procedures, when would be the earliest date you could fit her in?" Clearly Jamie had been a shit hot secretary in a past life.

Mr Barnes casually flicked through a large diary on his desk. "As luck would have it, I had a cancellation this morning for a similar procedure in a few months' time. I can do it on the thirty-first of October."

Kate burst out laughing as she emerged from behind the curtain. Both Mr Barnes and Jamie glowered back at her.

"Hello? Halloween? You can't seriously expect me to have surgery on that day?"

Jamie frowned back at Kate, mouthing a silent 'shush.'

Mr Barnes ignored the comment. "Perhaps you'd rather have some more time to think about it? There's no rush. We can easily sort something out for the beginning of next year." He stood up, signalling the end of the consultation.

Kate couldn't stop thinking about the eight centimetres difference and, in a moment of empowerment, fearful that she might change her mind, blurted out, "October thirty-first is perfect. Let's do this." She had to do this. She'd spent a lifetime hating her body. Enough. Jamie was speechless for the first time that morning.

Mr Barnes smiled and said, "Lovely, we will get that booked in for you then Mrs Buchanan, and send you the paperwork for the deposit."

Kate had forgotten to ask how much it would cost, but surmised that it couldn't be as much as a new car. Jamie guided the now-dressed but dazed Kate out into the reception area and back onto Harley Street.

"Bloody hell, Kate, you were incredible." Jamie was clearly brimming with excitement; her voice had taken on a high trill.

Kate, suddenly returning to the real world. "Oh my god. Oh my god, Jamie. I can't believe I just did that. Shit. I need to call David now."

"Yes you did. And I thought he was just sensational." Jamie turned her full attention to navigating herself and a somewhat dazed Kate across Baker Street. Thankfully, it was such a beautiful day as they'd planned to go and hang out in the park. Kate couldn't wait to get there, there was too much noise and cars and it felt bigger and more intimidating than it ever had before. She needed space and nature … ASAP.

"I liked him … but Halloween, Jamie? I mean, I'm not superstitious or anything, but surely having major surgery on a day famed for ghouls and witches isn't ideal?" Kate couldn't help but snigger.

"Stop being so bloody ridiculous. It doesn't matter what day it is. Besides, I think it's quite apt. You'll be wrapped up like a mummy anyway, so consider yourself dressed for the occasion." Kate looked at Jamie and the pair exploded into fits of giggles.

"Anyway, October is perfect timing. You'll be able to recoup over the winter and be all recovered and fabulous for next summer. Just picture it. No more swimsuits, Kate Buchanan, in a bikini. Actually Kate Buchanan in only little bikini bottoms with glorious upright titties thrusting proudly out for all to see. Yaaaaay."

Crikey, Jamie was persuasive, just listening to her made Kate want it all the more.

"Plus, you've been wanting this for years and now he's had a cancellation. It's a sign. Why don't you call David and see what he thinks too?"

"Okay, okay." Kate was caught up in Jamie's exuberance. Just being around her friend brought her previous feelings of empowerment surging back. She wanted to have upright titties, she wanted to wear a bikini. Goddammit she wanted to feel sensational and proud and fabulous and not like the freak that she currently felt she was. Yes. Yes. Yes. She'd call David immediately and ask him. No, she'd call David and tell him. Better. She was Kate Buchanan, woman supreme, ruler of the universe. *Ahhhhhh*, this was sooooo much fun.

Reaching for her phone, Kate dialled home and waited impatiently for David to pick up.

"Hello?" David eventually answered.

"It's me," Kate said, a little breathlessly.

"Sweetheart. How are you? How did it go?"

"Well, the meeting with the consultant was good; I liked him … a lot. And I really want to do it and he has a cancellation for October and I think I should have the boobs done at the same time as the stomach because it seems silly to have a lovely stomach that you won't be able to see because the boobs are hanging eight centimetres down from where they should be and therefore obscuring it." Kate's words poured out of her mouth at a million miles an hour. She barely stopped to take a breath.

Jamie was making faces and thrusting her boobs out and Kate was giggling. Being with Jamie was like being a teenage girl with no worries in the world; she was very infectious.

"I think you should do it," he proclaimed without hesitation.

"You do realise that it's a six-week recovery time?"

"I think you should do it."

"I'll have to stay in England for at least two weeks."

"I think you should do it."

"I won't be able to drive for six weeks."

"I think you should do it."

"We won't be able to have sex for months."

"I think we should think about it a little more."

"Are you being serious?" Suddenly Kate wanted it more than anything; no sex for months and no guilt either … just fabulous. Yes, she wanted this operation now more than ever.

"No, I was kidding, really, Kate. If you want this and you trust this guy, then I'm behind you one hundred percent. Got to go, got a game in ten mins. Book it."

"Love you."

"Love you too; just want you to be happy." And the line went dead.

Jamie looked at Kate. "Well?"

"He said, YES." Kate grinned, but the realisation of this actually happening was also overwhelming. Whilst the anxiety bubbled away, Kate was determined to keep it at bay. She would not think about the operation, she would only focus on the result and she entered a dream-like state, trying to capture the image that Jamie had so beautifully portrayed. Her on a beach, in bikini bottoms.

"Kate?" Jamie was nervous that Kate was going to change her mind. "Are you alright?"

"Uff … yes. Sorry. I'm processing."

"Don't change your mind, Kate. Please."

"I'm processing quietly," said Kate, and then seemed to break out of her reverie, "Remind me again, why are we opting for a non-alcoholic moment?"

Jamie laughed. "Because I've got to go into the agency later and … I think I'm drinking too much."

"And you decided that the day I was going to be traumatised by the image of a larger-than-life me, was the day that you needed to rein it in? Bloody marvellous."

Jamie linked arms with Kate as they entered Regent's Park.

LIFELINE

"This way, this way." Jamie was pulling Kate by the hand as they scurried towards the shade of a large oak tree.

"Why are we hurrying? What's the rush?" Kate knew they still had a good two hours before Jamie had to leave for her agency and was amazed at how her friend could move so fast in heels. There she was, sensible Kate, going at half the speed in her trainers whilst Jamie was practically sprinting in skyscraper objects of torture. To be fair, Jamie's legs did appear double the length of hers, so Kate attributed the difference in speed to this.

"Duh, the midday sun darling. Wrinkles, wrinkles. If we don't stay out of it, we'll be going back to Malcolm Barnes for a full face of Botox too."

Kate looked flatly at Jamie. "This is friggin' London, not Mallorca, we're lucky it's not raining."

"I know, I know, but I'm seeing my agent, tempestuous Tabitha, afterwards. She'll only find more reason to have a go if I turn up with a red face too. And besides, extra wrinkles won't help keep me at twenty-five."

"I don't want to burst your bubble Jamie"—Kate huffed, out of breath, finally at the tree—"but Madison's pushing eleven, unless you were having underage sex, you can't be twenty-five. No, No, I don't even want to know." Kate pulled a face, as the pair fell about laughing.

Taking out a neatly folded pale blue scarf from her bag, Jamie laid it carefully onto the grass. If she was going to see her agent, the last thing she needed were grass stains on her bottom. After Jamie had texted Kate suggesting the park, Kate had dashed into Marks & Spencer's stocking up for what she hoped would be an impromptu picnic. Not that she expected Jamie to eat, but she sure as hell was going to, especially now that Malcolm Barnes was going to rebuild her.

Kicking off her three-inch Louboutin heels, Jamie stretched out her long legs, as her feet touched the grass beyond the scarf. "This is actually nice, Kate. I rarely do this." Jamie cast her eyes around the wide green expanse. A little slice of nature right in the heart of London. Just sitting on the grass, the birds singing and with Kate by her side … Jamie exhaled.

"How come you have a scarf in your bag?" Kate was curious.

"It's my cover up. You never know when someone might ask you to take your clothes off, and there isn't always a changing area, so I always keep a scarf with me—just in case."

"Oh." Kate looked dumbfoundedly at Jamie. It did make her think, though. There she was half an hour earlier having full-blown palpitations about removing her clothes behind a black curtain, and here was her friend, having to strip off for strangers. They really did come from two different worlds.

Jamie settled on her scarf as Kate sat cross-legged opposite her, peering into the Marks & Spencer's fabric tote. Pulling out a trio of sandwiches, Kate waved a single triangle under Jamie's nose "Want one?"

"Not just yet, hun. Maybe later." Jamie also knew turning up to the agency with even the slightest extra bloat would not go down well. She'd always pee first too; every drop counted.

Having failed to tempt her with the sandwich. Kate pulled out a small pot of hummus with some carrots and celery. "What about this?"

Jamie shook her head.

The moment was now. Kate returned the crudité back to the bag and looked Jamie squarely in the eyes. Jamie backed away. She had a feeling she knew what was coming. Kate was going into mothering mode.

"Jamie, this is ridiculous. You have to start eating. You're fading away." Jamie failed to respond. "It's ageing you know."

Jamie gave her a dirty look.

"This is nuts. I'm sorry Jamie, but you're going to make yourself ill. Maybe I'm not one to talk. I fully acknowledge that I have an eating disorder. I think about my weight and food all the time. But … I control my eating disorder and from the looks of it"—she said softly—"you're letting yours control you."

Jamie looked glum. "Maybe it is an eating disorder, but it's not being controlled by me. It's being controlled by the industry I'm in."

Kate picked up another piece of sandwich and, not taking her eyes off Jamie, munched away at it, allowing Jamie the space to continue. Jamie looked up at the sky and sighed. "I know it's hard to understand. You see me as this skinny girl, and I get that's how I look to the outside world. But I don't work in that world. They don't want us to look like everyone else. That's the whole point. They tell me I could lose more weight off my thighs, that my face could be more angular." Jamie sucked in her incredibly chiselled cheeks to make a fish face, and lighten the mood somewhat. "But the thing is, I have to be this thin to work."

Kate continued nodding, worried that if she spoke, Jamie might stop.

"Okay, think about today. How you felt stepping behind that curtain. That's me every time I step into the agency or go to a casting. Every inch of me is being scrutinised. They might as well have me under a magnifying glass. They see everything. And trust me, the lighting is never flattering. Sure you get used to it, the stripping off, the weighing, the measuring, like a piece of meat, but that's really all you are. A commodity for them to use to sell stuff. And once you don't look how they want you to look, there are thousands of girls, younger, slimmer, hungrier, waiting to step into your stilettos. So when I say I can't eat. It's because if I do, my family won't."

"Blimey Jamie." Kate suddenly felt guilty for having a go at her friend. She never imagined it was that hard.

"People don't get it. They see what they want to see. The clothes, the travel, the pictures in the glossies. You tell them it's hard and sometimes they just laugh at you, saying. 'Oh poor you, having to pose in front of a camera all day.' Unless you're in the industry, you don't know the industry. The industry owns you until you're no use anymore and then it spits you out." Jamie continued, feeling more despondent by the second.

"Okay hun. I get that you're not controlling this, but it's just not good for you and, as you said yourself, it can't last forever. Maybe you don't have control over this world you find yourself in, but you do have control over your life and the world you choose to be part of. Have you considered what else you might be able to do?"

"Sometimes I fantasise about taking my laptop and just writing for one of those travel or fashion magazines ... but this has been my career since I was seventeen. Everyone books me for the way I look. I don't know how to be anything else." The reality of her predicament felt heavy on her shoulders.

"Jamie, do you remember on the beach when I was feeling guilty about Salsa Man? You gave me the pizza analogy, and that made perfect sense."

Jamie nodded, and a smile crossed over her face at the memory of that blissful day.

"Well, that conversation changed everything for me. What you did with all your pizza talk was open up another perspective," Kate said, noticing Jamie's eyes wandering as she clocked a group of young men playing volleyball nearby with their shirts off. "Stay focused," Kate said laughing. Once Jamie had peeled her eyes away from the topless guys, she continued. "Allow me to return the favour. Because, my darling friend, sometimes when we're in a situation, we can't see the answers ourselves and that's why we have friends."

Jamie was now fully focused on Kate, who put down the sandwich. She didn't need to be spitting food at Jamie whilst imparting her wisdom.

"Jamie, you're not twenty-five."

"Ouch. Are you trying to make me feel better? It's not working."

"I'm not trying to make you feel worse. I want you to face the truth. The key to a fulfilled life is to sample as many experiences as you can, but also not to get stuck."

Jamie looked blankly, and Kate wished she could find a metaphor like Jamie's pizza one.

"Look, Jamie, what I'm trying to say is this. Life is like a mountain and sure, we're all trying to get to the top, but it's not just about reaching the top. It's also the journey." Kate noticed that she now had Jamie's complete attention. "The top of your mountain at this moment is earning money, and the path you've chosen is modelling—a path filled with potholes and bushes that are tearing at your skin. But if you just stopped and looked around, you might see that there is another path. A path with roses on it. There's even a pizza shop," she said jokingly and Jamie laughed.

"Because Jamie, you're not enjoying this path and you're so, so wrong in thinking that modelling is the only thing you can do. You've just got to stop for a moment and … throw some spaghetti on the wall."

"Throw some spaghetti?"

"Yup. So somewhere, probably in Italy, to check whether spaghetti is cooked or not, they throw it on the wall and if it sticks, they know it's ready. What you have to do now is throw some spaghetti at the wall. The spaghetti, in this instance, being other employment opportunities. Jamie, you have to because this is killing you, and if you continue, your family won't eat nor will they have you."

"Throw some spaghetti? I don't recall my mother ever throwing spaghetti?" Jamie looked bewildered but Kate could tell that she was beginning to get through to her.

"I don't know Kate, I'm just lost. I don't know what to do or where I'm supposed to be. I thought if I moved back to London, work would take off again and life would be more exciting, but it isn't; I feel more alone and more isolated than before."

Kate nodded her head in silent understanding, encouraging Jamie to carry on.

"It's just that everything feels so wrong. Madison isn't happy being back here. She misses her friends and the carefree way of life, and my mum seems miserable as well. And then there's me. I just hate everything at the moment, not just the modelling. Hate being in the cold and the rain, the constant fear of crime which I never felt on the island. And what's more, I even hate the one thing I was looking forward to—the so-called excitement. The fabulous parties with all the 'fabulous' people. The truth is they're not fabulous. It's all so empty. But what do I do now? I've literally uprooted my family for this. I clearly need to throw some spaghetti, and fast."

Kate squeezed her hand and spoke softly, "I won't pretend to know exactly how you're feeling, but I can tell you I've had my moments where I've felt lost too. The thing is, when I feel like that, it's usually my instinct telling me that somehow I've taken the wrong path in my life and I need to change direction."

Jamie nodded, relieved that Kate understood; that she was able to be open and honest with her friend. They were both silent as they contemplated the conundrum that Jamie was in.

"Ooh," Kate said suddenly with excitement, clapping her hands.

"What?"

"Ooh. Ooh." Kate jumped up and dusted down her jeans, then started walking in circles.

"What? What?"

"Wait …" Kate held her hands up to her face in a prayer-like manner and started tapping her chin with her hands, as if she was trying to access a thought before plonking herself back down again, so close she was practically sitting on Jamie's lap. Grabbing hold of Jamie's hands, eyes wide, she grinned. "I think I've just thought of the spaghetti for you."

Jamie felt a shudder of anticipation. *Oh God, please let Kate have the answer* because she knew without a shadow of a doubt that Kate was right. She had to quit.

Kate started fumbling in the Marks & Spencer's bag and pulled out her phone.

"Why is your phone in the food bag?" Jamie looked horrified; she'd never known anyone to use a grocery bag as an actual bag.

"Not important now, Jamie." Kate started tapping away at her phone. When she was done, she put the phone down and winked. "Let's put this conversation on hold for a moment. I've just thrown some spaghetti for you."

"Okay, so back to what we were talking about earlier." Kate darted her eyes left to right in case anyone might be in earshot, then whispered the word "Sex." Her face turned a subtle shade of scarlet. "How's things with Cameron?"

Clocking Kate's blush and prudish manner, Jamie laughed. "Oh Kate, since you asked, I think I might be done with him. Of course the SEX"—she shouted loudly, secretly enjoying Kate grimacing with embarrassment—"is incredible. Like make you TINGLE in your LOINS incredible, but I'm just bored. I always get bored." Jamie watched as Kate's face took on a peculiar expression. It was somewhere between embarrassed, intrigued and slightly envious. The thought of hot, rampant sex reminded her of Robert, and her cheeks betrayed her.

Kate paused in contemplation. "It's interesting, when it comes to men, you have no problem letting go. You need to be the same way with work. Think of modelling like a man that no longer serves you." Why hadn't Kate thought of this before? Men were a far better metaphor for Jamie than food.

"And Karl?" Kate questioned, "Stop rolling your eyes. You do that a lot. It's a valid question. On the beach, you kept going on about how old he is and not your type, but why don't you just give him a chance? You said that he was mid-thirties. I'm older than that. Do you think I'm old?" Jamie shook her head.

"Is he ugly?"

"God no, not ugly. I suppose for an older man, he's rather attractive."

"Grrrrrr."

"You do know we haven't even met properly or had a proper conversation, he just happened to be at the same restaurant as me twice. We're text buddies, that's all."

"Sounds like fate to me. Y'know, sometimes what we really need is staring us right in the face."

Jamie smiled. She knew Kate was only trying to look out for her best interests. "Okay, I won't rule it out. I just don't want to spoil the friendship, that's all. And besides, I don't know what to make of him yet. I mean, look at this ..." Jamie reached inside her large black portfolio bag and fished out a book.

"Wow, I'm impressed." Kate read the cover, *"Raising Good Humans."*

"What on earth possessed you to pick that up? I imagine it's a tad far removed from your normal reading material, isn't it?"

"That's what I mean. Karl suggested I read it."

Kate groaned. Jamie could quite possibly be the only person in the universe who would be motivated to read a child-rearing book because of a man.

"I like this Karl. This is good. And actually hun, I have an idea. Why don't we text him now?"

Jamie gave Kate a death stare.

"Hear me out before you look at me like that." Kate continued to ignore Jamie's glaring.

"I can help you text him. I might have a better sense of what to write to a non-Cameron type of guy. Let's set up a meeting. Not a date … just a coffee or something … to discuss the book? C'mon Jamie, I'm going to be cut open. I think you can survive meeting up with a potentially nice guy." Jamie continued to glare. 'Nice guy' was always an oxymoron in her book. She was yet to meet one.

"I've never texted a guy first in my life." Jamie looked almost horrified.

"I get that, but if you keep doing the same thing, you're going to get the same result. Come on, give me your phone." Kate reached out her hand, but Jamie instinctively pulled her phone away. "Please, Jamie. I'm doing this for you."

"Okay, but don't send it. Please. You can write it, but don't send it."

In possession of Jamie's phone and searching through the contacts, thankful there was only one Karl and not twenty, Kate started tapping away.

> Jamie: Finished the book. Thought-provoking. Would be good to discuss. Let me know if you're going to be around this week and maybe we can meet for a coffee. Jx

Kate held the phone up for Jamie to see but without relinquishing it.

"I can't send that. You've even put a kiss on it," screamed Jamie, "He'll think I'm chasing him."

"Don't be ridiculous. You can make it clear when you meet him if there really is nothing more than friendship. Just drop in an imaginary boyfriend if you need to."

With that, Kate started edging away. Before Jamie had a chance to grab her phone back, Kate pressed send. Jamie buried her face in her hands. "I can't believe you did that."

"Well, I had to. You wouldn't have and I've just got a feeling," Kate said, putting Jamie's phone down next to her on the scarf. "Sorry," she said innocently, "It's for your own good."

Jamie appeared to be in shock and there was silence. Neither girl spoke. Kate started to worry that perhaps she'd gone too far, when suddenly, 'Beep. Beep.' Both girls looked at each other before making a frantic dash towards Jamie's phone. Jamie won and with a look of relief. "Not mine. Do you know how to delete a message once it's sent?"

"I don't think you can," Kate said whilst rummaging again in the Marks and Spencer's bag to retrieve her own phone. As she read the text, a huge smile washed across her face. "Jamie, I want you to listen and be open-minded. You know you said that you didn't think you had any other skills other than modelling?"

Jamie nodded.

"When we were in Malcolm Barnes's office, you were so organised, taking notes and everything. Well, the text I sent before was to a friend of ours. He's a big collector, mostly art. Really old, early forties," Kate said jokingly, followed by, "Very gay too and not remotely your type." Just in case Jamie's mind wandered; she knew 'gay' alone wouldn't be enough to deter her horny friend, who'd likely see it as a challenge. "Anyway, he has this huge collection of art and watches and vintage designer bags worth absolutely millions. He's been buying for decades, but it's a total mess. He's looking for an assistant, someone with good organisational skills, to help him get it all categorised. To begin with, the job would be to sort out the existing collection, but he wants to grow it and is looking for someone to run around to auctions and be his representative. It's perfect for you!" Kate's excitement was infectious. She was grinning, looking at Jamie earnestly.

"Art collection?" Jamie was intrigued. "Vintage bags, watches?" Shivers ran down Jamie's spine. This was almost too good to be true.

"Yup, an amazing collection. But it's all over the place. Everything needs to be put onto a spreadsheet, indexed, descriptions for each piece written … and you love writing, you just said before you'd love to travel and write. Jamie, this is serendipity. It's not nine-to-five either. You can work the hours you want and be around more for Madison. I didn't think of you immediately because the job would be in Mallorca. Nigel is an island friend. We met him years ago. He's totally nuts, incredibly eccentric, but has a heart of gold. When you mentioned that you miss Mallorca, that's when it came to me. What do you think?" Kate was bubbling with excitement. Jamie could return to the island. The thought was so blissful she just prayed Jamie would feel the same.

"What do I think?" Jamie beamed, goosebumps rising across her body. "I think you're my angel. When can I meet him? How do you know he'll like me?" The thought of finally getting out of modelling was like being set free; shackles being ripped away from her body. Jamie lent over and, with a huge sense of relief, gave Kate a huge hug. "I would love, love, LOVE that job. I adore art, vintage bags, and all things expensive. Oh my god Kate, really? Would he hire me?" A moment of anxiety washed over Jamie.

"Jamie, the job's already yours. Look." Kate finally relinquished her phone so that Jamie could read the text.

Nigel: She sounds perfect. Give her my number so we can connect and discuss details.

Jamie could have cried. A small tear did slip out of one of her beautiful green eyes. She was already on the new path.

GRABBING LIFE BY THE BALLS

"Hi it's me, Jamie," she whispered into the intercom as she was buzzed into the building. Walking through the long, narrow corridor towards the main office of Hurricane Modelling Agency, Jamie glanced up at the 'Hall of Fame' with Iman, Lily Cole, Yasmin Le Bon and other Supers all gracing the latest covers of Vogue and her heart sank. This was the end of an era. She was going to be thirty-two soon, so retirement was fast approaching, unless you happened to be one of the chosen few. Despite the daily rejection and unkind comments from the inside, to the outside world, you're put on a pedestal. The doors that open, the members-only lists that don't apply; there was no denying that being a model and looking a certain way had its definite perks. But then comes the flip side … and for Jamie, there was no getting around it anymore.

Swinging open the doors into the main room, Jamie swallowed hard and entered on autopilot. "Hey, guys." Eyes, teeth, dazzle, dazzle.

"Hello, darling." It was Jemima. One of the new bookers, an ex-model herself whose modelling days were over at twenty-seven despite still having the looks—five foot eleven with long dark hair and feline deep-set brown eyes. Jamie figured that would likely be her next job if Kate's offer didn't pan out. Just the thought made her heart sink a further twenty feet. It was a great proposal, but she hadn't even spoken to this Nigel yet. She'd have to keep tight-lipped and not get too excited until the job offer was confirmed. Besides, Nigel hadn't even met her.

"Nice cardi. Zadig&Voltaire?" Quizzed Jemima.

"Celine, actually." Jamie corrected as she wrapped it tighter around her body. The air conditioning was on max and she didn't tolerate the cold.

"Sorry, sweetheart, just had to take that call," Tabitha, her booker, uttered from her seat at the main table, somewhat flustered. The phones never stopped ringing; it was like being in one of those old-fashioned telephone exchanges. Jamie air-kissed Tabitha, who briefly stood up to greet her. She was impeccably dressed as usual, and her slightly frozen expression suggested she'd just recently had her Botox topped up. Jamie had to give it to the woman. She was almost fifty, forty to everyone who didn't know, and at least she was getting by on freezing alone.

"So, darling, I just wanted to call you in for a little chat." Tabitha looked concerned. A model's booker was like a surrogate mother; there to find them the best jobs, secure the highest rates, and of course, offload to. Break-ups with boyfriends, dead goldfish, haircuts from hell—all part and parcel of the counselling service. But it wasn't genuine concern.

Tabitha's phone started ringing once again. "I'll be right with you, darling. Just give me two minutes." Tabitha began what seemed like a full-scale assault on some poor unsuspecting male model called Jared. By the sounds of it Jared had messed up his addresses and turned up for a shoot at the wrong studio. Tabitha was not impressed. One more mistake like that and he could be struck off the board. That is, unless he managed to quickly secure himself a lucrative campaign of course.

Jamie walked over towards the men's board, where all the z-cards are kept of each model—A5 composites of their best work. She tried to scan the massive display in an attempt to figure out which Jared was getting an earful. *Mmmm, there's only one Jared ... with a body to die for. Oooh, and just look at Zane over there ... his eyes, his lips ... perfection.* Lost in the beauty before her, Jamie almost didn't hear Gavin, Head Booker of the New Faces division.

"Jamie, hello? Are you with us today?" Gavin had been filing away copy books at the back of the agency. These were duplicates of every model's portfolio kept in-house to show any clients popping into the agency. Noticing Miss King was in a trance-like state, he took it upon himself to come over. "Good to see you, angel. How's tricks?" Gavin beamed from behind his red-rimmed glasses as he planted a kiss on her cheek. He wasn't stereotypically good looking, but he had a quirkiness about him that made him rather adorable, especially when his crooked smile showed off unexpectedly remarkable teeth. Considering they were granted from heaven above and not courtesy of one of London's leading cosmetic dentists, it was somewhat of an anomaly.

"I'm good. How's things with you?" Jamie made small talk, but her mouth and brain were operating in two separate dimensions. She was feeling extremely uneasy, as she knew Tabitha hadn't called her in for a friendly chat, and all she wanted to do was escape this industry. Gavin began to chatter about his recent dates; all unsuccessful. His beloved cat Rupert, his hangover from the weekend. Jamie glazed over, her mind everywhere but there.

"I'm free, poppet," Tabitha finally called out, having clearly wiped the floor with the poor but rather yummy Jared and was pumped up and raring to go. Well, as pumped up as her willowy frame would allow. "Let's go and sit somewhere more comfortable, shall we? Would you like a drink or something? Water perhaps? You're looking a little dehydrated." Tabitha was already examining.

Keep smiling, you can do it.

Nestling into the large red sofa situated in the corner of the office, Tabitha and Jamie began their tête-à-tête.

"I'm worried about you, sweetheart." Tabitha leaned towards Jamie, her eyes carrying out a quick head-to-toe inspection now that she was at close range.

"Worried?"

"Yes, darling. What's going on with you these days?"

Jamie tried to intercept. "What do you—"

But once Tabitha started one of her monologues, there was no stopping her. "It's just that some of your clients haven't been as happy as they should be. George Humphries from Marie Claire said you weren't bringing your usual energy to the shoot. Said you lacked stamina, looked grey, tired and, frankly … ill." Tabitha's missile was aimed and fired.

"Oh, you know how it is, Tabitha. Flying, early starts, takes it out of you after a while." Jamie tried to placate her, but it wasn't working. And why wasn't Tabitha commending her on her weight loss? Her cocktail of well, cocktails, the occasional powder play with India and practically zero solid intake had her at the exact weight they wanted. So what if she was a little pale? What the hell were makeup artists for?

"Yes, darling, but still. It's your job to look your best at all times. Too many late nights, perhaps?" Tabitha wasn't stupid. She was all too familiar with the cycle.

Pulling her cardigan tighter still, Jamie racked her brain for some way to get out of being in trouble. But all retorts eluded her. In fact, her mind was one vacuous bubble.

"Well, darling. I just want to make sure there isn't anything going on in your life that you might need to talk to me about? If it's just a few late nights, we can take care of that. I want you in bed by ten every weeknight from now on, okay? Oh, and one more thing …" *Here it is. Tabitha always leaves the best for last.* "George said you were looking a bit puffy in the shots, too." *And annihilation commences.* "You might want to eliminate gluten, or just carbs in general. Of course, I want you to eat healthily, but just make sure it's not causing any water retention. The camera adds enough pounds as it is, we don't want to add any more." Translation: 'I don't care what you have to do to lose weight. Just make sure you lose it but also look incredible.' The bottom half of Tabitha's face moulded like Play-Doh into a faux smile.

"Oh my god, that's IT." Jamie stood up abruptly, casting off her cardigan, as something inside her snapped. "Look at me. Do I look bloated to you? I'm a size four. There's no room to be bloated. Even my daughter has more curves than I do. I can't do this anymore. I'm sorry, but I can't. I can't live avoiding the sun, and food, and getting older. This is insane."

"Jamie darling. Calm down." Tabitha didn't tolerate outbursts unless she was the one doing the bursting. "You know how this industry is. We're selling dreams. If you looked like everyone else, you wouldn't be getting paid. It's my job to give you the clients' feedback, so they keep booking you."

"I'm sorry Tabitha, I just can't take this nonsense anymore. It's not right. My daughter eats more than I do. I'm scared to sit in the sun in case I get wrinkles. One day I will get wrinkles and that should be okay too. This industry is messed up. Looking this way isn't sustainable. Not if you're not twenty anymore. And I'm not twenty, nor are most women I know."

Tabitha's already high eyebrows arched as high as the Botox would allow. "Sweetie, you're obviously having a bad day or something. Why don't you just go home and have a lie down? You're an amazing model. We've been working together for years. But as you get older, it just gets harder. I'm just trying to keep you working for as long as possible. I'm thinking about you, poppet, that's all."

Thinking about how much more money you can make out of me before you spit me out more like.

"Actually, no. Look around; so many agencies are adding diversity to their roster; curve models, mature models, trans models. Isn't it time you got with the programme? This industry is changing; it has to, and so must we."

Tabitha's left eye started to twitch. The scarlet flush around her neck and chest gave away what her botoxed brow could not.

"Tokenism. This is all just pressure from social media, but that's not what the big clients want. Plus, those models rarely get paid the top rates. You're either a model or you're not, and being a model means looking a certain way."

"Well if that's the case, then I don't want it anymore." Picking up her cardigan from the red sofa, heart racing, Jamie suddenly felt a surge of empowerment. She'd wanted to talk back to Tabitha for years. Talking to Kate had finally given her the strength to stand up for herself; the courage to find another path. One which didn't involve full-blown starvation, or death—she'd heard the stories. "I'm sorry Tabitha. I'm done. I'll work out any commitments I have, but then I'm out."

"Darling, if you walk out you know there won't be any coming back." Tabitha's face had stopped trying to smile.

"Perfect. I don't want to come back." And with that Jamie marched out of the office, past the other bookers who she couldn't help but notice were smiling discreetly, hoping not to be seen by Tabitha. Jamie finally had the nerve to say what so many others wanted to say, but rarely did.

Bursting through the door onto Cadogan Gardens, the warmth of summer hit Jamie. Turning her face up towards the sky and closing her eyes, she exhaled deeply for the second time that day.

Holy crap, she needed to call Kate. But Kate had gone straight to see family before she headed back to the island. Reaching into her bag, Jamie fished out her phone only to find several unopened messages. *Karl. Shit. Karl.* She'd forgotten all about Kate's crazy antics.

Karl: Good to hear from you. Yes, I'd love that. I'm away this week but any day next week is good. Let me know and we can meet at The Brasserie. Karl x

Jamie noticed he'd replied with a kiss, too. *Shit. Fucking Kate. Fucking crazy, but ever so adorable Kate.* What had she started? Oh god … her head was spinning; her life was spinning. Yup, she sure as hell was on a new path alright. One where she didn't have a map. Suddenly, an image of Kate emerging from behind the black curtain and booking her surgery there and then entered her mind. She remembered feeling in awe of Kate's decision to just go for it, and now she'd damn well done the same; taken control. It felt liberating, terrifying. Her blood was pumping fast around her body. She'd taken an almighty leap and now she just needed to grow some wings. God, she hoped the job with Nigel worked out.

Furiously tapping onto her phone, she composed a new text.

Jamie:	Hey what you up to? Need to burn off some frustration!! Wanna help?

Almost immediately, 'Beep. Beep.'

Cameron:	Of course! Just finished a meeting. I can leave now. Where you at?
Jamie:	Just leaving the agency. Meet me upstairs at The Bluebird. Heading there now.
Cameron:	On my way!

Jamie stopped by the roadside on the Kings Road. Resisting the urge to do any window shopping, she held out a hand to hail the next approaching black cab and jumped in. "Bluebird Please." London traffic was appalling and the cab ride took ten minutes just to go down the road. Pulling up outside the Chelsea institution, Jamie handed the driver a ten-pound note, shouting—"Keep the change"—as she jumped out and headed into the building.

Perching on a high stool around the large upstairs bar, Jamie wasted no time in ordering a Porn Star Martini for herself and a Mezcal Old Fashioned for Cameron, adding, "Can you make those with double shots please?" Flashing her wide infectious smile at the young barman who grinned back coyly. When Jamie needed a distraction, two things did the trick—men and alcohol, and the two combined were simply magic. But Jamie couldn't help but worry what might happen if this job didn't materialise. She'd just quit her career for goodness sake. Taking out her phone, she decided it was time to take control, in every aspect of her life.

Jamie: Hi Nigel, this is Jamie, Kate's friend. She told me about your amazing collection and that you need some help. I am the queen of organisation and just adore beautiful fabulous things. Can we jump on a call soon to discuss further?

Just as the barman returned with the drinks, in walked Cameron—perfect timing. As he strode into the room, Jamie's stomach did a quick tumble with excitement. The other punters in the bar followed with their eyes as his tall, athletic frame walked over to her, a cheeky smile planted on his face. Damn, he looked hot, even in simple blue jeans and a plain white T-shirt. In fact, he looked even better by day, as she realised it had usually been after-dark when they met. She could see the golden glow of his sun-kissed skin, further accentuating his incredible take-me-to-bed blue eyes.

As much as she'd started to tire of him, Jamie hadn't grown tired of the chemistry. As she stood up to greet him, Cameron lifted her off the floor in his strong embrace and planted a kiss on her lips. All eyes were upon them.

"Got you a drink. Want to do a shot, too?" Jamie twirled a curl of her hair around her fingers, as she gazed intently into his eyes. Conversations, which were thin on the ground, often centred around alcohol.

"Sure, I'm down. Don't have to be back in the office until tomorrow, anyway." Sitting down on the stool next to Jamie, Cameron placed one hand on the base of her back, fingers reaching down, just above her G-string line. Jamie raised an eyebrow at the barman, who immediately rushed over, but didn't seem quite as jovial since Cameron's arrival. "Two B-52's please." Jamie hadn't eaten, and this was basically three meals in one.

Jamie's mind started to blur as the vodka from the first drink quickly reached her bloodstream, especially since she'd cut back on her drinking. Sitting this close to Cameron, the rest of the bar faded into insignificance. Her heart was still racing, but this time for another reason. As the shots arrived, Jamie dipped one of her long fingers into her shot glass and sucked the sweet liquid slowly off her finger. Cameron watched intently. Then, taking her finger again, she ran the wet digit over Cameron's lips before knocking back the lot. As the heat rushed through her throat and into her body, Jamie leaned closer and whispered, "I need to go to the little girl's room; I'll be about two minutes." And with a knowing smile to Cameron, Jamie slinked off her stool and swanned deliberately across the bar, swinging her hips as if she were on a runway, and straight into the Ladies. She was relieved that there was neither an attendant nor any other women inside. Taking the last cubicle at the end of the long room, Jamie bolted the door and started to unbutton her white jeans when she suddenly heard footsteps and a deep sexy voice whisper.

"Jamie?"

"At the end," Jamie whispered back loud enough to be heard and unbolted the door, pulling Cameron inside with her. The second the door was bolted, their lips struck each other with force, their bodies so close they could feel themselves fusing together. Cameron was an amazing kisser … Jamie practically devoured his mouth, biting his lip, and tugging at his hair, all at the same time. His hands were already inside her vest top and suddenly he'd yanked it up to reveal her small but perky braless breasts. His mouth came off her lips, licking and sucking as he went south, taking turns to lick and suck each nipple until they had hardened and sprung out like torpedoes. Jamie grabbed a mop of his hair and yanked him back up to her face, attacking his lips again, before grabbing his belt and quickly unbuckling it.

Staring directly into his eyes, she took one hand and lunged it into his jeans, grabbing hold of his cock above his underwear, cupping its long hard shaft. "Fuck you're horny," he mouthed before going in for another assault on her lips. As they kissed hard, their bodies charged with passion, Jamie dove her hand inside Cameron's pants and slowly but surely began teasing his already wet penis as she ran her fingers around the rim, then down the shaft, playing around his balls, and back up again, as she started to build up momentum. "Take my jeans off!" Jamie was ready to burst.

"Yes, ma'am." Cameron was only too happy to oblige. Jamie surrendered his penis as she allowed him to peel down her tight white jeans, whilst she took out a condom from the side zip in her bag. As he reached the bottom of her legs, she took one foot out of her stilettos at a time, removing the jeans and then putting back on the heels—she didn't want to be barefoot in the loos.

"Now sit down." She closed the seat of the toilet, one of the few that still had a lid in London. Cameron obeyed. In just her vest top, G-string, and heels Jamie straddled gracefully across his lap, with one slender leg on either side, holding a plié position like a trained ballerina, hovering ever so intentionally above his rock-hard member. Taking the condom package in her mouth, Jamie gently bit the corner of the wrapper to open it and pulled it out. With the other hand, she slowly caressed Cameron's erect penis as he grabbed the centre of her minuscule panties and pulled them to one side, trying to pull her down onto him. "Steady on, cowboy," Jamie purred, as he stared lustfully up at her.

"I believe you're the cowboy today, missy." He grinned just as Jamie adeptly slid the condom onto him and carefully edged it down the shaft, before launching straight down onto his hard cock, letting it penetrate her. Instinctively, she placed her feet up against the wall, granting even deeper access. Cameron placed his hands on her waist and assisted as she manoeuvred herself up and down, harder and harder. It was an incredible lower body workout. Jamie couldn't help but think of the multiple benefits.

Suddenly, the main door opened and two women entered, chattering and giggling. Jamie sniggered as she put one hand across Cameron's mouth to stifle his moans, whilst she slowed down her movements without stopping. She enjoyed the added thrill of being caught. She also liked the feeling of power she had over men. They were such simple creatures. He was practically putty in her hands right now… or rather, a helpless cock in her powerful loins, as Kate would put it.

Once the coast was clear, Jamie took her hand off his mouth, which had been taking little bites at her fingers, and held on tightly behind his back. His eyes glazed over as he stared up at Jamie. "You're a fucking sexy bitch, you know that?" Jamie smiled. She knew. Knowing no one could hear them, Jamie began to move faster again, up and down, up and down, thrusting her hips as she arched and curved her lower back in order to create the necessary friction she needed to stimulate herself. Her thigh muscles burned as they held her in position, but she kept going until spasms of electricity shot through her, her thighs finally trembling from their workout. Not waiting for him to finish, she lifted off the delicious, and rather flushed Cameron and back into her jeans, as his hands and lips continued to grasp at any inch of her skin still left exposed.

"Where are you going? We're not done." Unbolting the door, Jamie walked out, giggling, leaving Cameron in the cubicle as she washed her hands, and headed out the washroom. Just as she was exiting, another woman entered, seeing Cameron as he emerged, her face looked alarmed. "Sorry, took a wrong turn." Cameron laughed and she couldn't help but smile. It wasn't every day you set eyes on a beautiful specimen like that.

Jamie was standing just outside the main room above the stairs, ready to go down, just as Cameron burst through the doors. "You left me in the Ladies." He was pouting but Jamie just sniggered. Clocking the stairwell going up towards the 'private access only' section, Cameron immediately grabbed one of Jamie's hands and pulled her up the stairs, pushing her against the wall the moment they were out of sight. "Fuck you drive me crazy, Miss King." As he launched on her lips again, Jamie's hands reached out behind his head. Grabbing onto his hair, whilst she lifted one long leg and wrapped it tightly around him, bringing him in closer. Their bodies pressed up against each other, she could feel his racing heart against hers as it pounded through his top as their tongues explored deep within each other's mouths ... Jamie had planned to leave, but in the heat of the moment, it was hard to resist such yummy excitement. "I'm starving," Cameron announced, pulling away momentarily, "How about we continue this elsewhere?"

THE CAVE
Mallorca, Spain
(Two Weeks Later)

"We're here," Kate announced to Jamie, as she slowed down outside vast dark redwood gates that nestled within a high white stone wall. Jamie had been uncharacteristically quiet on the drive and Kate, finally halting to a stop and turning off the engine, took hold of Jamie's arms so that she was looking her squarely in the eye.

"You've got this."

"What happens if he doesn't like me? What ha—"

"We've been through all this, Jamie. He's going to love you. He's going to adore you."

"But—"

"Stop it." They'd been having the same conversation since Jamie's arrival the previous night, and Kate's patience was wearing thin. She appreciated that her dear friend was very much out of her comfort zone, but nevertheless, this was happening and she had to snap out of it.

"Look," said Kate, a little softer as she leaned over pulling Jamie into a hug, "You are Jamie King, woman supreme, you are not just a pretty face and you're the most ridiculously anal, organised person that I know." She pulled back again looking at Jamie, her blue eyes sparkling, "Well, other than me." And Jamie chuckled.

Kate opened the door, made her way around the car and pressed the intercom whilst Jamie sat rigid, nodding her head up and down. *I've got this. I've got this* on a loop; as if saying it enough times, she might actually believe it.

There were no other cars on the road, nor had there been any shops or signs of life as they'd driven up the steep hill. Jamie wondered how she was going to manage without a car if she got the job. She couldn't exactly ask Kate to drive her to work every day. Also, if she did get the job and was able to move back to the island—just the thought made her heart sing—she'd want Madison to be able to return to her old school, which wasn't exactly close. But without her modelling income, she didn't have the budget to buy a car. Jamie's anxiety started to creep up again.

"Hola," said Nigel, in a very trill English-person-trying-to-speak-Spanish voice, through the intercom.

"It's us, Kate and Jamie."

"Darling girls. I'll open the main gates and you can drive up." Nigel had now aborted the Spanish. The main gates creaked into action. Kate jumped back in the car.

Jamie's face was flushed as she attempted to smooth down her now frizzy hair, grumbling, "I can't believe your AC isn't working, how are you going to manage?"

"Oh, I'm not," Kate said with glee, "I'm getting my new car next week. A Range Rover. I got a new car and the operation." She'd played it beautifully, which was fortunate given the Volvo was on its last legs. Fearful that it didn't have enough oomph to make it up the steep incline to Nigel's house, Kate started rocking back and forward as if her motions would somehow propel the dying car to the top.

The villa itself was hidden from view by a series of magnificent, tall palm trees that towered far above the roof of the two-story villa. As they reached the top, the property became visible—a stunning mixture of sleek modern lines and Neoclassical architecture with nymphaeum statues, fountains, and cascades. Perched on the edge of the highest point of Sol de Mallorca, it was breathtaking. Nigel stood by the front door, grinning. As the girls exited the car, he first hugged Kate, who then ushered Jamie forwards. "And, this is Jamie King." Presenting her with pride as if she was showing off a prized possession.

Letting go of Kate, Nigel grinned at Jamie and held out his arms. It seemed like the most natural thing in the world to just walk into them, so she did. Nigel wrapped his arms around her, kissing the top of her head. Then he pulled back and held Jamie at arm's length, still grasping her hands, and surveyed her from head to toe. Turning to Kate, "Oh, you didn't exaggerate darling," then continued his survey of Jamie. "You are stunning, absolutely divine."

Jamie blushed. Not that she wasn't used to this sort of accolade, but this was her new path and being stunning wasn't a prerequisite.

"And she's the most organised person I know," Kate exclaimed, knowing that Jamie had experienced enough focus on her appearance to last a lifetime.

"She doesn't have a car," Kate suddenly blurted out.

"No car?" Nigel, aghast with horror.

Jamie laughed a little awkwardly and flashed Kate a warning look. She didn't want to be a problem. She hadn't even started yet.

Relinquishing Jamie, Nigel turned his head and yelled into the vacuous hallway, "Ben, she doesn't have a car."

Nigel was tall and skinny, but his presence was notable. His greying hair flopped over his face, which he kept swiping to one side before pulling a hair band off his wrist, scraping it all into a ponytail. He had a beautiful face, now unobscured by the hair. His eyes glistened aquamarine, and there was a softness about him that melted away any last fragments of Jamie's anxiety.

Ben materialised and stood next to Nigel. He was significantly shorter and significantly rounder, his head was clean-shaven bald. Ben ignored her hand, and like Nigel, drew her into his arms.

"Hey Ben." Kate waved as she made her way back to the car. She was running late for her optician's appointment. "I'm going to leave you. Call me when you're done with your induction and I'll come pick you up." Before Jamie had a chance to stop her, Kate jumped back into the car, mouthing, "You've got this."

"Shall we lend her The Chameleon?" Nigel was now talking to Ben.

What? A pet? I don't want a chameleon. Why do they want me to have a chameleon? "That's so kind of you, but Kate didn't mention I'd be looking after any animals. I'm not sure I'm the best person." Jamie didn't want to insult their kind welcome gift, but the last thing she needed was to care for an animal—a reptile at that.

The men laughed and Nigel grabbed her hand, pulling her towards what appeared to be a garage at the side of the main house. Pressing a remote that he took out from his shorts, three doors lurched into action, rising to reveal a vast expanse filled with cars. A Porsche, a Jaguar. And was that an Aston Martin? Jamie's eyes gleamed. They were all beautiful. Weaving their way through the vehicles, they arrived at the far end of the garage, where one car was covered. Nigel reached down to the front of the car and peeled back the tarpaulin to reveal an old Renault. Jamie gasped. It was fluorescent green with red and turquoise stripes.

"The Chameleon," Nigel and Ben spurt out in unison.

Jamie gawped. She'd never seen anything like it. Ben and Nigel both seemed excited. They loved to shock. Jamie gulped down her gasp, shuddering at the thought of driving around in something so far from inconspicuous.

"She's our first car," said Nigel, "We never use her now, but she goes like a dream, and you're welcome to borrow her until you sort something"—Nigel hesitated—"less vulgar."

"You are over twenty-five?" Nigel continued, and whilst it pleased Jamie that this was even a question, she nodded her head, still finding it difficult to speak. "That's great. We won't even have to get you different insurance. Anyone over twenty-five can drive it." Nigel walked to the wall and opened a box where a multitude of keys were hanging. "Please take her, you can't walk here," he said, passing the keys to Jamie. Whilst it filled her with horror to be driving around in something so blatant, needs must.

"I don't need it yet, but thank you," Jamie said with genuine appreciation, passing the keys back to Nigel whilst praying she would soon be able to afford something here. Anything but The Chameleon.

"Okay, no worries, it's here for you when you arrive properly. When is that?" Nigel passed Jamie the remote to the garage.

"Well, I was waiting to see if you wanted me."

"Want you? Of course we want you. The job's already yours, darling. Get yourself packed up and back as soon as you can. And you'll need this to access The Cave." Nigel passed Jamie another remote, whilst Jamie stood with her mouth open. *The Cave?* She couldn't believe this was really happening. Kate genuinely was her fairy godmother, and now she had two more.

"Ohmygosh." Jamie's words blurred into one. "Are you sure? Really sure?" But Nigel wanted her to start immediately, and she wouldn't be able to move back properly until after Christmas. She handed the remote back to Nigel. "I know you want me to start straight away, but I have some existing bookings that I need to fulfil. I can't let people down."

She watched Nigel's face register a flicker of disappointment. "But from the sounds of it, there's a lot I can start remotely. If I gather all the information today, then I can make a start on it in London."

"Well, it's waited about two decades to get organised. I know we'll make it work. Now let's show you around." Nigel walked back into the garage as Jamie followed, tears threatening to escape as the reality of the situation hit her, but she held them back—she didn't want to be a blubbering wreck as well as a frizzy one.

Nigel stopped at the back wall, pressing a sequence of buttons on an alarm pad which shifted the wall to reveal a secret sliding door before disappearing back into the wall, revealing a spiral staircase. It was all very James Bond. Lights flickered on and illuminated the stairwell that appeared to be carved out of stone. Gripping the rope that acted as a handrail, Jamie followed Nigel down the winding stairs. At the bottom, an iron gate blocked the entrance to what Jamie could now see was indeed a massive cave. Pressing the alarm pad again, the gate sprung open, and more lights lit up the vast room. Jamie gasped. The Cave, much like the stairwell, was made of rock, and in the centre, a large glass desk was home to a new Mac, pens, pads, a camera, and was that a label maker? Two long red velvet drapes hung to the far right, and for a moment Jamie imagined she'd entered some sort of 'Red Room,' but reassured that Nigel was Kate's friend and that he was gay shook away any thoughts of being held captive.

Nigel seemed to relish in Jamie's reaction, watching her face with pleasure. "It's quite something. Kate's wonderful David designed it."

As they walked through the gate, Jamie's eyes scanned the space. To the far left, they'd carved shelves out of the rock, each lined with red velvet and enclosed by glass doors. Jamie smiled with delight as she cast her eyes across the many handbags ensconced within their glass homes; each glass cabinet with its own alarm pad. "The glass is reinforced," Nigel exclaimed. "Bulletproof too." He was proud of the security. Forcing her eyes away from the bags, Jamie followed Nigel to the far end of the cave. Pressing another button, shutters rose to reveal a terrace. The sun streamed into the cave and the lights flickered off. As she walked onto the balcony, she was stunned into silence. The panoramic view was breathtaking: small coves enclosed by shady pine forests, rugged rocks and cobalt crystal waters. To the far right of the terrace, there was a small covered kitchenette and bar with stools. Nigel reached down to a small fridge and produced a bottle of champagne. "It's induction day, let's make a toast because"—he winked mischievously as he paused searching for the right words—"Jamie King, you are my life saviour."

Taking the glass flute he proffered, Jamie corrected, "Actually Nigel, you are my life saviour." And they both clinked their glasses, grinning at each other like school children. As the sparkling liquid caressed the back of Jamie's throat, she could have purred with delight. Everything was going to be alright after all.

Nigel stared out to sea. "No, really Jamie. I need you. I'm out of control. I buy things, print out the invoice and shove it in a box. Ben's going crazy; he's worried I'm going to drop dead and he'll be left with this huge collection with no idea of what is what, the value or anything. He's banned me from buying any more until I get all this categorised, and I do so love buying." He grinned cheekily.

Jamie was equally excited. "I can't wait to get started on those gorgeous bags, but Kate mentioned you collect watches and art too?"

Nigel knocked back the remnants of his glass before placing it on the bar. "Follow me," he said, walking towards the interior of the cave. "The most important thing for me was to have someone I could trust." He looked Jamie squarely in the eye. "Kate says you're like her sister and trusts you implicitly, and that's good enough for me." Jamie held his gaze. She felt honoured to be offered this position. "And once we get this lot sorted, then we can start on stage two of my master plan—sending you off to various auctions and fairs to advance the collection." Nigel's excitement was contagious and as Jamie imagined all the incredible shopping she'd be doing; it was as if all her Christmases had come at once.

Walking towards one of the red velvet drapes, Nigel pulled the long gold cord, as the drapes swished to the side, unveiling a safe. As he pressed a sequence of buttons, the safe door popped open, revealing a large interior, shelved with various trays also lined with red velvet. Pulling out one tray, he walked back towards the glass desk and placed the tray of watches on top, lovingly running his hands across them. This was about the beauty of the watches; the craftsmanship, and Jamie felt a tidal wave of respect towards Nigel for trusting her with this precious cargo that obviously meant so much to him. Nigel picked up a watch. It was a rose-coloured gold bracelet ladies' dress watch. The mother of pearl dial with Breguet-style numerals, unlike anything she'd ever seen before. Nigel held the watch out to Jamie, as she took it, mesmerised.

"Do you know anything about watches?" Nigel didn't tear his gaze away from the watch nestled in Jamie's hands. "No, to be honest I don't." She glanced up at him. "But I will, Nigel. I'm going to learn everything there is. It's simply exquisite."

"It was my mother's. A Rolex. It dates back to 1914. I have no idea what it's worth now, but it's the most precious thing I own." He had tears in his eyes as he spoke and Jamie felt a rush of warmth towards this gentle giant with a heart of gold, as Kate had accurately described him. Jamie carefully placed the watch back in Nigel's hands, which he lovingly stroked before returning it to its velvet nest.

Jamie wondered what memories were being evoked in him. "I'm going to learn everything there is, Nigel. I'm going to get all of this." As she waved her hands around the cave. "All of this, photographed and categorised. I'm going to research and find current values and …" She was actually quite lost for words. Nigel looked up and smiled. "I know you will, dear."

Picking up the tray of watches, Nigel returned it to the safe, before announcing more jovially, "And, last but not least—the art." As he pulled the gold rope on the other red velvet drape, a second iron gate was revealed. Pressing the alarm code again to release the door, lights flickered on to reveal another slightly smaller cave. A humidifier buzzed, and Nigel explained how the art had to be kept at a certain temperature. Large metal storage trays with plastic sleeves filled this cave. "I'm sorry, this really is all over the place," Nigel explained, a tad embarrassed, "Ideally, I'd like all the art from a particular artist to be categorised together. They're all limited editions." He leaned in to whisper like a conspirator, "But I want to start buying originals." His eyes twinkled with excitement as he flicked through the plastic sleeves as one might flick through the pages of a book. "Damien Hirst, which is Pop Art and … you might want to make a note of this."

Jamie was already on it. Reaching into her buttery soft brown leather satchel, she fished out a small cream notepad.

"I absolutely love street artists. I think everybody should appreciate art, and all these artists started on the streets, not just for wealthy buggers like me." He chuckled. "Make a note of these names. Pure Evil," he said, stopping at an image of what appeared to be a mixture of a bunny and fingers.

"Aptly named, isn't it?" Jamie noted that he had several 'bunny fingers' in various different colours; she liked the pink and glitter one best.

"Most of the artists have their own tags. Pure Evil has a bunny tag which appears on all his work. What's important is what number edition it is, out of how many were produced, and whether the artist has signed it. A signed print increases the value." He continued to flick the plastic sleeves, settling on a rather terrifying image.

"That's Jack Nicholson," Jamie said with glee, recognising the brightly coloured image.

"Yes, the artist is Invader. Write that name down too." And he pointed to the bottom right-hand corner, "You see it says thirty-two of a hundred? That means a total of one hundred prints were produced and this was number thirty-two. The value of the print is often determined by the number in the run."

Jamie looked somewhat confused but kept nodding, furiously making notes.

"So most often the lower the number in the edition, the more valuable the piece." Flicking to another image. Nigel pointed to the right-hand corner that was marked 'AP.' "That means it's an artist's proof; these are the most valuable of all as there are very few of them. The AP is an impression of a print taken in the printmaking process to see the current printing state of a plate while the plate is being worked on by the artist. Sometimes the artist alters the main run, which is what makes these AP's rare and its rarity increases the value."

"And the tags?" Jamie was eager to show Nigel that she was fully engrossed.

"This sort of art comes from the street. Often, the artists are looking to express themselves. It gives a voice to the unheard, the invisible, the nobodies who want to be somebody; there's a feeling of satisfaction and not feeling so hopeless." Nigel resumed his list of artists: Hewlett, Cauty, Nick Walker, as Jamie furiously tried to scribble the names down, fearful she might not be able to read her writing afterwards.

Nigel continued flicking the plastic sleeves until he settled on one piece. Lifting the plastic sleeve out of the tray, his eyes gleamed with delight as he made his way to the glass desk and laid it out flat. Reaching down to the desk drawer, he pulled out a pair of white gloves. "When you handle the art, you need to please use the gloves." Having slipped his hands into the gloves, he reached into the plastic and gently eased the print out. The image was simple, a young girl with her hand extended towards a red heart-shaped balloon carried away by the wind.

"This of course, is Banksy," he said, not taking his eyes off the image.

"Oh gosh I love his work, always so powerful. And"—Jamie said, noting the scrawled Banksy signature at the bottom right of the print—"it's signed, so these must be really valuable."

"Exactly," said Nigel, pleased that Jamie was catching on; not just a pretty face after all. "Some say it's a symbol of lost innocence, others believe that the girl is setting the balloon free."

"It's beautiful. Always been one of my favourites," Jamie said, entranced.

"All of his works are simple, but genius, really. He's very political and his art gives a message about the society we live in. I wish I'd bought more of his prints or some originals but it's too late now; you can buy a house for what they cost." His eyes flickered with excitement. "But as I said, Ben's banned me until I get all of this into shape." Then clapping his hands together in a prayer-like fashion. "So, please Miss King, can you help me get this sorted?" he whispered before gently slipping the print back into its plastic sleeve and replacing it back in the metal tray. "I'm sorry, it's such a mess."

"Good god, don't be sorry. If it wasn't, then you wouldn't need me and Nigel ..." She hesitated, trying to find the words that would convey her genuine excitement. "Nigel, this is the most exciting opportunity that anyone has ever given to me. I am going to love sorting this all out. I won't let you down."

"I know you won't." He could tell by the way Jamie carried herself that his babies were in good hands. Walking back to the desk Nigel reached underneath, flicking open the top of a large wicker basket, piled to the brim with paper. "The invoices."

Jamie laughed. "Brilliant Nigel, I'll have this sorted in no time."

"The only invoice that isn't in there is my mother's watch."

"Lunch is served," Ben yelled down the stairs, interrupting their conversation. Nigel pointed to the entrance. "There's an intercom over there but Ben won't use it. I think he just likes to yell at me. Now please come and join us for lunch so you can tell us all about yourself," surveying Jamie up and down. "You do eat, don't you?"

Jamie grinned. "I do now."

NIP/TUCK

London, England

"David, wake up." Kate glowered over David's inert body. "David, helloooooo?" Her irritation escalated by his lack of response.

Kate always marvelled at David's ability to drop off for a 'power nap' as he called it. Any time, any place, anywhere. No matter how inappropriate the moment. But why did 'anywhere' have to be on her hospital bed? And why was 'any time' now, when she needed him most? She felt sick. She was never sick, not even during pregnancy. God forbid she ever relinquished any of the food she consumed. *Grrrrrr*, this was so frustrating! Not how she'd imagined it at all. She'd played the scene over and over in her mind many times; she'd be lying peacefully on the bed, patiently awaiting her surgery. Her black hair spread dramatically over the pillow, as if she were Snow White. David would be one of the adoring dwarves, likely Dopey or Bashful, but surveying his motionless body, she settled on Sleepy and she was no longer Snow White but Grumpy.

In her obsessive imagining of this precise moment, she'd be calm and composed. Confident that the correct decision had been made; that this surgery was going to be the making of her. David would be standing over her, whispering loving words of reassurance, stroking her and kissing her, filling her with love and support.

"David, wake up. I neeeeeeed you," she shouted deliberately in his ear, her patience running out as she nudged him forcefully.

"Uch. W-w-what's the matter? What's wrong?"

"I feel sick."

"Go to the toilet then." He rolled over to resume his sleep, his back now facing Kate. No doubt he was having his favourite dream, the one where he was drinking and playing pool down the pub with David Beckham.

Kate wished she'd left him at home with the kids and brought a friend to the hospital instead. A girlfriend would have given her the required level of moral support. A girlfriend would've sat there and listened to her now-growing list of anxieties and concerns. She should've asked Jamie. She certainly would have been supportive, and no doubt taken her mind off the impending surgery by amusing her with all of her wonderful stories. But Jamie was now juggling two jobs as she finished off her modelling commitments and was buried in research for Nigel. She had enough on her plate, so Kate hadn't even asked. She glanced back at David, now curled into a ball, dead to the world.

His gentle snores were exasperating. Kate went into the bathroom to escape the noise. Once inside—and with the door firmly shut—she pulled down her tracksuit bottoms until they sat in a pool by her feet, lifted up her jumper and took off her bra to survey herself in the mirror. How was it that most of her friends who'd had kids didn't have a disgusting body? How was it that two pregnancies had ravaged her body to this extent? Yet there was no mystery involved. Most of her friends had seen pregnancy as a means of having offspring, whereas she'd seen it as a reason to eat whatever the bloody hell she liked for nine months without feeling guilty. She never understood those women who craved apples and carrots. No, not her. Only full fat, full carbohydrate and anything else of the highest calorific value that she could possibly shove down her gob.

Everybody had nodded sympathetically and mentioned something about water retention, but Kate had seen the look in their eyes. She knew deep down that she couldn't be carrying four stones of water and one stone of a baby. Five full stones she'd put on, not once but twice. Was it any wonder her body had ceased to regain its pre-pregnancy shape? Like an elastic band that had been stretched too much, her elasticity had been decimated, and all that was left was this revolting, crinkly mass. No amount of dieting and exercise could ever rectify the situation, and she simply couldn't live with it anymore. Surgery was the only way forward. She was definitely doing the right thing. Or was she?

Pulling up her tracksuit bottoms and replacing the jumper without bothering to put on her bra, Kate continued to stare at herself in the mirror. What if something went wrong? What happened if she never woke up from the anaesthetic and for what? For vanity? She could potentially die and all because she didn't like the way she looked? She had children, for Christ's sake, she was a mother and a wife; she had responsibilities. David loved her just the way she was. Or did he? After all, it was his idea that she had the surgery. Her daughters loved her, irrespective of what she looked like, so why was she leaving them to do this? Was she a bad person who had her priorities all screwed up? Would David manage alone with the girls? What sort of mother was she to leave her girls for two whole weeks? Fear. Guilt. Fear. Guilt. *Arrrrgggghhhh.*

David was only staying for a couple of days whilst she had the surgery and then would return to the island with the girls whilst she recuperated at her parents'. No doubt David would just sleep with the two girls in their king-size American bed. They'd have breakfast in one of the many cafés near the school and dinner out every night. They'd probably love it, freed from the shackles of Kate. Yes, there was no doubt in her mind that her carefully constructed routine would fly out the window, but she had no right to dictate what went on during her absence. She only prayed that when she returned, she could reinstate order to the chaos that would no doubt become her home.

Shaking away thoughts of neglecting her children, Kate pulled herself together and reminded herself that she was doing the right thing. She left the bathroom and slammed the door. Still no movement from David. Going in search of her phone, Kate decided to return Jamie's text from the night before. Settling into the chair next to the bed, Kate plonked herself down and put her feet up on the bed, accidentally on purpose knocking David in the process. He momentarily stopped snoring, wiggled further away from her, and then the annoying sound continued. It was too early for anybody to be up; she was truly on her own. But then magically, 'Beep. Beep.'

Jamie:	Good luck hun, thinking about you. Don't worry, morphine is better than vodka!!
Kate:	Thanks, feeling sick as hell but too late now, hope you're right about the morphine
Jamie:	Let me know how it goes. Can I come visit you tomoz? X

Kate:	Will text you after the op. But think I might even be going home and you have enough on your plate. How's the research going?
Jamie:	In 7th heaven. Finished researching all bags, now working on watches. Bit daunted by art section though but Nigel is hysterical. He texts me about 100 times a day. I love it!
Kate:	I knew it ha ha. You're welcome.

Suddenly, the door to Kate's hospital room opened and in walked a pretty nurse. She took one look at David's lifeless body and gave Kate a sympathetic glance. "G'day, Mrs Buchanan, I'm Summer. Just came to see if you've settled in okay?"

"Thanks. Yeah, I'm fine, just nervous and wishing it was all over. Do you have any idea what time my surgery will be?" Kate said meekly.

"I believe you're the second one in today. Mr Barnes will come and see you shortly and then after that the anaesthetist will have a quick chat with you, so you'll probably go down around ten."

Kate groaned; that would be another four hours. Another four hours without food. She couldn't do it; she was starving already. One would think that nerves would've diminished her appetite, but apparently not. The nurse looked at her sympathetically. "Please don't worry, you're in great hands." With that, she passed Kate a regulation blue hospital gown and a pair of paper knickers.

"When you're ready, you'll need to put these on. And Mrs Buchanan, don't worry, it'll be over before you know it." Nurse Summer reassured Kate as she left the room.

Having been disturbed from his slumber by their talking, David raised his head and grinned sheepishly, then, looking at the garments muttered, "Hmmmm, sexy."

Kate had the urge to whack him, but recognising that this whole situation was self-inflicted, simply flicked her head dramatically as she'd seen Emily do a thousand times, and marched off to the bathroom. When she re-emerged, she noted that David had now moved from the bed to the armchair by the window and was noshing on a sandwich whilst on his phone. Kate looked at him incredulously. For a man who primarily left all the organisational stuff to her, he'd done remarkably well at preparing himself with provisions for his morning stint in hospital. Knowing full well that she wasn't allowed food or drink until after the operation, he at least had the good grace to look guilty when he was caught red-handed. Quickly shoving the rest of the sandwich into his mouth in one go, David muffled something like, 'Sorry.' Which came out more as a "Sooooorrrhhaaahhaaahaaay." As he laid eyes upon Kate in the hospital gown with the customary gaping back, showing off far from attractive paper knickers, which were four sizes too big. It wasn't her best look.

Kate didn't have time to respond, as seconds later, Mr Barnes entered the room.

"Morning Mrs Buchanan. How are we today?" Kate felt the desire to launch into her concerns but instinctively recognised his question had been rhetorical.

"Fine," she lied.

"Lovely, just lovely, now let's have a look at you." Mr Barnes signalled for her to remove the hospital gown whilst holding up a black marker pen menacingly. Kate remembered the marker pen. She hated that marker pen. Cringing, she dropped her hospital gown and sat on the bed, resigned to the fact that she was about to become a human canvas. She watched as he drew markings around her breasts and stomach, noting with some amusement that he'd drawn what appeared to be some sort of Mr Men face on her body. Her nipples had become eyes, her belly button a nose, and on her lower stomach a huge big smile stretched from one hip to the other. Well, at least she was Mr Happy instead of Mr Sad. The reality that these were incision marks caused another wave of nausea. Could she possibly ask for the morphine now, before she'd even had the operation?

The door banged open again and in walked the anaesthetist. Thankfully, this was the man she needed, he was the man who could give her drugs.

"Morning Mrs Buchanan." Another cheery, happy person. Perhaps they put morphine in the hospital's ventilation system!

"Oh dear"—looking at her face—"nervous are we?"

No. Kate thought. *I'm nervous but 'we' are not.* At least she hoped he wasn't nervous, seeing that her life was now in his hands.

"Not to worry, dear," he said, picking up her chart without even looking at her. *That's okay. Patronise me all you like, just give me drugs. I want pre-meds. Give me something NOW.* As if with sheer mind power alone, Kate transported these thoughts directly into his head as he turned to Nurse Summer and spoke the magic words, "Think we should give something to Mrs Buchanan to take the edge off her nerves."

Yes, yes, yes. You clever clever man, give me something, great idea. Kate looked over at David, who miraculously seemed to have put his phone down at the mention of drugs; Kate knew he was thinking about the gas and air he'd kindly shared with her when she was having Emily. A small white paper cup and two little white pills were thrust into her eager hands. She gratefully chucked them into her mouth before David could ask her to share them with him, swallowing them down with the water. Only after they'd been swallowed did she ask, "What were those?" Although anything was better than nothing.

"Temazepam, they'll just make you a little sleepy."

Kate lay on the now vacated hospital bed and tried to relax. She looked around the hospital room, which was ugly and plain and clearly hadn't been refurbished since it was built and god only knew when that was. There existed within her an absolute conviction that the pills wouldn't work, which was why it was so amazing when her following thought was disrupted by the door being flung open and Summer coming in.

"Mrs Buchanan, it's time to go down now."

Kate didn't believe she'd slept the last three hours, but the wave of relief was quickly superseded by a wave of irritation at being woken up. Why the bloody hell did they have to wake her up? Why couldn't they have just wheeled her down and given her the anaesthetic without waking her?

David was quickly at her side. Kate looked terrified.

"It's going to be just fine," he whispered, kissing her forehead.

"Will you stay here? Please? Don't go anywhere, please. Will you be here when I get back? Please, don't leave me." She was waffling, still half asleep and feeling drugged.

"I will never leave you, never," he whispered into her hair as he kissed her gently along her hairline. He stroked her forehead and stared deeply into her eyes. "Never." And then she didn't feel alone anymore.

Lying on her back as she was wheeled down to the operating room, the ceiling lights were shining in her eyes. One light … two lights … three lights. Kate desperately tried to distract herself from the panic that was mounting inside. Four lights … five lights. However, for some strange reason, counting lights as one is being wheeled down to an operating room for a five-hour procedure curiously didn't seem to offer any distraction. Thankfully, as she arrived in the pre-operating room, the anaesthetist was smiling kindly. Unable to speak, Kate had become catatonic. Inside, however, she was screaming, *I want to go home. I've made a terrible mistake. I want my mummy.* The anaesthetist was still smiling. What did he have to smile about? Perhaps he was a sick, sadistic psycho? Kate remained silent. *Shit, what happens if it doesn't work? What happens if it sort of works and I look like I'm unconscious, but really I can feel everything? Arrrrgggghhhh.*

"Mrs Buchanan, you'll feel a little prick, then I want you to count to ten."

She wanted to voice her concerns. She wanted to discuss a back-up plan. She wanted to ask the anaesthetist to watch her toe, and she'd find a way to wiggle it so he'd know that the anaesthetic hadn't worked, but all she squawked was, "One … two … " Blackness.

* * *

"Mrs Buchanan, Mrs Buchanan, wake up now. Mrs Buchanan, can you hear me?"

No, go away. Leave me alone. I'm trying to reach an unconscious state so that I can have my surgery. Stupid people. Why are they always interrupting me when I'm trying to sleep?

"Mrs Buchanan? Kate? Can you hear me?" And then something was being pushed into her hand.

"The operation is over, everything went fantastically. If you're in pain, then press the button on the remote I've just put in your hand, and it will administer some morphine."

Still unable to speak out loud. *Pain, what pain? What are they talking about? Haven't had the operation yet, just about to go down, got to count to ten. One ... two.*

Oh Fuck. Oh holy mother of ... owwwwwwwww! That would be that pain, that excruciating unbelievable some-werewolf-had-just-ripped open-her-body pain. No, worse than that. Some alien-that-had-been-incubated-in-her-body pain. Now ripping its way through her stomach-spilling-intestines-and-kidneys-and-other-organs-in-its-wake pain. Someone said something about pain, morphine, yes, what did she have to do? Oh yes, click the button. CLICK. *Aaaahhhhhhhhh* better.

Kate liked the clicky thing; it was fabulous that the werewolves and aliens had disappeared so quickly. She felt a little confused and opened one eye. David was still sitting in the armchair, and as if he'd been stuck in some time warp, still eating and still reading.

"I don't believe it," he said, "I've been kissing your forehead and stroking you for hours and only just sat down now. Honestly." And somehow she knew this was true, she'd felt it, and she smiled.

"What do I look like?"

"An Egyptian mummy, a beautiful Egyptian princess."

"Not Snow White then?" She felt confused, she'd planned a Snow White look not a Cleopatra look, especially not a dead mummified Cleopatra look. Glancing down, she noted that from under her chin right down to her thighs, she was totally encapsulated in bandages. Jamie had been right after all; she looked perfect for Halloween. Not really feeling any pain, but just in case, CLICK. No point in taking any chances.

Her legs were raised under the knees by a special bed which contorted depending on which body part needed to be supported, and the back of the bed was at a 120-degree angle to her legs. One tube seemed to be coming out of her stomach, and another two tubes, coming out from each breast. Kate had no idea what these tubes were for and noted that there were an additional two further tubes. One she presumed was a catheter for her wee—oh thank god, that meant she didn't have to worry about going to the toilet—and the other one she traced back to a bag which housed the morphine. She liked that tube the best, so much so that she actually didn't care about all the other tubes. CLICK and nothing hurts at all, no pain, just happiness. She felt as if she were floating amidst a sky of pure cotton wool clouds with enormous relief that it was finally over.

Summer popped her head around the door, she was mumbling something and Kate nodded in agreement, although she didn't have a clue what she was saying. Kate noted that Summer had an Australian accent, strange, she hadn't noticed before. *Ahhhhhh* how lovely; Summer was from the Land of Oz. This made Kate think about the yellow brick road. Summer gave Kate a little white pot of pills, which she dutifully took. It didn't really matter what they were. Summer was from the Land of Oz; she worked for the wizard, she could be trusted.

"Are you hungry?" David was talking.

Hungry? Is that what he asked? Am I hungry? No. It was strange not to be hungry. She shook her head.

"Are you thirsty?" David was still talking. Much better, he looked concerned and was paying her proper attention now; exactly what she wanted. Perhaps the number of tubes that were coming from her body freaked him out. He looked lovely. Nice, sweet, soft, lovely David. She loved him. Then Summer came in. She loved Summer, too. She loved the hospital room. It was pretty and CLICK. She loved this clicky thing. She really loved the clicky thing. What was it? Oh yes, morphine. She would call it Murphy, as she loved it sooooooo much. Summer was talking to David. What were they saying? David was worried that she was clicking too much. CLICK. *Shut up David. Shut up now.* CLICK. She'd better click a lot, just in case they took Murphy away. Oh please let Murphy stay. Murphy was her friend.

David was mumbling something about a football match, something about wanting to go, something about it being seven in the evening.

"Yes, go darling go. Click your heels three times, and you will be home," Kate said and David smiled, rushing out the door before Dorothy changed her mind. Kate was happy, sleepy and happy and on the yellow brick road where the Smurfs live. CLICK. Whoops. Hysterical, silly Kate. No Smurfs on the yellow brick road. Cleopatra the Egyptian princess on her way to the Emerald City. Blackness.

THE SIX MILLION DOLLAR WOMAN

Kate awoke with a start. In slow motion, confusion melted away as reality dawned. In a panic, she groped around the bed with her left hand for the clicky thing, as if she had entered a dark room, unfamiliar with where the light switch was. Panic subsided when she realised it was still clutched firmly in her right hand, like a child's comforter. Morphine. CLICK. CLICK. *Ahhhhhh*, immediate relief, and succumbing completely to the pleasure that her new friend Morphine Murphy gave her. She closed her eyes and wandered far away.

Suddenly, she found herself in Hyde Park, London, walking hand in hand in the sunshine. Her hand clutched in a strong grip, and a feeling of euphoria swept through her. She turned her face up towards her walking companion, and Robert smiled back at her. Robert? Salsa Man? Not David? Well, that was strange, but hey, what the hell, it wasn't real; it was all in her lovely, pure world of imagination. Happy and laughing as if they were good friends that had known each other for years, Kate found herself grinning as she looked up at him; as if a halo of sunshine was glowing around his blonde hair. She wanted to be there, exactly there, in that very moment, with him and nobody else. Contentment washed over her, knowing this was exactly where and who she was meant to be.

Deciding to take a diversion through the subway, all of a sudden they were no longer platonic friends, but far from it. They were lovers. Robert forcefully grabbed Kate and literally threw her up against the wall. Not even bothering to look around, he pressed one hand against her shoulder to keep her still whilst the other foraged up her skirt and went directly to base camp. Yanking her panties to one side, Robert explored inside … Kate gasped, *Oh my god*. It was so intense, so wild, so carnal.

Momentarily distracted by a coughing sound, Kate glanced over to her side to see a tramp lying on the floor several metres away from them. Empty beer bottles littered the floor beside him; if he didn't look so smashed to the point of unconsciousness, Kate might've felt embarrassed. But there was no embarrassment … not now … only passion–pure unadulterated passion. The danger of it all, notwithstanding the seediness of the situation, had Kate gasping for air. Robert helped … his fingers giving a whole new meaning to the word 'internal.'

Next, they were in a NCP car park in Hull. But in Hull, it was no longer sunny. It was a bitter winter's day and Kate was wearing a sexy, long, black leather coat lined with black faux fur. Kissing like a couple of sex-starved teenagers, Robert's tongue wasn't just French kissing, it was speaking goddamned Swahili. Releasing Kate from his vice-like grip, Robert spun her around to face away from him. Sweeping her coat out of the way, he wrapped his arms around her and dropped his pants. Yanking her in close, he pressed his groin against her and then, taking hold of her hair, pulled her head back towards him. Kate turned her eyes towards him, just as he began to thrust deep inside … she gasped again. Cars could be heard coming and going, just as he came and went inside her, over and over again.

Suddenly, she woke up. *Where did he go? Shit.* CLICK. *Bring him back.* CLICK. *I want more. Need more.* CLICK. CLICK. But this time, no Robert, just a picture of herself in a bikini. Itsy bitsy teeny weeny yellow polka dot bikini. Kate dragged herself into consciousness. *Oh my god. My breasts are huge. They look like two inflatable beach balls.* In and out of delirium, Kate kept looking down at where her new tits were situated, which scarily enough were significantly nearer to her face than was comfortable. Paranoia ripped through her. What happened if they'd made a mistake and gave her a breast enlargement instead of a lift? What would happen if she was now the proud owner of a pair of 34H tits? CLICK. *Well, that would be just lovely really, more for Robert to fondle and suck.* As lovely warm thoughts set to consume her, Nurse Summer entered the room, interrupting Kate's fantasy and announced the imminent removal of the various tubes from her body.

"G'day, Kate, how did you sleep last night?" Clearly, they were on a first name basis now.

"Quite good, thank you," Kate said politely.

"Excellent news and just look where your breasts are now, and how flat your tummy is," Summer said enthusiastically. Kate thought she must be having a laugh.

"I think my breasts look swollen and very high up," Kate said equally politely, not wanting to point out that she couldn't see her stomach as her now mountainous breasts were hindering the view. She wondered if it was just in her imagination that her chin was resting on her boobs.

"Nothing to worry about, they're just swollen." Summer confirmed Kate's suspicions as she bustled around the room, still chatting. "This morning, we're going to take out all those drips."

CLICK. CLICK. CLICK. She couldn't be serious? Kate looked at her imploringly.

"Not this one, not the morphine," she all but shrieked. Now in a major panic ... CLICK. CLICK. "I won't make a fuss about the others, but please let me keep the morphine one. I'm not ready," Kate beseeched, regressing to the age of five, and with the desperation of a heroin addict being dragged into rehab holding onto the entrance door, she held firmly onto the clicky thing.

Summer smiled; no doubt Kate was not the first to make this request. "No worries, you can keep that for a while. We'll take the other ones out first."

"Oh and not the catheter either." Kate didn't want to push her luck, but the thought of having to leave the comfort of her bed and walk the ten steps to the toilet seemed more than daunting.

"Okay, we can do that one later as well." Summer was so nice.

As Summer pulled out the tubes from each breast and then the stomach, there was a strange pulling sensation but no pain. Morphine. Kate loved Murphy the morphine. There was something extremely liberating about just lying in bed, with only her thoughts for company. She liked it. Her cogitations were vivid and varied, and they seemed to flow through her mind like an endless stream of mini epiphanies. She wished she had a notepad so that she could chronicle these pearls of wisdom; it was as if all of life's mysteries were being answered at once, the truth of her very existence being revealed.

Minutes turned into an hour, then a new nurse popped her head around the door. She was sturdy and scary looking.

"Time for the catheter to come out now, Mrs Buchanan."

Oh no. Where's Summer?

"Summer said I could keep it in," Kate whined.

"It really is best if it comes out now."

"Okay, but can I keep this one?" Kate indicated towards the morphine drip.

Sturdy, scary nurse smiled. "Alright dear." And then Kate loved, sturdy scary nurse as much as Summer. She'd simply not drink anything, nothing at all. If nothing went in, then it wouldn't have to come out. The nurse pulled out the catheter tube and headed back out of the room, saying, "Let me know when you feel the urge to go to the toilet and I'll help you get up. Don't try to attempt it on your own."

Duh. As if I'd try to climb Everest without a backup team. She just wouldn't think about the toilet or water. But no sooner had the nurse gone, her head was suddenly overflowing with images of waterfalls, and her thirst was monumental. All Kate could think about were fountains, seas, rain, lakes and her bladder swelled until she feared she'd wet her bed, or worse still, explode. Quickly, she pressed the buzzer.

Summer popped her head around the door. *Oh, great, Summer is back.*

"I need to go to the toilet. I don't want to get up. I can't get up. Can you put the catheter back in?" she asked, hoping that Summer would be more likely to grant her request than sturdy, scary nurse.

"No worries, I'll help you. It will be good to stretch your legs."

Good for who?

Summer lowered the lower half of the bed so that Kate's legs were almost straight. The bandages stretched to what felt like breaking point, and Kate felt like she was going to snap in two.

"Can I take Murphy with me?" Kate negotiated.

Summer looked momentarily confused until she saw Kate's firm grasp on the morphine drip and laughed.

"Yes, of course. Murphy can come with you. The morphine has to come with you—you're attached."

Summer grabbed hold of Kate's arms as she supported her into an almost upright position, whilst Kate slowly eased her legs to the floor. Now perched at the end of the bed. Kate took a look at the toilet door. It seemed very far away, but with Summer's assistance, Kate was able to hobble, no, shuffle, to the toilet. No longer a beautiful Egyptian princess but an old lady of ninety. Unable to stand upright, just hunched with age and riddled with arthritis, praying that she'd make it to the toilet in time.

* * *

Kate had her eyes closed when she heard the door creak open. Then David's voice, "Just be gentle with Mummy."

Small little butterfly wings landed on her face as Tali reached down to stroke Kate with her delicate little fingers. Without even opening her eyes, Kate knew her baby girl was there. As she prised open her eyes, she saw Tali held in David's arms wriggling, trying to escape.

"How are you feeling?" David put Tali back down as he leaned over to kiss Kate's forehead, lingering for a moment as he inhaled her.

"Good." She didn't want to voice her concerns, not in front of Tali, although she was desperate to share with David.

Now on the floor, no longer able to reach her mummy's face, Tali started to stroke Kate's arm. When she saw that her mother was awake, she beamed. "When you coming home, Mamá?"

Kate took hold of Tali's hand and Tali copied her father and dropped her nose down to Kate's hand, inhaling the scent of her mother.

Kate smiled reassuringly, stroking Tali's beautiful long hair and feeling relieved that most of the tubes were now out and Tali didn't have to see her like that.

Tali looked a little puzzled as she observed her mummy. "Where are da old boobies? The ones down there?" As she pointed to Kate's lower abdomen.

Kate and David both snickered. Although Kate's sniggers were muffled and accompanied by an 'ouch.'

"When are you going back?" Kate looked up at David.

"Tonight."

Kate felt glum. She knew David had to return to the island with the girls. They had school, and he had work, but it was going to be a tough recuperation without them. Sensing her apprehension, David was quick to pacify her. "Your parents are so excited about having you. Your mum's been cooking." *Great, Mum's going to make me fat. Feeding me and I won't even be able to run away. All this pain and suffering will be for nothing. God help me.*

"I know. It's just going to be hard. Two whole weeks without you and the girls."

"You'll be fine." David lent down to kiss her again. "It will be fine," he said more sternly, hoping to reassure her.

"And, you won't forget to feed the rabbits … and it's best to prepare the school lunches except for the sandwiches the night before … and Tali only has egg mayonnaise, and Emily decides in the morning, and you need to get them into bed by eight and …" Kate rattled off in a panic, just as David interrupted her. He took her face in his hands and squeezed her cheeks together so she couldn't speak.

"I've got this, Kate. If I forget, I'll just refer to the twenty page, laminated instruction manual you left on the fridge. There's nothing for you to worry about. We will survive without you. All you need to do is get better and come back to us soon."

"Did you text Jamie?" Kate hoped he had.

"Yes, actually, she's on her way now. I didn't know if you'd be up for visitors, but we have to leave soon and she's ..." He stopped searching for the word.

Kate finished off his sentence. "Very strong-willed. I know."

"Where's Emily?" Kate realised Emily wasn't with them.

"She's with your mum. They'll be here soon, as well," said David.

"What are they doing?"

"I think she said she was going to take her for a haircut."

"WHAT?" Kate was now fully alert as her morphine drip had been replaced with adrenaline. Kate had PTSD when it came to hair. She could only conclude from various family photos and a deep-rooted memory that was now fully triggered, that her mother had stuck a bowl on her head and cut around it. The young Kate had been severely traumatised, leading to a phobia of hairdressers in adulthood and one of the many reasons she now had hair as long as Rapunzel. Kate closed her eyes with misery.

"I had no choice," David said in defence, "You know what your mum's like."

Kate remained silent. David continued as the gravity of the situation sunk in. "It might be my fault," he said suddenly, concerned that Kate's mum could walk through the door at any moment and fearful that Kate, regardless of her constrictions, just might muster the energy to raise a knife and stab her a hundred times. "I happened to mention that I was concerned about doing the girls' hair in the morning, and Emily overheard me and she asked your mum."

Kate was still silent.

Suddenly the door burst open and Emily gushed in. "I've had a lovely haircut."

Barbara, Kate's mum, followed behind.

Kate looked at Emily, a wave of pure horror taking over at the decimation of her daughter's hair. Whilst she didn't look like a monk, her long, beautiful locks had been chopped. David looked at Kate, then at Barbara, who seemed oblivious to Kate's irritation.

"It's spikey." Emily was now touching her hair with her hands, showing off the new style, totally oblivious to the rage now enveloping her mother.

Kate's eyes suddenly grew wide, and David was fearful she was about to turn into a monster at any moment. "It looks lovely darling, doesn't it, Kate?" David stared with intent at his wife, hoping to diffuse the situation before Barbara ended up in bandages too.

Barbara approached the bed and bent down to kiss her daughter, much to David's horror, but thankful that Kate was in pain and unlikely to lash out. "I brought you some chicken soup and gave it to the nurses to heat up for lunch. Everything is ready for you at home. David said it was hard for you to lay down straight, so I got your father to bring in one of the reclining garden chairs and—"

"Thanks Mum," Kate interrupted, still wanting to throttle her but was thankfully too overwhelmed with tiredness, "I just need to close my eyes for a bit."

"Don't worry, David. We'll look after her. Sam and I are excited to have her with us. Two weeks will go by in a flash." Barbara turned her attention to David.

"Thanks, Barbara. We really appreciate it. I feel bad leaving her with you," David said, hoping this wasn't a terrible idea.

"Ah, don't be silly. We are eternally grateful to you for taking her off our hands in the first place," Barbara said with amusement. Kate winced at the memory. She remembered telling her mother that she'd met the man she was going to marry after her first date with David. Barbara had rejoiced, dancing around the kitchen, singing, "Hallelujah, praise the Lord."

Their voices became muffled, and Kate drifted back to the pleasant state of unconsciousness. The next thing she heard was Emily call out, "Jamie!" She opened one eye, and saw that Jamie had breezed in. Her mother and Tali were no longer there, just Emily and David.

"Really pleased to meet you," David said to Jamie, "I've heard so much about you. I hear you've introduced my wife to vodka and you're going to start working with Nigel soon?"

"Yes, I've already started, but I'll be heading back to the island by Christmas—and FYI your wife needed very little encouragement," Jamie said with a wink.

David chuckled, "Well, I know Kate can't wait to have you back," then David turned to Kate. "We've got to go now, darling. I'll let you have some time with Jamie."

Before she knew it, David and the girls had disappeared, and Jamie was dragging a chair so she could sit closer to Kate. "You look like a beautiful Egyptian princess."

"Thank you." Kate smiled. Jamie got her so completely.

"Are you in pain?"

"No, not really. The morphine is great. Can we find it on the black market in Mallorca?" Kate wanted to laugh at her own joke, but it was just impossible, so Jamie threw her head back and laughed for the both of them.

"Do you remember anything about going down?" Jamie continued her interrogation.

"To be honest, everything is just one big blur, other than …" Kate stopped. She wanted to tell Jamie about the strange fantasies she'd been having about Robert.

"What?" Jamie was now curious.

"I've been fantasising."

"Oooh. Tell me more." Jamie leaned in.

"About Salsa Man."

"Who?"

"You know, Salsa Man. The one who gave me the tingle."

"Ahh yes, the tingle."

"Yes. Jeez Jamie, it's not like I get the tingle every day."

Jamie just nodded, waiting for Kate to explain.

"It's not that I regret not going back to the class, but at the same time, if I'm honest, it was amazing to experience the way he made me feel. So sexy, so desirable and, dare I say it, so totally and unequivocally alive. Chances are I'll never bump into him again, although it does worry me that Mallorca is such a small island. Can you imagine the embarrassment?" Kate's face flushed red at the thought of bumping into him, especially now that she'd spent so many hours indulging in explicit fantasies.

"Don't be silly. Fantasies are harmless and you are not likely to bump into him. Stop fretting."

Jamie was right. The chances of her bumping into him were minimal.

"And how's Nigel's research going?"

"Oh, wow. I love it. I've got a few more modelling jobs, and then I'm done, and big news"—she paused for dramatic effect—"my mother isn't coming back to the island."

"Aw, you're going to be all grown up then and look after your own daughter like the rest of us," Kate said, safe in the knowledge that Jamie couldn't hit her.

"I do feel a little anxious about it."

"It will be fine and you've always got me." Kate realised that this was a big transition for Jamie, and joking about it probably wasn't a great idea.

"Yeah, my mum's going to go back to Italy to be with her sister, who's living just outside of Venice now, and honestly whilst I hit full-scale panic mode when she first told me ... she's right. I needed her to look after Madison when I was modelling, but Nigel is so amazing and I can work around school times. It's perfect."

"You'll be fine," Kate said. She felt like she was drifting out of her body and the energy to talk became more challenging, but she was enjoying being with Jamie and tried to rally on. "And Karl, what happened with that?" she mumbled. It was so hard to talk.

"You look tired, princess." Jamie avoided Kate's change of topic. "You get some rest. We can text or chat later."

"Thank you for coming," Kate managed to squawk out, aware that Jamie was leaning down to kiss her forehead in much the same way as her family had. Jamie felt like family now and a warm fuzzy feeling of being loved consumed Kate as if she were being coddled in velvet.

It felt strange to just be lying there. She felt guilty that her to-do list was being neglected, but by not being able to do anything, she entered into a new blissful, alternative reality. One where she didn't have to be responsible. She realised how much she carried for others and how exhausted she had become. Why had it taken surgery to reach this epiphany and how could she integrate this knowledge into her everyday existence? She couldn't keep having surgeries every time she needed a break. God, she was tired. So very, very tired. Blackness.

HONEST, HONEST

"Flippin' hell," Jamie exclaimed as the carefully filled biscuit tray of brownie mixture slipped from her fingers and onto the kitchen floor. "Shit," followed, as lovely chocolate splurge cascaded all over immaculate limestone tiles. "Bloody Kate," was also uttered as she mopped up the mess; after all, it had been Kate's fault that she was baking in the first place. Kate was the one who'd inspired her to try, making it look so effortless when she'd gone to stay with them in Mallorca, whilst juggling huge family dinners all at the same time. *Damn bloody Nigella too.* Jamie glanced over at the open pages of her latest tome, *How To Be A Domestic Goddess*, now covered in flour and chocolate chips, second only to, *Raising Good Humans*. How life had changed.

But it was the thought that counted, wasn't it? Jamie wanted to try to make lunch for her mother and Madison, who were out shopping together. But surveying the mess in her normally spotless kitchen, realised she had all the culinary skills of a domestic idiot; she hadn't even started on the main course. Glancing up at the clock on the oven, Jamie was alarmed to see there was less than an hour left before their arrival. There was just one thing for it—throw caution to the wind and risk lunch at The Brasserie again, and this time with Maria too.

* * *

"Hi Henri. Table for three, please." Jamie smiled at the head waiter, as she pushed open the large double-frosted glass doors to The Brasserie.

"Ahh, and this must be your ... sister?" Henri attempted to flirt with Maria, knowing full well she certainly was not. Jamie happily assumed Henri was referring to Madison being her sister, as was the norm, but when she realised it was her sixty-plus mother, not so happy, furrowing her brow at Henri.

"Actually ... mamma, but *grazie*, people say we look alike. She got my good genes." Maria flirted back coquettishly, enjoying the compliment, as she thrust back her shoulders and held her head a little higher. She was, after all, at least six inches shorter—and wider—than her daughter, on a good day.

Sitting down at one of the corner banquette tables at the far end of the room, Jamie was relieved to see the restaurant wasn't that busy. Madison was already perusing the menu, and Jamie hoped to God they had something new on there that she might agree to eat. She really didn't like taking her to McDonald's.

"I'm going to miss you, Nonna." Madison suddenly reached her hands across the round table to grab her grandmother's, as Maria's big brown eyes started to tear up.

"Oh *bambolina*, I gonna miss you too"—clutching her granddaughter's hands—"but I will come visit you, and you come visit me too. You will love Italy ... all the pizza, pasta and gelato." Maria's face lit up, radiating pure love and warmth, and Madison couldn't help but smile. "I will Nonna, I will."

"Me too Mamma. Honestly. I am going to miss you, and I just wanted to say how incredibly grateful I am for everything you've done for us, helping me with Maddy, being there for her, for me and even your crazy ways that drove me batshit crazy so many times, but I do love you, so very very much." Jamie reached across to grab both her mother's and her daughter's hands in the middle of the table. All three of them were quiet. Then suddenly Jamie snatched her hands away as quickly as a Labrador scoffs down its breakfast as she fumbled for the menu.

"Don't look," Jamie whispered, holding up the menu in front of her face, with only her eyes peering over it. Jamie was wedged between her mother and daughter on the circular banquette table, facing directly towards the bar.

"Where?" Maria said a little too loudly for Jamie's liking and started to scan the room in search of what she wasn't supposed to be looking at. Jamie hunched her shoulders and crouched further forward, so that the menu covered her entire face. The waitress scurried over and planted a water bottle on the table. It was a brown glass 1942 tequila bottle. Jamie wished it was tequila. Nevertheless, a cool idea to recycle. Madison was now playing with the salt.

"Careful," Maria said to Madison as little flecks of salt spilled out of the mill.

Madison put it down. "I really don't like it here, there's still nothing on the menu that I like." Folding her arms once again in protest.

Jamie seemed impervious to the mess Madison was making and her complaints.

"Where, what ... you hiding from?" Maria returned her attention to Jamie and leaned in closer, trying to figure out why her daughter was acting so strange. Jamie just shushed her and dropped her head even lower after taking one more peek over the top of the menu, towards the bar.

"Don't look," she commanded, as she nodded her head through the menu in the direction of the bar. "That guy over there."

"Where?" Maria's voice raised even louder.

"At the bar, glasses, wearing dark blue jeans and a grey jumper over an untucked white shirt," she whispered. *Nice jumper, cashmere. Weird that he's here every time I am, does he live here?* Jamie recalled how smart he'd looked in his suit the first time she'd seen him. She noticed his jeans sat snuggly over his bum that was resting on the bar stool, his back towards them. As if on cue, he swivelled round on the bar stool to reach down to retrieve something in his rucksack, Jamie clocking his original Adidas trainers, before swivelling back again without detecting the trio.

Maria finally realised who Jamie was talking about and slumped down so that she was also behind the menu. "Oooh, *bello*," lowering her voice, finally, much to Jamie's relief.

"Stop it, Mamma," Jamie scowled, "Please stop it, just keep quiet and he won't notice us."

"And no want him notice us, because?" Maria's question hung in the air.

"He's not my type. We've just texted a few times. But I didn't answer his last text, so can you please not draw attention to us. Please?" she begged.

"Pah," Maria exhaled. "*Ragazza Stupida!*" Of course not your type. He real man. Not little boy. Is Italian? Look at hair." Maria sat back on her seat and stared directly at Karl's back, willing him to swivel around again so she could get another look.

"His name is Karl, and he has a son the same age as Maddy, and it's not like that," Jamie continued to whisper, still hiding behind the menu. "And I doubt he's Italian, Mamma," she said feeling annoyed, although his hair did seem to have grown since the last time she'd seen him, he really did have quite the head of hair. "Anyway, that's not the point."

"What is *il punto?*" Maria was confused.

Madison looked up. Following her grandmother's gaze, she rested on Karl. "Ooh," she exclaimed. "Mum, is that the guy who was here last time? Ooh, Mum, his son is super cute." Jamie and Maria both stared at Madison.

"I thought you were too busy having a meltdown to notice?" Jamie was quick to retort.

"Oh, I noticed him." Madison had a cheeky glint in her eye. Maria gave Jamie a look as if to say, 'like mother, like daughter.'

"Where are you going? Sit down," Jamie barked as quietly as barking at someone in a whisper could be achieved.

"To *il bagno*. What, *no permesso* go to *il bagno?*" Maria wiggled out of the booth before Jamie had a chance to rugby tackle her back into her seat. Smoothing down her long skirt, she walked in the direction of the toilets. Jamie reached out, trying to draw her back, but just ended up swiping the air. Too late. Maria had escaped.

The entrance to the toilet was right by the bar. Jamie watched with trepidation as Maria sauntered over, praying to god that she was indeed going straight to the toilet. Maria stopped just as she reached behind Karl and turned back to look at Jamie, winked, and then much to Jamie's complete horror, tapped Karl on the shoulder. Jamie felt her stomach sick with embarrassment as she watched Karl turn around. He'd grown facial hair too. She hated facial hair. Her first instinct was to drop to the floor under the table, but realised that would make it seem even more like she was trying to avoid him. She lowered the menu, so she was no longer hiding behind it, and pretended to study it whilst cursing her mother. She managed to nudge Madison to stop staring in Maria and Karl's direction and pointed something out on the menu. She dared not look. She was going to kill her mother. Never had a menu been scrutinised with such intent. Finally, Maria returned … with Karl.

"Hey." He smiled. He did have a lovely smile. Nice teeth, very white.

Then planting on one of her old agency smiles. Dazzle. Dazzle. "Hey," Jamie said sweetly, glancing up at him briefly, desperate to avoid eye contact. She looked at the table, the 1942 tequila bottle, and then finally picked up the salt mill and started playing with it, praying that Maria wouldn't tell her off, embarrassing her even more.

"I've not seen you." His voice penetrated from afar. He didn't sound annoyed at all.

Jamie, not usually lost for words, felt awkward. "Erm … I'm sorry, I—"

Maria interrupted her—"She been very *occupata*. She got a *nuovo* job you know"—before sitting back down in the booth, leaving Karl standing. Suddenly she started patting the seat beside her, inviting him to join them. Jamie kicked her underneath the table. *"Ahia!"* Maria yelped and turned to Jamie. "Why you kick me?" For heaven's sake, did her mother really have no filter? Karl was laughing and Madison seemed rather mesmerised.

Placed in an incredibly difficult position being caught out kicking her mother, Jamie decided that honesty might be required. "Mamma, you're embarrassing me. Just stop." Then she turned to Karl. "I'm so sorry, but my mother is right. It has been hectic. I'm changing careers and—"

"Come sit with us," Maria interrupted again as she shuffled along the banquette to make room. Karl slid in next to her, placing his rucksack on the floor. "I can't stop for long. I've got to do some research for a job coming up next week."

Jamie was relieved to have moved on from the awkward conversation, and somewhere in the mix, found her manners. After all, it wasn't as if they were complete strangers.

"You sent me a text to say you wanted to chat about the book and then you disappeared?" Karl was laughing; not annoyed at all at being ignored, before taking off his glasses and wiping them with a spare serviette. Jamie noticed his eyes for the very first time. They were a kind of golden brown, similar to the tones in his hair.

Jamie couldn't exactly say that it was her barmy friend Kate that had sent the text, so she just kept quiet and blushed.

"Honestly, it's not a problem. It's been pretty hectic my end too. My divorce got finalised and—"

"You *divorciato*?" Maria cut in. God, could that woman not just keep a lid on it and stop interrupting everybody.

"Yes, thankfully …" He hesitated, as if processing whether he should elaborate. "I was married to a model. Terrible experience, I can tell you. She ran off with another photographer."

Madison, who'd been uncharacteristically quiet up until that point, suddenly blurted out, "My mum's a model."

Karl's smile dropped like it had just done a bungee jump off a two-hundred-foot cliff, and was it Jamie's imagination or did he seem to back away? Jamie was startled by his reaction. Usually men became even more intrigued finding out that she was a model, she'd yet to have one back away.

Quick to defend herself. "I was a model but"—glaring now at Madison—"I'm no longer a model. Sorry about your divorce."

Karl still seemed hesitant but then recovered. "I'm not judging, it's just …"

Maria patted his arm and once again, much to Jamie's embarrassment, finished his sentence, "*Bad divorciato, sì, sì*, is like fire on body all over," in her own spirited way. And Karl and Maria seemed to share a moment with both their heads, nodding up and down like a couple of those bobbleheads that sit on the dashboard of a car.

Karl shook his head and roused himself out of his reverie, turning his attention to Maria. "Yup, that about sums it up. It was like being burned alive, never to be repeated." Then he turned to Madison, finding his smile again. "Except I got Max, and he's probably the best thing that's ever happened to me."

Jamie noted that when he spoke about Max, the tension seemed to lift from his body.

"We're going to live in Mallorca," Madison piped up, wanting to squeeze herself into the conversation having been bestowed with Karl's attention.

Karl looked at Jamie and raised his eyes inquisitively. Jamie decided it was time to take control of the conversation. "Yes, as I wanted to explain before my mother and daughter interrupted." She turned her head side to side, giving both mother and daughter the 'enough' look. "I've just landed a new job back on the island."

"Back on the island?" Karl seemed genuinely interested.

"Long story, we used to live in Mallorca, then we left and now … now we're heading back." Jamie smiled at the thought but then somewhat uncharacteristically, wanted to defend the profession she'd given her life to. "Not all models are evil witches, you know."

Karl smirked. He didn't look convinced and started to make an origami aeroplane out of the serviette in front of him.

Maria, now aborting her English, turned to Jamie, grabbing her hands. *"E' un vero uomo. Sensibile. Bellissimo. Se non fossi così vecchia e grassa lo prenderei per me."* Jamie giggled. Her mum had said, 'He is a real man. Sensitive. Gorgeous. If I was not so old and fat, I'd take him for myself.' Jamie felt a rush of blood hit her face and Karl was shaking his head as if he didn't understand and Jamie translated, "I am an old and fat lady with a big mouth, but even I know you deserve better."

Karl laughed and started nodding in agreement, and for a moment, Jamie thought her mother was going to see this as an invitation that old fat women were his thing and sit on his lap. She seemed to be shuffling closer to him. This had to stop right now.

Karl passed the origami aeroplane to Madison, who smiled sweetly and then he looked at his watch. "It's been lovely meeting you ladies properly, but I've got to go now, do my research for this next project."

Jamie found herself intrigued. She was entering strange and new lands and not used to men walking away from her. She found herself wanting him to stay. "What do you do?"

"I'm a photographer."

Ah yes, he said his wife ran off with another photographer. Jamie involuntarily shivered. She'd had enough of that world and being pulled and pushed around by photographers. Karl seemed to understand her reaction and without her even verbalising he added, "Not all photographers are manipulating wizards." They all laughed.

"What job are you researching?" Jamie's curiosity was fully aroused. She remembered him wearing a suit. She'd never met a photographer who was so smartly dressed.

As if he read her mind he said, "I own my own agency, The Karl Kaphlan Agency, just over there across the road." He pointed to a shop with black and gold awning. "We do all sorts of photography: weddings, families and we also work with some leading papers and journalists. I usually delegate the commissions. I'm the one meeting clients and getting the jobs in but"—he paused as his golden eyes began to sparkle—"occasionally a job comes in that's too juicy, so I nab it for myself."

"And what's this one, then?" Jamie was genuinely interested, enjoying the passion he clearly had for his work.

"It's from The Daily Mail, their Weekend supplement magazine. They're doing an exposé on Shoreditch and the Urban Art Scene. It's one of the hotspots for emerging street art. If there's a free metre of space, a wall, a building, a fence, anything, then it's a canvas."

"That's what my mum's doing," Madison said enthusiastically.

Karl turned to Jamie and looked confused. "You're a model-come-graffiti artist?"

Jamie laughed and proceeded to tell Karl all about the job with Nigel. After months of researching, she was now able to talk with some knowledge about some of the graffiti artists. Madison and Maria were unusually quiet, just watching the two engaged in conversation as if they were watching the finals at Wimbledon.

"I really have to go or I'll lose the light; there's a lot of ground to cover." Karl stopped and seemed to cogitate for a moment. "Do you three want to join me? I'm only doing a recce, to familiarise myself for the shoot next week."

Jamie was about to decline when Maria took control, putting on a more authoritarian voice, "Jamie, you go. I take Madison to McDonald's."

Jamie was embarrassed that Maria had put Karl on the spot. The invitation had been for the three of them and here was her mother practically shoving her onto him.

"No, Mamma, don't be silly. Karl doesn't need me hanging around."

Maria was already sliding across the banquette so that Karl was forced to stand up, and before either Karl or Jamie could voice any protests, she reached over to Madison and pulled her up from the table.

Madison turned to Jamie. "Please, Mum, I really want to go with Nonna, and there's nothing I like here and you never let me eat McDonald's and Nonna is leaving us soon. Please."

"Yes, Jamie. I spend special time with my granddaughter, you go with nice man. *Ciao ciao*. Lovely to meet you Karl," she said, giving him one of her cheekiest smiles.

But before anyone could voice any protests, Maria marched out of the restaurant, Madison in tow, not before winking once again at Jamie.

"I'm sorry about my mother. She's very Italian. Big mouth."

Karl laughed. "You haven't met my mum." He was still standing up, looking down at Jamie.

"I've got to go. Come on, why not join me? You seem to know your stuff and it might be useful." As if sensing Jamie's hesitancy, "Can I be honest, honest?"

Jamie found this amusing. "Honest, honest? Not just honest? Are there different levels of honesty?"

"Honest, honest? Jamie, is that when I first saw you, I thought you were a beautiful woman for sure, and I should have guessed that you were a model, I mean obviously"—he looked her up and down—"but I'd just split up from my wife and all my friends were telling me I had to get out there …" he paused never taking his gaze of her. "But, honest, honest, now that the divorce is settled, plus the fact that you're leaving to return to your island. I'm not looking to start anything that can't go anywhere," he said wistfully. "But …" He perked up and smiled, and Jamie noticed that his smile was tender and unthreatening, with small wrinkles appearing by the side of his eyes and dimples on his cheeks. "Honest, honest, I'd really love your company if you have time. We can have that conversation about the book and the challenges of being a single parent."

Jamie laid her palms flat on the table and leaned in. "Honest honest?" she echoed, and he nodded; his smile never leaving his face. "That suits me just fine. Friends?" And she held out her hand and Karl took it, shaking it like they'd just made a deal.

"Friends."

MILLENNIUM FIREWORKS
Mallorca, Spain

Kate perched on the rocks at the far end of the sea wall. The wall, which encircled the exclusive yachting enclave of Puerto Portals, was a man-made construction; built to protect the hundreds of sleek and stylish boats from the openness of the Mediterranean Sea. As the sun beat down, Kate smiled with contentment and revelled in the joy of missing out on grey, murky mornings so characteristic of England at that time of the year. Staring out across the bay, Kate focused on her breathing, which was laboured and erratic. This morning marked the first time she'd run the entire length of the wall without a single break.

Kate had started running as soon as she was given the all-clear after the surgery, and she amusingly cast her mind back to her first attempt. Enthusiastically, she'd adopted a determined starting position, with her lovely new chest thrust forward and her eyes firmly fixed ahead. Only seconds later, however, it was game over as after a mere twenty steps, she'd crumpled into a very un-sporty heap. However, clutching at her side, with a stitch so painful she was convinced she'd developed acute appendicitis, Kate had refused to give up. Slowly but surely, twenty steps turned into a hundred, a hundred turned into half the sea wall, which led her to the tremendous achievement of that morning.

The sea wall had become Kate's favourite place to go running. She loved the peace and tranquillity with nothing but the sound of the waves and the wind whistling in her ears. When she'd finished running, she would sit at the end of the wall, looking out to sea. She would stay for ages watching the magnificent boats come in and out of the port; wondering who owned them and imagining what it would be like to be out on one of them, losing herself in the fantasy of being in a different world of complete freedom. So deep in thought was she, that at first she didn't hear him.

"Kate, is that you?" A voice called out from some unidentifiable location.

Who could that be? She wondered, trying to trace the source.

"Kate!" yelled the voice once more, this time closer, "Kate, it's me, Robert."

Kate's jaw dropped and the blood once again started to pump fast around her body. Robert, the man from Salsa. Robert, who'd made her body tingle. Robert, who, unbeknown to him, had often played the leading role in her fantasies.

"Robert," Kate gasped in surprise. Shit, she looked like crap now; all sweaty and with no makeup on. *Bloody hell*, why did she have to bump into him now? She'd visualised their meeting many times before, especially as she lay alone in her bed, her hands delicately touching herself, the very thought of him making her wet. She shot up with a start and began to look around for him. Finally spying him clambering down from a stunning, sleek, sexy-looking yacht—the Luciana—forty-five feet of freshly varnished teak and sparkling chrome and then ... then there was Robert, exactly as she'd imagined him. *Oh God.*

Grinning as he jumped athletically over the rocks, Robert was edging his way closer to her. *Bloody hell. Holy fuck.* There really was no escape, so Kate did what any self-respecting woman who found herself cornered would do. She sat back down, fixed a grin on her face and called out in what she hoped was a nonchalant way, "Robert, how nice to see you again." *Help.*

"You okay?" he said approaching, as if they were old friends. "What are you doing here, sitting on the rocks all by yourself?" He moved in to plant a kiss on her cheek, flirtatious as ever. Nothing had changed. Kate didn't know what to do. She looked into his eyes; those big, beautiful eyes. Big mistake. Suddenly she found herself melting all over again, just as she had when they were dancing in the Boomba Bar. *Uno, dos, tres ... cinco, seis, siete.* Everything about his face was as she remembered it, exactly as she'd envisioned it. Oh so many times. Kate averted her eyes in a futile attempt to regain her composure and instead focused on his lips. Full and red and plump; perfect for kissing. *Arrrrgggghhhh*, this was useless.

Aware that she was staring at him a little too intently and further aware that an answer was required to his question. "Running," she finally squawked. *Running?* Is that all she could manage? She had to do better than that. "Running the sea wall," she elaborated, somewhat breathlessly. Well, four words were better than one. In an hour she just might be able to produce a whole sentence. "What are you doing here?" she finally said.

"I've been here for the Ruta de la Sal Regata, but I'm leaving tomorrow for a trip around the Greek Islands." As he spoke he stared at her as if he'd noticed something was different but wasn't quite sure what. Kate recognised this as she watched him trying to process what had altered and then he focused on her breasts.

"You look different," he finally announced, curiosity having gotten the better of him.

"Boob job," she said innocently. *Bugger.* Did she really just say that? What on earth was wrong with her?

Robert laughed. "That's what first struck me about you, Kate, your honesty; you say it how it is. I like that."

Ignoring the compliment and desperate to regain some semblance of dignity, Kate clarified, "When I say boob job, I mean boobs lifted, they're all mine." With that she jiggled up and down, tits bouncing, in an attempt to illustrate that there was no silicone in residence.

"Actually ... boob reduction," she corrected. Much better; men like big boobs. Hopefully she'd be awarded bonus points for having such womanly, huge breasts that she just had to make them smaller.

Robert sat down next to her and for a moment, there was calm, silence. Nothing but the sea and the wind and the sun shining down on the two of them, where nobody else existed and nothing else really mattered.

"You never came back to Salsa," Robert said slowly.

Lie, Kate, don't tell him the truth, just don't. "It scared the living shit out of me." *Fuck, Fuck, Fuck. What's wrong with me?* She blushed. Had he noticed? She became flustered; irritated that she had such a big mouth and couldn't just lie and make small talk like every other normal human being. Suddenly Kate's momentary calmness had gone, and the tingle was back and making its presence known like never before. *Go away. Go away.* As if it were thrusting itself through steel iron gates and abducting her helpless body. DESIRE. *How can this be? Impossible.* Kate doesn't do desire. Kate doesn't do the tingle; she's put it away, packaged it securely and put it up where the vibrators live, in the top cupboard, collecting dust. *Stop looking at him, Kate. Stop acting like a little lovesick schoolgirl. Make your excuses and just go.*

"I ought to be getting back. David will be wondering where I am." Finally, some common sense.

"How is your dance partner?" Not that Robert really gave a damn.

"Good." But Kate didn't want to talk about David, either.

"How is Latka, or is it Ingrid?" Kate attempted to be polite, if a little sarcastic.

"What were you scared of in Salsa then?" Totally ignoring her question. Tennis ball successfully hit and firmly back in the opponent's court.

Lie, Kate, just lie, hit the ball back over the net, then get the fuck out of there.

"You," Kate announced, honesty making a full singing and dancing performance that afternoon. *Brilliant Kate, just brilliant, straight into the net. Arrrrgggghhhh.*

"The dance?" he questioned, yet he knew the answer even as he asked it.

"Yes, the dance and the non-kiss."

"The what?"

"The non-kiss. You know, in the rain."

"Ahhhhhhhh."

"Yes. Ahhhhhhh," she agreed, and they nodded their heads in unison.

"You weren't the only one to feel it, you know."

But she didn't know, she didn't know anything. *Make small talk, keep the conversation going and then extricate yourself without making a complete and utter prat of yourself.*

"Beautiful boat," Kate said, averting her eyes over to his yacht. She shifted uncomfortably on the rocks, conscious of his proximity. Stunned by the intensity of the physical feelings she had for this man, this stranger practically. She couldn't look at him any longer and gazed out to sea.

"Yes, she is," said Robert flatly, making it sound about as glamorous and exciting as a trip to the supermarket. His eyes still on Kate. "I'm going to miss her."

"Where's she going?"

Reverting his eyes back to the boat, "I'm trading her in for a power boat after this trip."

Kate wanted to ask why but just kept silent.

"How about you?" Robert turned the focus back on Kate.

She ignored the question and stood up. "I need to leave. I've been here for ages and I should be getting back. Lovely to see you." *Yes, that's it girl, you're doing well. Now retreat. NOW.*

"Sit a moment longer ... I always wondered whether I'd bump into you again."

No, Robert, no, please don't say that. On command, Kate sat back down, but this time she felt even more awkward as she'd unintentionally plonked herself down even closer to him than before; she could smell him for Christ's sake. Freshly baked apple pie with a dollop of cream couldn't have smelt better at that moment. It was intoxicating, pulling her in as she fidgeted uncomfortably on the rock.

Robert edged in closer still, his leg now grazing hers, the pounding in the pit of her stomach increased by about twenty decibels.

"I'm sorry if I'm being flirtatious. It's very naughty of me. You just look so—"

"So what?" Kate interrupted. She wanted to know, needed to know.

"Beautiful ... vulnerable ... delicate ... edible."

Kate gulped. *Beautiful. Vulnerable. Delicate. Edible.* The words spun around in her head. She'd never seen herself as any of those things.

Kate was clueless how to respond; desperately racking her brains for an appropriate response. He shouldn't be speaking to her in this way. Her very own moral code dictated that even allowing a man to speak to her in this manner was not one of the principal ingredients in the pot of a successful marriage. Yet she wanted to hear more. For the first time, she'd met someone who saw another part of her; a part that had been buried and was now enthralled, after a lifetime of being invisible, at finally being acknowledged.

"Serene." Robert instinctively sensed her need, conscious of her descent into the melting pot. He was a pro, a 'player.' He'd played this game a thousand times before whilst she was a mere novice; naïve and ignorant of this world of seduction. She tried to get a sense of this man who seemed so genuine but surely couldn't be for real? Was she that naïve? *Get up Kate. Get up and go now. Run, run, as fast as you can.* Yet, she couldn't run. It was too late. Her legs had already turned to jelly; that and the fact that she was convinced a wet patch had emerged in the crotch of her grey running shorts.

She looked at the way he was dressed, casual but designer; a white T-shirt with jeans that fit perfectly. *Oh my god, there's a bulge in his pants.* Kate blushed and averted her eyes. Moments later, Kate's awareness of 'The Bulge' caused a curious turn of events. In the realisation that she was responsible for the swelling, 'Kate The Prude' was taken over by another Kate, the Kate who had appeared mid-dance with Robert all those months ago; a more sexually assured Kate. Kate, The Seductress.

Strong and confident, The Seductress spoke, purred even, "The dance was electric." Surprising the old, meek Kate.

"Yes, it was," Robert said with equal assurance.

"Why are you selling her?" The Seductress wanted to know.

"I want to start going to the Caribbean, and I need to get

something bigger, but I don't want a crew, so I'm switching to power. I like being on my own." Robert paused, but no longer than the time it took for the thought to enter his dick and travel up to his brain.

"Would you like to have a look around? She's a real beauty." What better ending for his last day in Palma.

Small talk. Is this small talk? Meek Kate wasn't sure but was instantly put back where she belonged, as The Seductress was running this show now and didn't care; she wanted to go and have a look at the lovely sailing yacht, which belonged to the man with the lovely bulge in his pants. "That would be fabulous."

They both got up, but he didn't touch her; he didn't want to scare her away, not while she was being so uncharacteristically calm. In silence, they walked to the Luciana; the air thick between them. As they descended the rocks to where the boat was moored, still no words were spoken. As Kate went to cross the gangplank, Robert reached out his hand to help her. In that moment, when his fingers touched hers, an electrical current ran through her entire body but Kate couldn't speak. The Seductress had implemented a ban of silence. Kate would've run, but The Seductress kicked off her shoes, thrust out her fabulous new tits and smiled.

"Would you like a drink?" He was the perfect host, smiling politely.

A pint of vodka would do the trick. "A glass of water would be lovely." Kate attempted to stay as calm as possible.

"That would be down in the galley. Come, I'll show you inside." Robert beckoned her with his eyes before disappearing down a ladder.

She followed him, making her descent whilst a little voice, a very small muffled voice, cried out, *no, no, don't go. This is a baaaaaaaaaadddddd idea.* But as conscious as she was of her meek inner voice, Kate's voice, she was also aware of a small ache deep within. It was an ache in her womb. In her womb? Conscious that Robert was down there somewhere getting her a drink, she took it upon herself to go and explore. All dark wooden panelling and doors in close proximity. She wandered down the small galley and opened the door at the far end and gasped. This wasn't a room; it was a bed enclosed by four walls. Quickly she pulled the door shut, but it was too late; he was behind her. Directly behind her.

She didn't turn, and she didn't speak. His breath was heavy on the nape of her neck. The ache in her womb had gone and now there was a small vibration; a pleasant, warm vibration. The vibration moved at a rhythmic pace, as if someone were playing the drum roll from Ravel's *Bolero*. Unable to turn around, she could feel him, smell him. She closed her eyes and gave in to the pure pleasure that his smell elicited. He placed what must've been an ice cube from the glass he was holding onto the nape of her neck, and suddenly, with the unexpected iciness, the drum roll got louder. Still, she did not turn around; still neither spoke. The ice cube was melting as he moved his fingers slowly in circles round and round her neck before sliding them down, massaging the length of her spine, vertebra by vertebra, underneath the now wet cotton of her T-shirt. The sensation was exquisite, but still she did not turn around. Still, there were no words.

The ice cube travelled down slowly, sensually, and then curled around to her front, magically finding each breast; lingering for only a moment before continuing its descent. The ice was now melting furiously as the heat emanated from her body … then, without stopping, it reached the bottom of her shorts. Ice cube fully melted, his fingers pulled at her shorts and stroked the base of her spine. She knew that she needed to leave. This was the moment they called 'the point of no return.' Kate would definitely be retreating, but Kate was no longer there; she'd left a long time ago. The Seductress had command of this army now, and she was enjoying this man running ice cubes up and down her body, his fingers fondling her silky smooth skin.

Still, with her back to him, Robert wrapped his arms around her waist and kissed the back of her neck—moist from sweat and ice—with soft little delicate rosebud kisses that sent electric currents through her body. Skin all goosebumps and eyes closed tight. Still she had not faced him; she was in a daze, hazy as he was kissing her. Top off. *Oh no. Please dear god no. Disgusting grey peacock patterned bra. Of all days.* It came off quickly, thankfully, and her sensational pert upright breasts sprouted forth, nipples outstretched, as if they were crying, 'touch me, touch me, suck me.'

Eyes closed he turned her around … and then … and then … the kiss. How could one possibly begin to describe the kiss? Just lips, touching, caressing, no tongues at first, just soft lips on soft lips; small short pecks brushing the side of her mouth and down her neck and then back up again, and then his tongue inside her mouth … firm … wet … soft … perfect. Kissing slowly, she moaned, even The Seductress whimpered. The kissing was overwhelming. Then his lips left hers to travel down to her nipples, her beautiful new nipples. *Oh thank god they'd been lifted; by now they would've been down to the floor.* But they weren't. They were just thrusting themselves into his mouth. He took one nipple and slowly kissed it as he gently held the other breast. Another ice cube … more wetness … more electricity. He stroked both breasts, giving them exactly what they required, what they deserved.

Strange, there seemed to be two hands on her breasts, one caressing her hair and yet still two more now tugging at her shorts.

Shorts now down—muggy grey full coverage knickers exposed—but who cared? Not her. Not at that moment. She cared about nothing except the pleasure. The wetness between her legs increased; should she be embarrassed? Was there such a thing as being too wet? She didn't know, she didn't care and then came the fingers, the fingers were inside her ... her legs crumbled ... he held her up with his fifth arm all the while the fingers were moving inside of her, slowly, with great precision, as if he were a surgeon performing open heart surgery. Such precision that Kate gasped. Her mind was void of thoughts except the exquisite, infinitely delectable, most extraordinary sensation that was now tearing through her body. And then it happened. Just with his fingers, just as if he were playing Bach's *Double Concerto* on the violin. Just with her standing up, knickers around her ankles. Kate orgasmed. Kate screamed as if a thousand fireworks had simultaneously exploded inside her body. The Millennium Trafalgar Square fireworks display had just taken place inside of Kate Buchanan, and with the explosion, her legs totally gave way.

She started to shake, slowly at first, but then her whole body convulsed as the force of their connection ricocheted around the far regions of her being. As the shaking took over her body, Robert lifted her up; the knickers thankfully dropped to the floor and she was naked but not ashamed. He carried her to the bed, and gently laid her down. She was not ashamed because she felt beautiful. Quivering, she lay there in shock, in complete and utter astonishment, trying to recapture the sensation, and then suddenly he was lying next to her. Speech was useless and resistance completely and utterly futile.

With a frenzy and a passion and an impatience that belied her, she lay back with her legs open, welcoming, inviting, without inhibitions, she wanted him inside her. She pulled at his clothes; she didn't even give a thought to her nakedness with this man who was all but a stranger. His jeans were slung across the cabin. Kate caught a fright, not even a pair of Calvin Klein boxers to be ripped down as he was going commando. His penis, which, having escaped from the confines of the jeans, stood proud and tall, like a sergeant major in front of his huge army on the verge of leading his troops into battle. More kissing, more sucking—deep, soft, sensual lips that fit perfectly with her own—pulling, tugging little nips that sent shivers up and down the entire length of her body. Smelling his smell, kissing his body, his face, they consumed each other, entwined around each other, like snakes, curling, stretching, folding, sliding into each other.

The vibrations started all over again in the pit of her stomach and then moved lower and lower until she knew she was going to have another Millennium fireworks display right there and then. The drums became stronger and harder. Boom. Boom. Boom. The big bass drum was deafening as he thrust himself inside her, expelling long, deep breaths as he strived to contain himself. She squeezed him, her legs wrapped around him never to let him go. They both held the moment and then he thrust again and then again and then suddenly she felt it; the explosion. She was oblivious now to where he was or what he needed, and selfishly for the first time in her life, she was consumed by her own joy. No longer Kate the wife, nor Kate the mother— just Kate. When she looked up to see the ecstasy on his face as he finally came, she screamed like she'd never screamed before. She swore, and she cried. She wrapped her arms around him as he lay shuddering on top of her. Then, from afar, she let out one final agonised howl as real tears streamed down her face onto his head buried within her breasts. It was a howl of pleasure and a howl of pain; it was a howl of just having experienced the most incredible thing she'd ever experienced in her whole life and a howl of knowing her betrayal.

Almost as quickly as The Seductress had appeared, she then disappeared … and it was Kate who was left lying naked, entwined around a man she barely knew, shaking and trembling uncontrollably.

THE BLACK HOLE

I know I'm in here somewhere. In this deep, dark, bottomless well. If I just try, look a little harder, a little closer, will I find myself again? Will I find a way out?

Kate sat in her car, staring at the steering wheel. Not that her brain was working. It felt like she was in shock. *It's so dark, it's so cold and I'm so alone.*

Kate leaned over the steering wheel and peered through the windscreen. She looked up at the sky. Not a cloud marred the vast, infinite blue, but Kate couldn't see it. She couldn't focus. She was barely aware of where she was. *Just a glimmer will do, just a small speck of light to let me know that there is a way out, that there is hope of escape.* Yet there was nothing, just blackness, as if she'd had acid poured into her eyes and was no longer able to see. *How will I ever be able to escape?* The wound felt so great. She tried to breathe, but her breath was shallow and each time she tried to inhale, it felt like her guts were being ripped in two. *What happens now?* Tears began to fall from her eyes, at first slowly, and then suddenly they poured out of her and she howled. Her whole body shuddered as if she'd been zapped with five hundred volts of electricity. She couldn't process what had happened, and the howling continued. Great, loud, dying animal sounds of pain, the wailing of lost souls in the underworld. She banged her head repeatedly against the steering wheel.

She was not alone there in the black hole. A feeling she had never experienced to this intensity before sat with her, pulling her down and blocking the light and her way out. *SHAME.* Dignity and Integrity, who once were her friends, now departed. They no longer existed. *SHAME. And SHAME mocks me, taunts me, teases me. SHAME covers every part of my body and I won't be able to sleep and I won't be able to eat.* Kate kept trying to focus. She needed to get out of the Port. Someone might see her and she couldn't face that. She needed to go somewhere quiet, somewhere she could be alone until she figured this out. *Keep looking up,* Kate opened her eyes wide and focused on an aeroplane that was making its way across the sky. *Take me with you.* But the seconds dragged on and the pain was excruciating.

The constant barrage of thoughts kept swirling round Kate's mind. *How could I have been so stupid? How could I have been such a huge fucking idiot?*

Eventually, her howls stopped. She continued to sniffle, and the tears kept falling like water from a burst pipe. Kate returned her gaze back to the steering wheel. She had very little recollection of what had happened after her 'experience.' They'd hardly spoken, and she'd practically stumbled away from him, without leaving her number—not that he'd asked—and there certainly was no talk of a second rendezvous. Thank god he was leaving the island; she'd never have to see him again. Her mind was one hazy blur where confusion reigned. She couldn't go home now. She couldn't. Instead, she decided to drive down to a secluded little cove, a favourite spot she'd sometimes take refuge on days when she wanted to get away from the world. It was beautiful. And it felt safe. Safer than anywhere else at that moment.

* * *

She arrived at the car park, situated conveniently right in front of the small beach that she knew would be empty at this time of the year. She eased herself out of the car and made her way to the bar at Cala Comtessa. Beyond the bar, the sea beckoned her, luring her in, its deep blue waters calling out her name. Perhaps she should just forget about the bar and walk straight into its inviting watery abyss, to be swallowed whole for the lying, evil, wicked woman that she was. At least then she wouldn't have to live this day or any other day. An adulteress for eternity.

Thinking about her girls, Kate wiped the dark thoughts from her mind and settled for taking a seat at the little beach shack instead, at least for now. Sheepishly, looking around, Kate noticed that despite its split-level layout, she was the only one there so far, except for the sun-weathered older woman who appeared to be in charge that morning. If it weren't for her unspeakable act, it would have been a truly glorious winter's day. Blue skies dominated above, the sea reflecting turquoise and calm, belying the turmoil that lay beneath and the weather warm enough not to need a jacket.

Taking a seat on one of the cheap white plastic seats on the lower level, Kate rested her arms on the equally cheap white plastic table. None of them seemed to have tablecloths, likely they were just wiped down with an old rag, if they were lucky, between customers. The thoughts came rushing back, infiltrating Kate's entire being. She momentarily recalled Lady Macbeth's soliloquy, 'Out, damned spot,' feeling the same burden of guilt, wishing she could wipe her whole self-clean somehow. She needed to come clean … to someone. But who? Jamie.

Jamie was probably the only person in the whole wide world who wouldn't judge her. Given her liberal views on sex, she probably wouldn't even think it a big deal. Yes, she needed Jamie. She desperately needed Jamie right now. But what would Jamie do? She'd probably tell her to have a drink and calm down. Vodka. Kate glanced at her phone. It was only eleven fifty-five in the morning. Oh fuck it, she needed to escape, she needed to pass out. She needed to get away from this terrible, gut-wrenching pain that enveloped her.

* * *

(Ten Minutes And Two Vodka Tonics Later)

Impossible as it seemed, the vodka made Kate feel worse, as her mind kept replaying the whole Robert experience. She kept seeing him, his firm, tight body descending onto hers. She tried to shake the image from her head, but she couldn't help cringing with the embarrassment that she'd laid herself so open to him. She knew that she had to talk this through and even if Jamie didn't totally understand, at least she wouldn't be judgemental. Plus, Jamie knew her well enough to realise how completely devastating this situation was. Taking out her phone from her bum bag, she typed with shaking fingers.

Kate: huge emwrgency need you now

Typing was proving difficult, even autocorrect couldn't help her. Hopefully it would be legible enough for Jamie to get the gist. Then the waiting. *Please be there, Jamie, please, please, please be there. I need you.* And then, just moments later she saw those amazing three dots she needed, and then … 'Beep Beep.'

Jamie:	What's up? What happened? You okay? The girls??
Kate:	no, nottook … fucked uo … need you come.. Awap
Jamie:	Fuck okay. Where are you?
Kate:	Cala comteeessssa. the bar … vodjaa
Jamie:	You mean the little cove next to Illetas beach?
Kate:	yess.. Pls comme now. Pls Jamiee
Jamie:	I'm just at Nigels. I'll be about half an hour. Don't go ANYWHERE!! X

Staring into the bottom of her plastic cup, now drained of any liquid, Kate's mind began to swirl even faster. An old gentleman appeared to have sat on one of the tables across the opposite side of the shack; she hadn't even noticed him arrive. A gentle breeze blew, bringing with it the fresh smell of pine from the surrounding trees, threatening to take the cup with it. Despite being two vodkas down, Kate managed to grab the cup before it flew off the table. *Wish it could whisk me away too. I can't go home. How can I ever face David again?* He'd be on-site today, oblivious that she had turned their world upside down. Would he sense that she'd violated everything that they both held so dear? The sanctity of their marriage had crumbled in one stupid, careless moment and no matter how much Kate turned it over in her head, she couldn't see a way out of the black hole that she had stupidly climbed into.

Glancing out from the little beach bar, Kate was taken aback by the view. It was truly breathtaking. Cradled by trees, which provided necessary shade, especially in the summer months, the little sandy cove was now home to a couple of toddlers playing by the shoreline; a woman several steps behind them, no doubt their mother, was watching. *Oh, what have I done? My girls.* She lived in frickin' paradise with a sweet, adorable husband and two gorgeous little girls. What was she thinking? She didn't want to think. Glancing over at the older woman, she yelled out, *"Uno más, por favor."* Not even bothering to stand up. The woman's wrinkled face cracked further with a smile, as if in acknowledgement of her predicament, and came over as quickly as she could with a refill, and kind, soulful eyes. *"Gracias,"* Kate managed to mouth out.

Knocking back her third vodka tonic, Kate waited for oblivion. It didn't come. How was she going to live the rest of her life? She'd have to tell David. She'd have to pray that he would show her mercy because the guilt was all-consuming and she just couldn't spend the rest of her life living this terrible lie. But if she told him, he'd never understand. How could he? Why should he? She didn't even understand it. If she told him, then he would be in pain and that would make it ten times worse. He would leave her; because once that trust was broken, he would never ever trust her again or forgive her. He was such a proud man and this would destroy him. It would destroy her. It would destroy the children. Oh, how could she have been so stupid?

"Kate." A familiar voice interrupted her tortuous thoughts. "Kate, Kate are you okay?"

It was Jamie, rushing towards her, like a mirage in the desert. Kate wasn't sure it was entirely real. Taking a seat next to her, Jamie reached across to take her hands. "Kate, I got here as soon as I could. Thankfully Nigel is away, so I just finished off what I was doing and came straight here. Tell me, what happened? You look dreadful."

Jamie didn't understand what it was like to love someone in the way that Kate loved David. But if Kate did love David, then how could she have done what she did? Was her marriage a lie? NO. NO. NO. She did love David; he was her everything. But then why had she managed to be with Robert in a way that she'd never been able to be with David? How could a stranger make her tremble and shake and quiver and yet David, whom she loved with all her heart, could not? What was she going to say to Jamie now?

"Done something terrible." Kate's words were slurred but understandable enough. Jamie had enough experience speaking to drunken friends to understand the dialect.

"Terrible? Like what?" Jamie was now looking Kate square in her eyes. She may as well have been looking into her dark, dirty soul.

"Jamie, I don't know what to do." Kate covered her face with her hands and her body started to heave again.

"Just try telling me what happened first." Jamie stroked Kate's back.

"So hard. So very very hard. Have fucked up. Not just a little iddy biddy fuck up, but a great big huge fuck up."

"Okay, I can't imagine what you may have done that's so bad, but I'm here hun, just tell me and maybe I can help." Jamie paused. "You don't need me to hide a body for you, do you?" Her big green eyes suddenly opened wider, hoping that was not the emergency.

"Had a multiple orgasm," Kate suddenly blurted out.

"Oh my god Kate, what the fuck? How is that fucking up? Halle-frickin'-lujah more like."

"Not with David."

"Fuck."

"Yes. I don't understand what happened. All seems so surreal. Also have to tell you that am pissed now. Trying to drown out the misery with alcohol."

"Yes, I can see that, but let's not panic. Just talk me through it slowly." Jamie was next to her, and Kate noticed that she had now taken the plastic cup and sneaked a little sip.

"I bumped into Salsa Man when I was doing my morning run earlier. Do you remember I told you about the guy who gave me the tingle? Oh my god, what have I done?"

"Shit. You had sex with Salsa Man? When? Where? How?" Jamie's face had now taken on a very different expression. Every muscle seemed to have been animated into action.

"I don't understand what happened. I was running along the sea wall and he had his boat moored in the port where I've started to run. I've cheated on David. I've been unfaithful. I've been an adulteress lying whore. I'm a—"

"Steady on. Just calm down for a minute." Jamie interrupted.

Kate did not calm down. "I hate myself. Don't know what to do. Can't breathe. I need another drink." Kate looked around for the older woman and started signalling a drinking motion with her hands. Jamie looked at the woman and gave a stern shake of her head and wiggle of the finger.

"Look at me. I want you to take a really deep breath." Jamie filled her nostrils as if to demonstrate deep breathing. Kate copied. "That's it. Now hold ... and now I want you to exhale ... slowly."

"Woooooooooo," Kate exhaled. It sounded more like she was in childbirth.

"Good. good. Let's do two more. I'll do it with you."

As the girls paused for breath, another couple joined the bar. They were younger, and judging by their clothing, were likely still out from the night before.

"Okay, so first things first. Does anyone know?" Jamie wanted to take control, as Kate was clearly incapable.

"No, it just happened NOW. I have to tell David. I can't carry this around on my own. I can't live the rest of my life with this."

"Stop it right there. First of all, you cannot tell David, not ever. Do you hear me?" Jamie had now taken hold of both of Kate's shoulders, which was a good thing as she was struggling to sit upright.

"No, have to. Can't live lie the rest of life. Will kill me."

"No, you don't and it won't. Trust me. Now I need to know something. Have you arranged to meet this man again? I'm taking that it was a one-off, a weak moment, right?"

"Weak moment? Fucking hell. Is that what you call it? Didn't feel like a weak moment. Felt like the most powerful moment of my life. Hate myself so much but it was incredible."

"Okay, not a weak moment then, but certainly not a normal Kate Buchanan moment. You have never done anything like this before. Stop panicking for a second and just let me figure this out.

So no one knows, right?"

"No one knows. Can only trust you."

"Does he have your number or know where you live or anything like that?"

"No, and he's leaving Mallorca today. Gone now and unlikely to return. Will never see him again. But what am I going to do? I've just cheated on David. I love David so much." The tears that had momentarily stopped, welled up again. "I just don't know how this happened. One minute I'm running, feeling alive, happy and content for the first time in ages, and the next minute he comes scrambling over the rocks and it was like I wasn't there anymore."

"Look, what happened, happened. Please don't torment yourself over the one, the only indiscretion of your whole life. You are not having an affair. It was not planned. It just happened. Okay?"

Snot ran down Kate's nose and in the absence of a tissue, she wiped it on her top. "He asked if I wanted to see his boat. I didn't, but this other person who seemed to take over my body took control, and I ended up on his boat and having the most incredible sex of my life. I never knew it could be like that."

"That's it." Jamie's face lit up as if she'd had a eureka moment. "Perhaps this needed to happen Kate, perhaps you needed to experience this? To learn how amazing sex can be, to know that you yourself are capable of those feelings."

"Why would I need to experience this? I was happy before and now I'm miserable. It's like tasting pizza for the first time. How am I supposed to live without it now? How am I supposed to live with myself?" Kate buried her face in her hands again. "Where's the vodka? I need that vodka!"

Jamie reached across to take Kate's hands and looked at her softly. "Look hun. This was one moment of your whole life and something happened that you didn't plan and didn't expect, but somewhere in that moment, you found something you'd been looking for. You found you. You found a part of you that you'd hidden for so so long. Perhaps this had to happen, to enable you to experience something so mind-blowing as to reawaken a part of you that you've suppressed for all these years. I am not going to let you torment yourself over this, and I'm not going to let you have another vodka either. This is what we're going to do." Jamie was in the driving seat now.

Kate looked at her, her eyes begging for a solution, relieved to not be going through this torment alone. "Give me your phone. I'm going to text David as if I'm you and tell him that you're coming to help me unpack some last remaining boxes even though you and I both know there are none haha, and then ask him to pick the girls up. Then I'm going to take you back to mine, make you a herbal tea, and you're going to sleep it off. And when you're sober, I'll drive you back to your car and you can go home. Okay?"

Kate looked back at Jamie, like a little girl who had been told what to do, and was happy to know she was being looked after by someone who cared. "Okay. I'm just pleased he's gone."

"Me too hun, me too."

"So to be clear, because I don't feel very clear. Are you saying that I should just forget it?" The little Kate within her looked lost.

"That's exactly what I'm saying."

"So I shouldn't tell David?"

"No, you should never tell David or anyone else. What for? You're not having an affair, for Christ's sake. My lips are sealed for an eternity. My advice to you is to do the same."

"Jamie, I know you'd never betray me." Still, Kate looked imploringly up at her friend, just needing that little extra splash of reassurance.

"I would never betray you, Kate, never."

"But ... what about the multiple orgasms? I was happy in my life not experiencing multiple orgasms ... I think? But then what worries me is that I didn't seem to have any control. It was like some huge out-of-body experience. I think I am schizophrenic."

"You're not schizophrenic, Kate. You've just been reborn into a more sexual being. Maybe you needed to let yourself go in order to feel it? Maybe, for whatever reason, you've never allowed yourself to let go with David. Perhaps all this time your mind has been closed to it. Maybe now you know you can, you'll start to share that passion with David? Perhaps something good will come out of this?"

"Perhaps. When will the sadness go?"

"The sadness will go in time, but you are a good, honest woman and you don't deserve to feel sad, not even for a moment. You're in control of when you'll get over it. Just tell yourself that it wasn't Kate Buchanan, 'wife.' That it needed to happen and then carry on as normal. Why don't we get out of here and go back to mine now? Start putting all of this behind you."

Kate leaned in and hugged Jamie. "Thank you. Truly. For everything. And I'm so sorry to put this on you. I can't even tell you how terrible I feel—"

Jamie cut her off. "I'll always be here for you, Kate. But there's nothing to be sorry about. It never happened."

Kate wiped the tears from her eyes. "It never happened."

PEACE

(Six Months Later)

"Kate, it's too hot. Get off me." David tried, not for the first time that night, to extricate himself from Kate, who was glued to him. The heat was stifling, even at three in the morning, and it felt as if they were enveloped in a hazy mist of mugginess. The sheets had long been abandoned, as had any nightwear, as they lay naked, entwined around each other. The sound of the fan clicking annoyingly kept them awake, and even more frustratingly, was proving ineffective at keeping them cool.

"Sorry, you smell so good." Kate nestled in further, snuggling deeper and deeper into David's soft, warm flesh. She found sleep easier when she was cuddling him, but it was so hot.

"Really, Kate, you gotta get off me. I can't breathe and I think I've just been bitten."

"Bloody air-conditioning unit, why'd it have to break now? When did the guys say they were going to get around to fixing it?"

"*Mañana*," David said nonchalantly.

"I'm in all morning but meeting Jamie for lunch. Will you be here?" Kate nestled in even closer, ignoring his request and throwing one leg over his.

"For what?"

"For the air con people."

"Yes, yes, I'll take the girls to school and then come straight back. I'm working from home all day. Go to sleep, and get off me."

"I can't sleep. I'm still thinking about doing the challenge next year."

"It's just the Inca Trail. It's not Everest." He disentangled himself to the sound of their skin squelching, sticky with sweat.

Kate couldn't fall back to sleep. Her mind shifted gears, as if she were doing a Formula One circuit. During daylight hours, she kept herself so busy that she didn't allow herself to overthink. But, it was in these moments, in the still of the night, with nothing to distract her, that the thoughts would sometimes slither back in.

In the early days, when the guilt would consume her, she blamed her low mood on hormones and, bizarrely, David seemed to accept this. Women's hormones were like a black hole where David was concerned. She found running helped, especially outside surrounded by the natural beauty. Just that week, she'd read an article about hiking the Inca Trail and, with a flash of inspiration, decided to put all the training to good use and signed up to do a charity challenge the following year.

"I'm too hot. I'm going to cool off in the pool," she whispered. Silence. Kate slithered off the bed, went to grab her bikini bottoms, and then thought better of it. Who'd see her at this time of the morning? She'd just go naked. A nice little skinny dip in the pool, do some lengths, think, ponder, plan her Inca Trail trip. Anything was better than just lying in bed. If she could cool off, then she might be able to sleep.

As Kate slowly made her way across the garden, the blades of grass tickled between her toes. She felt a rush of adrenaline as she enjoyed the liberation of walking starkers, the utter joy of feeling so secure within herself, wild, free and totally unabandoned. As she reached the edge of the pool, she stretched out her arms and reached for the sky. The stars illuminated the vast blackness, just one more stretch and she could almost touch them. Wanting to hang onto this feeling, harness it, consume it and never let it go, she reached higher and inhaled deeply. At that moment, everything felt beautiful, and calm. She exhaled, letting go of everything that had ever held her back. Life was good. This … this was peace.

The cool water stroked her body as she lay floating on her back, looking up at the stars, which seemed particularly bright that night; it was as if they'd cast a wonderful candlelit glow around the garden. Kate closed her eyes and revelled in the ecstasy of the moment.

After months of torment and agony, she'd finally arrived at her destination. The recalibration process was complete, and the pain had dissipated. For the most part, she'd exterminated all thoughts of Robert. The sexual ache she'd had for that man, constrained by her newfound passion for physical activity and dare she say it—her husband. The excruciating agony that was her betrayal was replaced with a dull ache. An ache that she'd have to live with for the rest of her life. A small price to pay to save her family.

She'd been an idiot; such an idiot that she could've lost David. Yet, without risking it all, without feeling that all-consuming fear those months that ensued her encounter with Robert, she'd never have realised how lucky she was. Jamie had been right. Kate recognised that Robert had indeed been instrumental in her evolution. Without him, she'd still be feeling restless and frustrated. Without Robert, she'd still be walking around, oblivious to the sheer joy of the simple things that already existed within her life. Everything she needed, she'd had all along; she just hadn't been able to see it. So, slowly, she'd stopped tormenting herself, stopped thinking of the incident as evil, and twisted it in her mind into something that had to happen; a wonderful and very secret encounter that had touched her soul and made her feel more alive and more beautiful than she'd ever felt before. Kate didn't want to waste her precious life with feelings of regret when something good had materialised out of this. She'd experienced a wonderful passion that was never meant to last and could never have been sustained, but in its moment was so natural and pure that it took her breath away.

Suddenly, Kate felt strong arms wrap around her, pulling her legs under the water, and she smiled. David had silently slipped into the pool. He didn't speak but also naked, came around swiftly, and folded himself around her.

"Mmmmmmmmm, thought you wanted to sleep?" Kate teased him, relaxing into his arms, slowly rubbing against him, and sensually massaging his body with her own.

"That was the idea, but images of you swimming naked woke me up."

"You mean woke a part of you?" Kate jested as she felt David's hardness brush against her back. Slowly, one hand circled her waist, keeping her afloat, whilst the other stroked her gently.

"Don't you have a tennis match tomorrow? Don't you need your sleep?" Kate continued to tease him as she turned around, wrapping her legs around his waist and nibbling his ear.

"I'm living for the moment. Isn't that what you've been telling me? Be in the here and now."

Kate smiled and as their lips touched, his tongue entered her mouth. She felt The Seductress come alive, but alive to the caresses of her husband, her best friend and now her lover.

ACCEPTANCE

"Hands off." Jamie slapped Kate's hand away from the triangle of Club Sandwich Kate had reached for. "You've already had two," she exclaimed.

"I think I preferred it when you were a model and starving," Kate said grumpily, still looking longingly at the sandwich.

"Ha bloody ha."

"Can we share it, at least? Now that I'm doing the Inca Trail next year, I've upped my training and I'm starving."

Jamie ignored her, grabbing the sandwich and shoving it into her mouth before Kate had a chance to wrestle her for it. "OMG I almost forgot, I have news!" Jamie blurted out in between chews.

"You're finally in a real relationship?" Kate said excitedly.

"What? No. Why would I need that? No, I mean real news!"

Kate looked at her blankly. "Well spit it out then, what is it?"

"I … I … I found my first grey hair!" Jamie's eyes grew brighter, as her smile grew wider.

"Ohmygosh what? Hahaha so I guess you're not twenty-five anymore then?" Kate winked. "So did you pull it out?"

"Actually no, I've decided to keep it. It's part of me and I don't see why I should feel ashamed of it."

Kate looked blankly at Jamie; the one she knew had clearly left the building. "So where is this grey hair then? I need to see this."

Jamie ran her fingers through her hair in an attempt to expose it. And just as she did, Kate leapt up and began inspecting Jamie's hair in the same way that she might inspect her daughters'.

"Get off me! We're not going to do this here. I'll find it later and show you," Jamie protested, swatting her friend away like a fly with her long slender arms.

Defeated, Kate sat back down, and Jamie attempted to regain her composure after being subjected to a very public head inspection.

"Sorry," said Kate.

"It's okay. I guess I've just been doing a lot of thinking recently. Not having to rely on my looks for work has made me question everything I've ever been taught. I mean, why are we supposed to colour our hair when it goes grey anyway? Who decided that? And why don't men do it? Well, most men. You know what I mean. In fact, have you seen some of those silver-haired beauties with flowing grey locks? I've started to follow some on Instagram and they call themselves the 'Silver Sisters' and they're just fabulous. So I've decided I'm going to be one too.

Kate looked at her friend. "Right, but I think you're going to need another few decades before you even get close to that." Jamie's face dropped and Kate realised her friend was actually serious.

"I'm sorry again. I suppose I never expected to hear those words coming out of your mouth. If anything, you've always tried to be younger, but I'm happy for you. Acceptance is a huge thing, and it's not easy for us women to accept ourselves exactly as we are." Kate reached over and touched her friend's hand. How things had changed.

Suddenly Jamie reached out with her other hand clasping Kate's with both of her own. "And I'm really sorry too, Kate."

"You're sorry now? For what?"

"I feel I owe you an apology."

Kate couldn't fathom what Jamie could possibly be apologising for. "Is it because you ate the Club Sandwich?" Kate said playfully.

"Haha no, of course not. I'm being serious. I've been thinking about that time we went to see the specialist and sat in the park afterwards."

Kate frowned and interjected. "That was a great day. What are you apologising for?"

"Yeah, it was a great day. It's for encouraging you to go ahead with the surgery. I feel like I pushed you into having it. I was just so clouded back then. You never needed to change anything about yourself. You were always beautiful just as you were. I guess I didn't see it. In anyone, least of all myself. And that's why I've decided to question it all now."

Jamie had nothing to apologise for. Jamie had empowered her to change something about herself that she didn't like. Nobody had cajoled her into the surgery, not Jamie and not David either. All they had done was support her in her own journey and she would do it all again in a heartbeat.

"Don't be ridiculous. That decision was all mine. And I don't regret it for a second."

"You don't?" Jamie's eyes widened as she gazed back at her friend.

"I don't. I did it for me, and only me. And even if you hadn't been supportive, I probably would have ended up doing it anyway. But thank you … for thinking I was beautiful."

"You'll always be beautiful to me." Jamie locked eyes with her friend and they both smiled. And in that moment, they knew their friendship would stand the test of time.

"Soooo ... back to my question on relationships." Kate stared directly at Jamie, her mouth now curled into a cheeky smile.

"I am dating Kate. I date all the time." It was true. Jamie had found a great babysitter and, whilst she didn't have as many sleepovers as she did when Maria was there, her sex life was still very much alive and kicking.

"Yes, I know and I love your stories, but I'm not talking about the shags. I'm talking about a relationship."

Jamie shuddered involuntarily and pulled a face. *Pah Relationship. Who needs a frickin' man full-time?*

Kate ignored her expression. "You know, somebody that I can meet. Someone from our generation. Someone, 'appropriate.'"

"Yeah, yeah. I'm sure I will. One day."

"Okay, I'll drop the subject. Just promise me that if you do get together with an appropriate man, you'll let me meet him. It would be so much fun to go on a double date."

"Okay, I promise." Jamie grinned mischievously before intentionally changing the subject. "What you up to now? Sure I can't change your mind about the Cosmopolitans?" They'd been there for over an hour and it was her fifth attempt at persuading Kate to break her 'no alcohol' stance.

"No, I can't Jamie. I'm training this afternoon. My body is a temple," she said with a playful yet stern look, indicating that the subject was closed.

"So you keep telling me," Jamie groaned, wishing for a moment that she could have the old Kate back. "You're so booooring. I took the afternoon off. I thought we were going to play."

"A temple."

Jamie pulled her mouth down, sulking, realising that her attempts to bring the 'new' Kate over to the dark side were in vain.

"We should get the bill." Kate looked around for a waiter.

"Yeah okay. I guess I'll see you in spin class on Monday then. And seeing as you won't play with me today, I think I'll go and have a walk instead."

* * *

Once Kate had left, the thought of ordering herself a Cosmopolitan floated into Jamie's mind, but then departed as quickly as it had landed. She didn't need it. She didn't need it at all. The walk would do the trick just fine, and she gathered her belongings and headed out.

As she meandered towards the end of the port, she took her time to take in her surroundings, which, to be fair, were pretty damn amazing. The luxury marina was home to boats of all shapes and sizes, from small MasterCrafts used for wakeboarding to luxury motor yachts, belonging to the rich or famous, or decidedly infamous. You never knew who you might bump into. Glamorous boutiques and an endless supply of cute cafés and chic restaurants attracted people from all over the world, and Jamie was struck by just how different her life was back on the island. She was surrounded by people who didn't live by the normal rules, people who paved their own paths, and that was exactly what she was doing now too—paving a new path for herself and Madison. As she reached the end of the marina, she decided to head towards the sea wall instead of the beach. It would be quieter there, plus she'd get an unobstructed view of the sea.

The path along the wall itself was deserted, and as she walked, she noticed everything from the jet skis making their mark across the waves like white lines of frothy fizz, to the solitary couple on top of the tiny, rocky island just across the way. Reaching the end of the wall, Jamie carefully eased herself down onto the flat side of one of the large, multifaceted boulders and stared out to sea. Closing her eyes, she filled her lungs with the fresh salty air as the glorious Mediterranean sunshine warmed every inch of her body. And then, slowly, she exhaled, and in that one breath it was as if all the stresses of the past year had been released and she realised she was smiling. She did that a lot these days. Her job was amazing. Madison was deliriously happy being back on the island. And she was happy, too. More than happy; she was free.

As she gazed at the vast blue expanse where the sky merged with the sea, Jamie felt peace. The sun cast golden ripples across the surface of the water. This was home. This little slice of paradise was where she lived. She wanted to pinch herself. How had she ever doubted it? The beautiful island offered everything she'd ever needed, ever really wanted, but she just needed to learn that for herself. It had taken going back to London to realise how empty that existence was, how much the modelling was destroying her, how the pace of life was just too frantic. Although one good thing had come out of it, and that was meeting Karl.

Since their afternoon together scouring the bustling area of Shoreditch, they'd found a real connection. The narrow streets had been alive with activity, cool coffee shops and small boutiques alongside incredible street art. Somewhere between the exploration and the conversation, she'd encountered a different sort of chemistry from the one she usually had with men. Karl wasn't like any man she'd ever met before. She loved that she didn't have to play games with him. He was just there for her in a way that she'd never experienced. And whilst she couldn't see him as often as she'd been able to in London, she'd miraculously grown to care for someone of the opposite sex for reasons other than sex. They were friends, and just thinking about him made her eyes sparkle.

Jamie was so deep in thought that she didn't notice the man walking down the sea wall until he was right behind her. He stood in silence, also taking in the outstanding natural beauty that was before them. Unexpectedly, he cleared his throat, making her jump up; startled that the moment was no longer a solitary one. Wobbling precariously on the rocks, she lost her footing, and the man reached out a hand to steady her. Surprise turned to a flicker of excitement as she turned around to face him. His blonde hair flopped over his eyes and, whilst he definitely wasn't in his twenties, there was something magnetic about him. He stepped back, realising he'd startled her and grinned, fine lines etching the corners of his eyes, further accentuating the rugged handsomeness of his face.

Hmmmm, she thought. *Appropriate.*

"I'm so sorry. I didn't mean to creep up on you," he said, releasing his hold on her. His golden hair glimmered in the sunlight as he took a finger to flick it away from his eyes.

"Oh gosh, don't worry. I'm the one that should be sorry, jumping up like that. I didn't hear you." Jamie returned her gaze back towards the sea. "Beautiful, isn't it?"

"Breathtaking," he said, and as she turned back around, she realised he hadn't taken his eyes off her. A slight blush crept onto her cheeks and she smiled, noticing that when he smiled back, his whole face lit up in a way that was quite simply, irresistible.

"Hi, I'm Robert …"

THE END

ACKNOWLEDGMENTS

What can I say? It's only taken us fifteen years! And holy moly, what a rollercoaster those years have been!

Mum, thank you for being the kindest, most selfless woman in the world. Thank you for always being there, for showing me what it truly means to be a parent, and for never letting a day pass without reminding us all how much you love us. If Mother Earth was ever personified, she'd be you. I'm also very grateful for your eye for good-looking men, which you graciously passed on to me! ;) I love you immeasurably.

My beautiful daughter, you are the one who made me a mother first and I want to thank you for all the lessons along the way. Having you at a young age meant that we had to learn and grow together. From telling everyone to "Go to the kitchen!" in your feisty younger years, to your equally feisty older years. I'm so proud of the strong, independent woman you've become. I love you more than you know.

My son, the sweetest, funniest, most loving boy, who continues to teach me about motherhood daily—the highs, the lows, and the everyday ordinary in between. You also took me by surprise by coming along when I least expected it and taught me that being a mother is the most important job of all, even if it means watching *The Diary of a Wimpy Kid* on repeat. Love you to the moon and back, my MooMoo.

It goes without saying that I want to thank you, Suzie. My friend, my co-author, my bonafide soul sister, for being by my side through it all. Even if no one other than us reads this book, it is the greatest testimony to one of my most incredible friendships, and this insane, crazier-than-any-fiction roller coaster we've both been on since it first began. I am soooo relieved to finally get our baby out into the world, so I'm sorry (really not sorry!) for the red hot poker; I know you love it really! Because without it, our baby would be preparing for retirement! Here's to writing many more books together (a future Suzie problem I know!) and perhaps one day we'll write the real, far crazier, stories we lived whilst we wrote this one, which has been both my lifeline and source of immense joy. It's been an honour. Thank you.

I want to thank our editor Sophie, for your patience and integrity, and helping us finally get this book out. And of course Jim, our epic cover designer and formatter, for jumping in and saving us at the end, and bringing our artistic vision to life, even if you do suffer from bunny-induced trauma for years to come! You've been a true star!

My darling sister, thank you for always having my back (you do realise I'll still be taller than you even when we're in our eighties haha!) and other members of my family, who've always been there; I love you all dearly. And last of all, I want to thank all of my incredible soul sisters and the odd honorary brother (you know who you all are!) for being on this wild ride with me, even if you didn't know about the book. Whilst we are connected to family by blood, it is our friends that we choose, and if we're lucky, some friendships last a lifetime.

Natasha

Life has been full of many roller coaster rides, but there have been unwavering constants who've walked by my side, shared in the joy and carried me in the darker moments. Without you all, I would never have had the courage to write this book.

First and foremost, I want to thank my husband. My Beau, my Doble and now my Crinkle. We have shared a life together of such richness and adventure. We started young, have grown together and you are my absolute world. Thank you for helping me with the storylines, for allowing me to discuss even the more uncomfortable plot twists, safe in the knowledge of our love.

To my children, seeing you grow into beautiful young adults, following your dreams, and evolving into adulthood with such integrity. Parenting you three has been the greatest achievement of my life (finishing this book a close second!), and I could not be prouder of what stands before me today.

To my outer inner circle (sorry Anthony) that would be my brother, my sister Lisa, and my parents. My parents, you are my greatest cheerleaders with your constant reminders that there's no such word as 'can't', even though I often didn't believe that whilst writing this book. You've encouraged me and believed in me, and what a gift that has been. For my sister Lisa and my brother Anthony, I love you and our friendship so much. We have shared so many adventures and life experiences, and as we now slide gracefully into old(er) age, knowing that we're together, is the most comforting gift of all.

I cannot acknowledge by name all of my soul friends, I've been truly blessed. For those who were with me from the very beginning and who I know will be there 'til the end. And to those I found along the way. We've laughed and we've cried, we've held each other and we've shown up. This is what true friendship is about; respecting that we all have busy lives yet knowing when to drop everything to be there for one another. And you've all been there with such love for me. I can only hope that you've felt that reciprocated as we travel down this winding road of life. Without my incredible soul sisters, this road would have had far less flowers.

I want to mirror Natasha's appreciation for Sophie, our editor, who without, we'd certainly be editing this book for years to come. I also want to thank our designer, Jim, for your patience with our many technical challenges and your reassurances along the way, we are so grateful - may we all continue to dream of bunnies!

And finally my co-writer, Natasha. I am without words ("Huh, now?" she says after spending the last fifteen years cutting my word flow by fifty per cent to avoid a *War and Peace* end product). Natasha, your unwavering determination, your constant drive and passion has carried me through this project. All gold stars go to you for not letting us give up. Your 'poker', whilst searing hot and unwelcome at times, is the only reason we finished this project, and if life is the journey and not the destination, then I wouldn't have had anybody else in my carriage. I hope we get to write lots more books together because this journey has been the light, it has been the escape and we have laughed more than anyone could ever imagine on a journey that had this many bumps. Thank you.

Printed in Dunstable, United Kingdom